UNDERSTANDING SUZAN-LORI PARKS

UNDERSTANDING CONTEMPORARY AMERICAN LITERATURE

Matthew J. Bruccoli, Founding Editor

Linda Wagner-Martin, Series Editor

Volumes on

Edward Albee | Sherman Alexie | Nelson Algren | Paul Auster
Nicholson Baker | John Barth | Donald Barthelme | The Beats
Thomas Berger | The Black Mountain Poets | Robert Bly
T. C. Boyle | Raymond Carver | Fred Chappell | Chicano Literature
Contemporary American Drama | Contemporary American Horror Fiction
Contemporary American Literary Theory
Contemporary American Science Fiction, 1926–1970
Contemporary American Science Fiction, 1970–2000
Contemporary Chicana Literature | Robert Coover | Philip K. Dick
James Dickey | E. L. Doctorow | Rita Dove | John Gardner | George Garrett
Tim Gautreaux | John Hawkes | Joseph Heller | Lillian Hellman | Beth Henley
James Leo Herlihy | John Irving | Randall Jarrell | Charles Johnson
Diane Johnson | Adrienne Kennedy | William Kennedy | Jack Kerouac
Jamaica Kincaid | Etheridge Knight | Tony Kushner | Ursula K. Le Guin
Denise Levertov | Bernard Malamud | David Mamet | Bobbie Ann Mason
Colum McCann | Cormac McCarthy | Jill McCorkle | Carson McCullers
W. S. Merwin | Arthur Miller | Lorrie Moore | Toni Morrison's Fiction
Vladimir Nabokov | Gloria Naylor | Joyce Carol Oates | Tim O'Brien
Flannery O'Connor | Cynthia Ozick | Suzan-Lori Parks | Walker Percy
Katherine Anne Porter | Richard Powers | Reynolds Price | Annie Proulx
Thomas Pynchon | Theodore Roethke | Philip Roth | May Sarton
Hubert Selby, Jr. | Mary Lee Settle | Sam Shepard | Neil Simon
Isaac Bashevis Singer | Jane Smiley | Gary Snyder | William Stafford
Robert Stone | Anne Tyler | Gerald Vizenor | Kurt Vonnegut
David Foster Wallace | Robert Penn Warren | James Welch
Eudora Welty | Tennessee Williams | August Wilson | Charles Wright

UNDERSTANDING

SUZAN-LORI PARKS

Jennifer Larson

The University of South Carolina Press

Published by the University of South Carolina Press
Columbia, South Carolina 29208

uscpress.com

Printed in the United States of America

Library of Congress Cataloging-in-Publication Data

Larson, Jennifer, 1977–
Understanding Suzan-Lori Parks / Jennifer Larson.
p. cm. — (Understanding contemporary American literature)
Includes bibliographical references and index.
ISBN 978-1-61117-107-5
1. Parks, Suzan-Lori—Criticism and interpretation. I. Title.
PS3566.A736Z75 2012
812'.54—dc23
2012028936

Chapters 2 and 4 appeared in a different form in *Reading Contemporary African American Drama: Fragments of History, Fragments of Self* (New York: Peter Lang, 2007).

CONTENTS

Series Editor's Preface *vii*

Acknowledgments *ix*

Chapter 1
Understanding Suzan-Lori Parks *1*

Chapter 2
"Three-ness" and "the Space in Between":
Imperceptible Mutabilities in the Third Kingdom and
The Death of the Last Black Man in the Whole Entire World *9*

Chapter 3
"Deliberate Calculation" in Money, Sex,
and Black Plays: *Venus* *26*

Chapter 4
What "Able" and "Angel" Mean to a
Welfare Mother: *In the Blood* *40*

Chapter 5
Folding and Unfolding History, or
Identity Fabrication: The Lincoln Plays *58*

Chapter 6
As We Advance Living: *Getting Mother's Body* *83*

Chapter 7
"This film has been modified from its original version": *Girl 6* and *Their Eyes Were Watching God* 102

Chapter 8
The Revolutionary Revised: Essays and *365 Days/365 Plays* 127

Notes 139
Bibliography 153
Index 157

SERIES EDITOR'S PREFACE

The Understanding Contemporary American Literature series was founded by the estimable Matthew J. Bruccoli (1931–2008), who envisioned these volumes as guides or companions for students as well as good nonacademic readers, a legacy that will continue as new volumes are developed to fill in gaps among the nearly one hundred series volumes published to date and to embrace a host of new writers only now making their marks on our literature.

As Professor Bruccoli explained in his preface to the volumes he edited, because much influential contemporary literature makes special demands, "the word *understanding* in the titles was chosen deliberately. Many willing readers lack an adequate understanding of how contemporary literature works; that is, of what the author is attempting to express and the means by which it is conveyed." Aimed at fostering this understanding of good literature and good writers, the criticism and analysis in the series provide instruction in how to read certain contemporary writers—explicating their material, language, structures, themes, and perspectives—and facilitate a more profitable experience of the works under discussion.

In the twenty-first century, Professor Bruccoli's prescience gives us an avenue to publish expert critiques of significant contemporary American writing. The series continues to map the literary landscape and provide both instruction and enjoyment. Future volumes will seek to introduce new voices alongside canonized favorites, to chronicle the changing literature of our times, and to remain, as Professor Bruccoli conceived, contemporary in the best sense of the word.

Linda Wagner-Martin, Series Editor

ACKNOWLEDGMENTS

I wish to thank the following people for guiding and supporting the vision and revision of this project: Trudier Harris, Bill Andrews, James Coleman, Philip Gura, Rebecka Rutledge Fisher, Linda Wagner-Martin, Beverly Taylor, Sandra Govan, Malin Pereira, Jeffrey Leak, Randi Davenport, Natasha Smith, Mary Alice Kirkpatrick, Kristina Bobo, Andei Williams, Molly Westerman, Colleen Thorndike, Leslie Davison, Amy Stitzinger, Rachelle Gold, Ben Sammons, Meredith Malburne-Wade, Joy Cranshaw, John Hannah, Pam Hamilton, Matt Luter, Maura D'Amore, Amy McGuff Skinner, Harry Thomas, Sarah Ficke, Kelly Bezio, Tara Fee, Elizabeth Kiem Harper, Anne Sclater, Katie Rose Guest Pryal, Amy Armbruster, David Darr, Glenda Noel, and Brice and Houston Barnes. I extend special thanks to my family—Doug and Colin Dorney, Nancy and Steve Shapiro, Bob and Bonnie Larson, Debbie Larson, Eli Larson, Meagan Larson, Emily Larson, and Jesse Larson—for their encouragement, patience, and love. And, finally, I must thank Larry Larson, who helped me find my voice; I miss him every day.

CHAPTER 1

Understanding Suzan-Lori Parks

Suzan-Lori Parks wrote in her essay "Possession" (1994) that "the history of Literature is in question. And the history of History is in question too." She then went on to explain how she sees her work as "a way of creating and rewriting history through the medium of literature."[1] Thus, Parks's attention to history and her signification on the texts, language, figures, and cultural events that shape our lingering and acquired perceptions of that history, from Abraham Lincoln to George Jefferson to the AIDS epidemic, is not surprising. Her works explore the simultaneously formative and deleterious effects that these texts, linguistic structures, figures, and cultural events tend to have on racial and individual identity.

Parks was born on May 10, 1963 in Fort Knox, Kentucky.[2] Yet her father's army service moved her and her family around the United States and the world to locations such as California, North Carolina, Maryland, and West Germany, where she attended high school. For college Parks chose Mount Holyoke. She majored in English and German, and in 1983 she took a short story–writing class with James Baldwin. Baldwin saw potential in her style and suggested she try writing plays. She therefore began crafting "The Sinner's Place," which would become her senior thesis project. The English department awarded the play honors, and Parks graduated Phi Beta Kappa in 1985. Mount Holyoke refused to stage the play, however, on account of its nonconventional form and content, and it later premiered at Hampshire College.

After college Parks studied acting for a year at the London Drama Studio before moving back to New York. *Betting on the Dust Commander* premiered a year later at a tiny New York venue called "The Gas Station," and the International Woman Playwrights Festival staged a reading of "Fishes."

Her first major play was *Imperceptible Mutabilities in the Third Kingdom,* which premiered at the Brooklyn Arts and Cultural Association (BACA) in New York in 1989 to unprecedented critical acclaim and subsequently won an Obie Award for Best New American Play in 1990.

Over the next decade, six new plays premiered—*The Death of the Last Black Man in the Whole Entire World* (BACA Theatre, 1990), *Devotees in the Garden of Love* (Actors Theatre of Louisville, 1992), *The America Play* (Yale Repertory Theatre/Joseph Papp Public Theatre/New York Shakespeare Festival, 1994), *Venus* (Yale Repertory Theatre, 1996), *In The Blood* (New York Public Theatre, 1999), and its companion *Fucking A* (2000, Diverse-Works). In this same period, she wrote three radio plays—*Pickling* (1990), *Locomotive* (1993), *The Third Kingdom* (1993)—and four screenplays—*Anemone Me* (Apparatus, 1992), *Girl 6* (40 Acres and a Mule Filmworks, 1996), *Gal* (unproduced, 1997), and *God's Country* (unproduced, 1997). She also taught at Yale University before becoming the director of CalArts dramatic writing program in 2000.

In July 2001 *Topdog/Underdog,* starring Don Cheadle and Jeffrey Wright and directed by George C. Wolfe, opened at the Joseph Papp Public Theatre. Parks married musician Paul Oscher, who once played in Muddy Waters's band, two days later. Earlier that year, she'd been awarded a MacArthur Foundation Genius Grant. In 2002 *Topdog/Underdog* was awarded the Pulitzer Prize, making Parks the first African American woman to win the honor for drama, and the play moved to Broadway in November.

Her next major dramatic work, *365 Days/365 Plays,* appeared as a play a day for a year, running simultaneously on stages across the county from November 16, 2006, through November 16, 2007. In the meantime Parks released her first novel, *Getting Mother's Body* in 2003, and wrote three more screenplays—the made-for-TV *Their Eyes Were Watching God* (Harpo Films, 2005), *Act V* (in production, 2005), and *The Great Debaters* (Harpo Films, 2006)—as well as a book for the musical *Ray Charles Live!* (2007). Most recently the Joseph Papp Public Theater staged in 2009 *Father Comes Home from the Wars (Parts 1, 8 & 9),* an adaptation of a group of plays from *365 Days/365 Plays,* as well as a new play in 2010, the as-yet-unpublished "The Book of Grace," which follows a Texas waitress, Grace; her domineering macho husband, Vet; and her sexually confused stepson, Buddy, with whom Grace has an affair.[3]

The historically focused elements of Parks's aesthetic position her as an author whose work challenges the ways readers imagine and experience history and/or receive recorded accounts thereof. These texts make history more visceral and relevant by asking readers to see the past as more personal and urgent: history and identity remain ever entwined, haunting each other while still seeking to redeem both the other and itself. Parks's texts represent this tumultuous relationship by revisiting, or, more accurately, by revising some of the most famous texts and contexts in our culture and history. These include Harriet A. Jacobs's *Incidents in the Life of a Slave Girl* (1861); the exploitation of the woman known as the Venus Hottentot; *Carmen Jones* (1954), *The Jeffersons* (1975–85), and other films and television shows with questionable representations of African Americans; Zora Neale Hurston's *Their Eyes Were Watching God* (1937); Nathaniel Hawthorne's *The Scarlet Letter* (1850); Tony Kushner's *Angels in America* (1991/1993); Abraham Lincoln's assassination; and William Faulkner's *As I Lay Dying* (1930) and *Light in August* (1932).

The "revision" inherent in Parks's aesthetic is by no means "revisionist." Indeed it could be read as the inverse of such an approach. Parks belongs to the group of writers and historians who revise history with an eye toward putting absent or neglected groups back into it. Even when she borrows themes or characters from Nathaniel Hawthorne, Harriet Jacobs, William Faulkner, or Tony Kushner, she does not tear these authors' texts apart; instead she builds on them, using them as foundations for a new text. And, through these new texts, we see the old text again. Even when Parks criticizes a past work, as we see *Girl 6*'s questioning of black stage and screen representations, her revisions do not seem to advocate that we wholly dismiss these earlier representations. Rather, her new version of the story suggests that we see these works again with more modern, more critical eyes—eyes that see beyond the surface of the work to the contexts that inform its creation.

African American literature, of course, has no shortage of rich visual metaphors, from W. E. B. Du Bois's double-consciousness in *The Souls of Black Folk* (1903), to Pecola Breedlove's wish for beauty and transformation through eye color in Toni Morrison's *The Bluest Eye* (1970), to John Edgar Wideman's prophetic "Eye" Isaiah in *The Cattle Killing* (1996). These metaphors link vision to identity, knowledge, history, and memory. Thus we would be remiss to forget that "revision" literally means to "see again." The relationship between seeing and writing is mysteriously codependent, as perhaps expressed best by E. M. Forster's often-referenced query from *Aspects of the Novel* (1927): "How can I tell what I think till I see what I say?"[4] Blind writers' composing processes, for example, can differ vastly from those of sighted writers,[5] and Parks herself insists that she maintain control over the way her texts appear on the printed page, regardless of the effect on publishing costs and book prices.[6]

Literary creativity, it seems, transcends normal vision. More than just seeing, it is "vision-ary" because there is inherent within it intent, hope, and the potential for transformation—for the creator and for the created works. The writer, the visionary, must create the sights, the sounds, the feelings of the imagined world so the reader can witness them anew with each reading, be it the first or the ninety-ninth. When an author revises a literary text, he or she asks us not only to see again, but hear again, feel again, experience again. The inevitable consequence of this re-vision, this "seeing again" of the literary world, is that the reader also "sees again" the world outside of the text, the "real world" that contextualizes both the act of writing and the act of reading. When Parks takes a re-vision to the stage/screen and the page, we begin to see again that which we took for granted or that we perhaps never saw in the first place. At the same time, Parks's efforts cannot be reduced to mere mimicry; they are still wholly innovative. Each re-vision creates a new text that connects to, yet remains distinct from, the revised text. Such an aesthetic is best called (re)vision-ary because it is both a seeing again and a wholly new seeing.

Kimberly W. Benston's 1990 article "Facing Tradition: Revisionary Scenes in African American Literature" describes the theoretical roots of this aesthetic. In his examination Benston analyzed important scenes of seeing, reseeing, and reflection in some of the most well-known African American texts, including Frederick Douglass's descriptions of Sophia Auld in his 1845 narrative, the protagonist's moment of racial awakening in James Weldon Johnson's *The Autobiography of an Ex-Coloured Man* (1912), Richard Wright's deconstruction of the father's image in *Black Boy* (1945), and Nettie and Celie's reunion in Alice Walker's *The Color Purple* (1982). Benston has argued that such scenes "present a simultaneous enactment and theorization of consciousness taking place at key textual moments."[7]

In the Douglass example, Benston focused on scenes in which Douglass described the changes he saw when looking on his once-angelic mistress Sophia Auld, who at first showed a "white face beaming with the most kindly emotions" and "did not deem it impudent or unmannerly for a slave to look her in the face. . . . Her face was made of heavenly smiles, and her voice of tranquil music."[8] Slavery, however, quickly undermined Sophia's goodness, and Douglass soon observed, "The fatal poison of irresponsible power was already in her hands, and soon commenced its infernal work. That cheerful eye, under the influence of slavery, soon became red with rage; that voice, made all of sweet accord, changed to one of harsh and horrid discord; and that angelic face gave place to that of a demon."[9] According to Benston, this seemingly unfortunate change actually proved beneficial for Douglass because "rupturing the illusion of reciprocity between Sophia and the hero implies the possibility of an unmediated confrontation with the face of mastery and the consequent liberation of vision from its framing apparatus" and moved him to "mobilize the narrative of self-perceptive emancipation."[10] The change and the growing difference between Douglass and Sophia Auld opened space for Douglass's identity and agency to exist outside of the influence of whiteness in general and the white gaze in particular.

In the revisionary experience, "African American identity looks on an image of being at once external and internal to itself, an echo or expression it must revise in order to see itself." For the writer then, "writing and reading intersect *as* tradition, (re)envisioning blackness as an immanent locus of expressive emancipation."[11] Because white, male, hegemonic power structures have subjugated and marginalized the black subject in life and in art, including text, stage, and screen, the very act of revising becomes a mode of revealing and/or complicating identity for the African American writer. The product of this revelation—the epiphany that accompanies the harmonious juncture of reading and writing, seer and seen—can signify the beginnings of a less oppressive literary tradition that will contain both what is read, both old and born anew, and what is written.

Parks, of course, goes beyond Benston's (re)envisioning because she does not simply engage the history or legacy that a text or context creates; she literally brings another text into her own. Rather than (re)envisioning (responding to/altering a reflection or manifestation), then, Parks's works are more directly revising, seeing the thing/text itself again. Her works thus even more intensely foreground reading, writing, and their impact on identity.

While Parks's texts can certainly stand as complete literary creations independent of their "ur-texts," in order to understand Parks's revisionary agenda most fully, one must read the history or the literature she has revised. The even deeper inherent call in Parks's texts is not just to have read the relevant text and compare it in hindsight to hers, but to read the old text again with the new sight provided by her revisionary work. As a result of this rereading, the old text, still intact, emerges more whole, more complete, and perhaps even more relevant than before it was subject to the revisionary impulse, because the reader's vision is clearer, more inspired, and more informed.

Such reseeing channels Anna Julia Cooper's notion of "the darkened eye restored" in *A Voice from the South* (1892). Describing the effects of suddenly hearing and understanding the black woman's voice after centuries of silence, Cooper observed: "The world has had to limp along with the wobbling gait and one-sided hesitancy of a man with one eye. Suddenly the bandage is removed from the other eye and the whole body is filled with light. It sees a circle where before it saw a segment. The darkened eye restored, every member rejoices with it."[12] Parks's revisionary works connect modern black playwrights with the ill-fated Venus Hottentot, question what became of the freedom promised in Abraham Lincoln's Emancipation Proclamation, and bring Faulkner's dead back to life. Parks removes the bandage that we too often use to hide or ineffectually salve histories or stories that are too complicated or too painful to engage, as well as the bandages we have used to cover the wounds that are gaping holes in history and literature—the stories that have not been passed on.

In "Possession," Parks wrote, "Since history is a recorded or remembered event, theatre, for me, is the perfect place to 'make' history—that is, because so much of African-American history has been unrecorded, disremembered, washed out, one of my tasks as a playwright is to—through literature and the special strange relationship between theatre and real-life—locate the ancestral burial ground, dig for bones, find bones, hear the bones sing, write it down."[13]

Considered alongside Cooper's manifesto, Parks's description of her artistic agenda, which also echoes Alice Walker's description of unearthing her foremothers in *In Search of Our Mothers' Gardens* (1983), becomes all the more imperative. In both Parks's and Cooper's writings, sight and sound combine to create a more complete story, to reveal the invisible, to resurrect the forgotten. For Parks they also create an original text—a text that is simultaneously new and old. Parks asserted specifically of the bones in "Possession" that "their song is a play—something that through a production *actually happens*—I'm working theatre like an incubator to create 'new' historical events. I'm re-membering and staging historical events which, through their happening on stage, are ripe for inclusion in the canon of history. Theatre is an incubator for the creation of historical events—and, as in the case of artificial insemination, the baby is no less human."[14]

This resurrection and creation Parks has described in her essay is especially notable because it follows a clear, step-by-step process. It begins with excavations—with finding and revealing the "truth" about those stories and people previously lost to history. Then there is pause as we hear the bones, and finally there is writing. This second step though, hearing the bones, is more complicated than first impressions might suggest. Hearing the bones singing involves more than just listening, because "their song is a play," and a play must be heard, watched, and, ideally, read. This hearing and watching creates Parks's "new" history—as well as a broader understanding of historiography and its role in identity politics.

But, again, this watching and listening to "hear the bones singing" is not the last step in Parks's revisionary process; the play as production is only the penultimate stage. Next the writer/artist has to "write it down." Once history is created and the baby is born, the witness to this history must record what he or she sees and hears. We often assume that playwrights create a production to be staged, but Parks seems to be telling us in "Possession" that her aesthetic is more circular, and perhaps even infinitely so, than this traditional model of playwriting suggests. Her writing (the written version of the play) actually records an already staged event—historical or literary. In the case of Parks's plays and screenplays then, when the written play is staged again, the original staging—the bones singing—is actually born again, thereby leaving room to let other writers to pick up the story and make it their own old/new story, as if it were a kind of textual-dramatic call and response. For Parks's novel, *Getting Mother's Body,* such a theory of inherently dramatic composition opens countless new avenues for interpretation, most especially for comparative analysis with Parks's earlier works, for even a prose narrative would, according the paradigm she has established, be based on "a play" that was once the bones' song.

Parks also has asserted, "As a playwright I try to do many things: explore the form, ask questions, make a good show, tell a good story, ask more questions, take nothing for granted."[15] And why would she expect anything less from her readers/performers? The underlying message of "From *Elements of Style*" then both inspires and instructs: "This essay is intended primarily for the next generation of theatre makers" (20), for she is both guide and sage to the up-and-coming dramatists. The critics—although they may hungrily hang on her every word—are merely an afterthought.

This dismissal, however, should not discourage critics, but rather encourage them to establish their undeniably vital role in uncovering new dimensions of and beginning new conversations about Parks's works. They can mimic Parks's approach to playwriting in their approach to analysis: "explore the form, ask questions" then "ask more questions, take nothing for granted" (6). In so doing, their arguments at times collide with Parks's assertions about her own work. But rather than hinder the discussion, these moments of disagreement embody the beauty of Parks's revisionary aesthetic. Parks's revised works show that the texts and contexts on which she signifies are still relevant; their histories are still open to interpretation, and new ideas and new players can still be written in. So it is with Parks's own works. Their meanings are not fixed, but open to interpretation, questioning, and even reenvisioning/revising, allowing their importance and their relevance to remain undeniable.

Overall Parks has been and will remain an undeniable force in the African American literary tradition, even if she never writes another word. For as long as Americans are haunted by their histories, they will continue to dig for the bones of their ancestors. For those willing to listen, the bones will always sing. Then those who come to love the songs will write them down, and they will become revisionaries.

CHAPTER 2

"Three-ness" and "the Space in Between"

Imperceptible Mutabilities in the Third Kingdom and *The Death of the Last Black Man in the Whole Entire World*

Critics give Parks's early plays disparate labels: descriptors range from "obtuse," "complicated," and even just "difficult," to "postmodern," "experimental," or simply "poetic." More important, though, these early plays, specifically her first two major productions—*Imperceptible Mutabilities in the Third Kingdom* (1989) and *The Death of the Last Black Man in the Whole Entire World* (1990)—caught the dramatic and literary worlds' attention, and they define and shape Parks's innovative aesthetic, even though she has claimed in essays and interviews that she does not necessarily have one.[1]

The critics' labels do correctly suggest, though, that these two early plays are perhaps most relevant, both individually and as keys to understanding Parks's oeuvre as a whole, because of the ways in which they are *about* language. They do not just use language as a vehicle for other narrative purposes, and linguistic signification is not just a device for revealing larger tropes. The plays instead reveal the ways in which language shapes and is shaped by time, space, and identity—and therefore narrative. These plays examine language through a lens that resembles a kind of "triple-consciousness," a deeply metaphorical and historicized approach to understanding identity that explodes the duality of Du Boisian double-consciousness and reveals the fractured and cavernous liminal spaces in between each side of the "two-ness" described in *The Souls of Black Folk,* as well as between other potentially distortive binaries, including the written/spoken (or page/stage), literal/figurative, and linear/circular.

Imperceptible Mutabilities in the Third Kingdom

Parks's first major work, the Obie Award–winning *Imperceptible Mutabilities in the Third Kingdom,* opened at the BACA Theatre in Brooklyn, New York, in September 1989, to an audience of fewer than one hundred people.[2] According to Shawn-Marie Garrett, the play "signaled the long awaited arrival in the American experimental theatre of a politically minded new playwright of originality and substance, physically possessed by words, mindful of their shapes and powers, and heedful of their long half-lives."[3] It contains five sections—parts 1–4 and a reprise of part 2. Each part introduces new characters—or "players," as Parks has labeled them here—in a new drama; lines often repeat, and in performance actors are often "recycled" as other players in different parts.[4] Part 2, "Third Kingdom," and its reprise provide the strongest framework for understanding the play's approach to language and its impact on identity. These sections, set in the Middle Passage, feature a chorus of "seers"—Kin-Seer, Us-Seer, Shark-Seer, Soul-Seer, and Over-Seer—that together try to make sense of sentiments that seem to exist beyond language.

Kin-Seer articulates the imagery that conjures the slaves' perilous passage across the Atlantic as well as the complicated metaphorical descriptions of the divided self. The player explains a dream in which "I was standin with my toes stucked in thuh dirt. Nothin in front of me but water. And I was wavin. Wavin. Wavin at my other me who I could barely see. Over thuh water on thuh uther cliff I could see my uther me but my uther me could not see me" (38).[5] Kin-Seer is haunted by the divided "me," represented by a visual disconnect. This haunting evolves later in the section when Kin-Seer goes on, "My uther me then waved back at me and then I was happy. But my uther me whudhunt waving at me. My uther me was waving at my Self. My uther me was waving at uh black black speck in thuh middle of thuh sea where years uhgoh from uh boat I had been—UUH!" (38). Here appears a third division, the capital-S *Self,* who both Kin-Seer and his transatlantic counterpart (who Kin-Seer eventually labels "Me") can see, a shared "Self" characterized by both color and time; this Self is "black black" and "years ago." The third self is also situated in a "middle," albeit vast, space, and this space is communal: Kin-Seer "had been" there too.

In *The Souls of Black Folk,* Du Bois wrote that African Americans are "born with a veil, and gifted with second-sight in this American world,—a world which yields him no true self-consciousness, but only lets him see himself through the revelation of the other world. It is a peculiar sensation, this double-consciousness, this sense of always looking at one's self though the eyes of others, of measuring one's soul by the tape of a world that looks on in amused contempt and pity. One ever feels his two-ness,—an American, a Negro; two souls, two thoughts, two unreconciled strivings; two warring ideals in one dark body, whose dogged strength alone keeps it from being torn asunder."[6]

Kin-Seer's dream engages Du Bois's "vision" on visceral and temporal levels. First, Kin-Seer, like the other Seers and most of the other players/figures in Parks's early plays, lacks "true self-consciousness." They are "adrift in time, space, and consciousness," and "their history is scattered, confused, lost."[7] Here Kin-Seer does not even recognize "Me" as part of a "self" until the Over-Seer—the representative of "the other world," the white world—confirms this identity: "thats your *self* youre looking at!" (38). Also both Du Bois's and Parks's paradigms racialize the "body" of the self (one as "dark," the other as "black black") to highlight the legacy of violent disembodiment, both literally and figuratively—that both led to and emerged from this divided identity.

Yet Parks's players do not feel a two-ness; they feel a three-ness. As Kin-Seer continues to try to make sense of this dream, Over-Seer alternately warns that the other seers will be jettisoned (38)—thereby living the historical legacy of the slave ships' barbaric white overseers—and evaluates and interprets Kin-Seer's dream. He declares first, "The second part comes apart in 2 parts," thus making three (38), and ultimately, "Half the world had fallen away making 2 worlds and a sea between. Those 2 worlds inscribe the Third Kingdom," the play's first articulation of its title (39). The Third Kingdom evolves from the fragmentation of one world into two with a fluid space in between. But the Third Kingdom is not just created; it is inscribed—indelibly written or carved—which firmly tethers its existence to language.

The second articulation of the play's title comes from Shark-Seer, who revises the declaration to "In between thuh folks is uh distance thats uh wet space. 2 worlds: Third Kingdom" (39). This confirms the fluidity of the in-between space while also equating the two worlds with "thuh folks," indicative of black history and vernacular culture. The description follows Shark-Seer's more enigmatic articulation of his own dreamscape: "I dream up uh fish that swallowin me and I dream up uh me that is then becamin that fish and uh dream of that fish becamin uh shark and I dream of that shark becamin uh shore. UUH! And on thuh shore thuh shark is given shoes. And I whuduhnt me no more and I whudunht no fish. My new Self was uh third Self made thuh space in between" (39). James Frieze has explained that this dream "evinces, not particular identity positions, but the dynamics of relational identity. In the paradigm of Shark-Seer's fish story, identity is made visible only after it has been swallowed."[8] The Shark-Seer doesn't know what the self is, but he knows what it is not. The Shark-Seer's self emerges somewhere between the (great white?) shark's perception of the fish, which is its prey, and the evolutionary results of the shark's stepping from the water to walk on land. The third self is a product of change and struggle, a struggle not unlike that against the "unreconciled strivings" and "two warring ideals" Du Bois's subject survived through "dogged strength." As Frieze indicated, the third self evolved from the fractured binary of not-fish and not-Me because "nature and ideology both abhor a vacuum [so] the 'space in between' is bound to be filled, to become a interstice in which a new identity is built."[9]

Evolution, of course, implies mutation, and this provides a valuable outline for understanding how language and identity coexist in this section and throughout the play. The "mutabilities" of the play's title also support an emphasis on mutation, even though, as Deborah Geis has noted, Parks's own (perhaps sarcastic) explanation for the play's title refers only to the most basic dictionary definition for the words in the title.[10] This "Third Kingdom" section alone, however, suggests much deeper meanings, beginning with this brief nod toward evolutionary rhetoric.

First, the "imperceptible" here, and in the other parts of the play, implies a disconnect with consciousness. While the word literally signifies that which is barely noticeable because of its size or increment, insomuch as it derives from the verb "to perceive"—which applies to understanding, interpretation, and awareness, especially that which comes from the senses—it calls our attention to the players' struggles with understanding their world and their "selves." So, when Parks's long-time collaborator Liz Diamond asserted that in the world of the play, "change is happening all the time, but evolution is imperceptible," she was linking two of the play's most important themes.[11] As the players react and adapt to changes around them, they cannot immediately understand the effect of these reactions and adaptations, especially the effect on consciousness and therefore, identity. "Mutability," with its roots in the verb "to change," implies a similar openness to changes and to evolutionary mutations; however, since it contains "mute," it also reminds readers of the silencing that often accompanies such changes, especially changes in power and written history.

And because the "imperceptible mutabilities" exist in "the Third Kingdom," the text points to part 2: "Third Kingdom" as the central interpretive space in the play. All the title's interpretive implications for consciousness and evolution within the three-tiered vision of identity, the triple-consciousness, are outlined in this section. Thus it is especially significant that part 2 gives readers the first occurrence of one of the play's major sight/sound wordplays: the double meaning of "kin" as both the modal verb "can" and the noun that signifies relation.

Shark-Seer, the evolutionary mouthpiece, says it first: "How many kin kin I hold. Whole hull full" (39). "Kin" does not appear in this section again, outside of the labels for Kin-Seer's lines; however, it plays a major role in part 3. Philip C. Kolin has given these wordplays the concise label "puns," and he has called them "subversive, explosive." He connected them to Rep & Rev, Parks's jazz-based approach to linguistic signification, and has posited that they function as a tool for "encouraging audiences to see double or triple around the edges of white fictions that have enshackled African Americans."[12] While this pun literally points to the shackles that bound the enslaved in the hulls of slave ships, metaphorical possibilities also abound. Parks claimed that the inherently poetic "Rep & Rev are key in examining something larger than one moment. Rep & Rev create space for metaphor & c."[13] In other words, the linguistic evolution from "kin" to "can" and back again creates an in-between space reminiscent of that which birthed the Third Kingdom.

In this particular pun, the space conjures the Middle Passage and the pestilent suffering caused by the tight-packed slavers. Overall, in fact, the Seers "image a form of seeing which is unwittingly poetic, and display a visionary capacity which is startlingly vivid but horrifyingly incomplete."[14] That is to say, the in-between spaces of language and expression are productive, but they are still limited—perhaps because they help reveal how much is still missing: so many stories of slavery, the Middle Passage, Jim Crow, and other systematic racisms.

Looking back to part 1 of the play, echoes of double-consciousness and the evolution into a triple-consciousness emerge already as productive paradigms for understanding the play's message vis-à-vis language: players both rely on and struggle with language as the mode to express the in between spaces of their fragmented identities. Part 1, subtitled "Snails," follows five main players: three friends, Molly/Mona, Charlene/Chona, and Veronica/Verona; a researcher and "exterminator," The Naturalist/Dr. Lutzky; and a robber with no name and "no speech, who the women have dubbed "Mokus" (26). The women believe that their apartment is infested by a giant cockroach, but the bug is merely The Naturalist/Dr. Lutzky's disguise in an attempt to "conceal himself and observe the object of study—unobserved" (27).

Molly, who is considering suicide (à la Ntzoke Shange's "colored girls" in *For Colored Girls Who Have Considered Suicide When the Rainbow Is Enuf*)[15] at the scene's opening, reflects, "Once there was uh me named Mona who wondered what she'd be like if no one was watchin" (27). This line, a version of which is also spoken by the anonymous shooter in *Topdog/Underdog* (1999), is followed later in the scene by the slightly, but significantly revised, "Once there was uh me named Mona who wondered what she'd talk like if no one was listenin" (28). Garrett has pointed to this later line especially as "a concise rewording of DuBois' double-consciousness and its consequences, with a crucial temporal dimension added."[16] Thus Molly's ability to see herself at alternate points in time—expressed through a channeling of the "once upon a time" structure of traditional narrative—allows her to express and explore the crucial third element of her triple-consciousness, time. Molly's combination of first and third person in these reflections underscores this temporal element's impact on identity. Like Kin-Seer, she sees "me" in "the past" as well as another self, "Mona," who is different still than Molly, the name the play gives her lines.

The shift from "watchin" to "listenin" grows in part from Molly's realization that the cockroach, the disguised white Naturalist/Lutzky—representative of the "other world"—is indeed watching her. Molly struggles with the performative nature of language and its relationship to identity throughout the scene. Specifically her depression seems linked to a teacher's kicking her out of school for her inability to recite requisite lines from a version of "Mary Had a Little Lamb," a plot element that represents the epitome of rote "white as snow" narratives. She explains, "I diduhnt quit that school. HHH. Thought: nope! Mm gonna go on—go on ssif nothing ssapin yuh know? 'S-K' is /sk/ as in 'ask.' The little-lamb-follows-closely behind-at-Marys-heels-as-Mary-boards-the-train. Shit. Failed every test he shoves in my face. He makes me recite my mind goes blank. HHH. The little-lamb-follows-closely behind-at-Marys-heels-as-Mary-boards-the-train. Aint never seen no woman on no train with no lamb. I tell him so. He throws me out. Stuff like this happens every day y know? This isnt uh special case mines iduhnt uh uhnnn" (25).

Molly's construction, with pronunciation-key accuracy, of "'S-K' is /sk/ as in 'ask'" shows her nuanced awareness of and proficiency for language, so a lack of skill cannot account for her "failure." Kolin has argued that when "she is called upon to recite/repeat/valorize white codes and symbols, Molly's mind goes 'blank' because she cannot comprehend or accept the racial fetishization of the totem animal of white purity and salvation. There is no record in Molly's deep racial memory of white icons, but her teacher insists that she dis-remember her black heritage to obliterate any black voices inside her."[17] Molly's "deep racial memory" rejects that which she has not directly witnessed because the lack of witnessing conjures a memory of forced white supremacy, that is, segregation: Mary and her lamb likely did not ride in the Jim Crow car.

This subtle linking of communal memory and racialized history further demonstrates the relationship between identity and temporality that contributes to the "three-ness" the players feel. Since memory and history are inherently hyper-aware of time—based in the past but ever-shaped by the present—Molly and the other players intuit that "history can quite concretely be used against you. . . . Their understanding of the workings of power may be partial, but Parks's figures are historically minded themselves."[18] They know their own present, their own past, and a shared past. And as the scene progresses, Charlene revisits the "Mary Had a Little Lamb" narrative so that the lamb "put uh hex on Mary," and when Mary dies, "thuh lamb was in thuh lead" (27). Here Charlene taps into the hoodoo traditions of African American folk culture to subvert the white narrative's deleterious effects.

Molly's initial reflection about the "Mary Had a Little Lamb" incident comes in scene A of part 1, and the stage directions—minimal in Parks's early plays—that open this scene indicate that Molly and Charlene should share the stage with a slide show containing "images of Molly and Charlene," such that "Molly and Charlene speak as the stage remains semi-dark" (25). Geis observed that this slide show "reveals a gap between what we are told are 'images' of them (Parks leaves the director to choose the images), and their conversation about Molly's leaving school and considering suicide."[19] Similarly Charlene reports later in the scene that despite the fact that the police have "Ninety-nine different versions" of the robber Mokus's picture "on file" none in fact "looked like he looked"; the images are unable to capture his likeness just as a name is unable to signify his—or any one in the play's—identity (28).

A photographic image may perhaps be the epitome of "looking at one's self though the eyes of others," all while time seems to "stand still": the present subject looks at his/her past self through the "lens" of a specific history, memory, or other temporal foundation. By exposing the limits of these images, according to Garrett, "Parks strips away the aura of authenticity surrounding these images, insists that photographic evidence is always constructed through interpretations and dramatizes how distorting and distorted the conclusions drawn from such evidence can be. It makes no difference if the characters try to assert control over the way they are represented by the camera."[20] Thus these images are not without real power, especially over the ways in which history remembers and records identity. Mokus's erroneous mug shots, for example, recall "the history of false accusations and lynching of blacks in America,"[21] and Verona's anxiety over the seeing *Wild Kingdom* host Marlin Perkins "SHOOTING THUH WILD BEASTS!" with a gun on television calls attention to "Perkins's most dangerous weapon," that is, "the lens of his camera that portrayed blacks as savages, part of the jungle landscape in which he identified and defined them."[22]

Photographs play an even more significant role in part 3, "Open House." This section begins with a "double-frame slide show" featuring images of an enslaved woman named Aretha with her charges Anglor and Blanca. The first scene enacts the "photo shoot" that produced these images, and the dialogue here reveals that Aretha is leaving her job as Anglor and Blanca's caretaker. The ensuing scenes chart Aretha's journey to emancipation and her struggles to understand its implications.

Aretha places great faith in the malleability of the photographic images. In the first and last scenes of this section, she is collecting the pictures for her scrapbook, but in both scenes the children are crying. About this, Aretha simply asserts at the end of the section, "Dont matter none. Dont matter none at all. You say its uh cry I say its uh smile. These photographics is for my scrapbook. Scraps uh graphy for my book. Smile or no smile mm gonna remember you. Mm gonna remember you grinnin" (54). Memory makes meaning fluid; Aretha will see what she wants to see in the pictures.

And while this section's stage directions provide somewhat more detail about what types of images should appear in the opening slide show, the lack of tangible specifics here and in part 1 about what photographs the director shows in a production adds to the play's rejection of photographic "evidence." If the photos are really are as important as Aretha's obsession suggests, then the choice of images—and the amount of narrative/temporal disconnect between the photographs and the action in the play—could radically change the play's meaning. Thus the ambiguity implies that what is said (the language) and the presence of the images in juxtaposition to that language (thereby revealing the images' inadequacy) is by far more valuable for understanding the play's meaning. Indeed Aretha's interest here seems to lie not as much in the quality or authenticity of the image, but rather in "the idea of archiving."[23] In labeling them "graphy," she actually equates the images with written, rather than visual, traditions.

The most important written text vis-à-vis identity in part 3 is "the book," a nebulous, fluid, and destructive record that functions as "the undisputed text of empowerment and erasure."[24] The play links the book to the players' triple-consciousness by having the book answer the central query Shark-Seer first poses in "Third Kingdom" and that Mona poses here in "Open House": How many kin kin I hold. Whole hold full" (42).

Miss Faith, a quasi-religious messenger, reads and interprets the book; she also brutally pulls out all of Aretha's teeth and takes pictures of them to archive in this "great chronicle" (46). As Aretha ponders how she is going to accommodate the kin and strangers she plans to meet, Miss Faith first responds with a series of "footnotes" citing historical data on an "English slaver, the *Brookes*"—including the size of the hull (3,250 square feet), the number of slaves transported (600, "although it only has room for 451"), and the ratio of male to female slaves (2:1) generally on board (43–44). These footnotes/citations situate the text as part of codified written history, and while this text seems at first to include valuable information about the African American experience, it soon becomes the tool that Miss Faith uses to extend the *Brookes*'s atrocities to Aretha's visitors. She tells Aretha, "You give the facts. I draw from them, Maam. I draw from them in accordance with the book. Six hundred will fit. We will have to pack them tight" (44). When Aretha protests, Miss Faith replies, "We know well that 'she who cheateth me out of some valuable square inches shall but cheat herself out of her assigned seat aside the most high.' We are familiar with Amendment 2.1 are we not, Mrs. Saxon?" (44). The legal and faux-Evangelical tone of these passages thus parallel the book with religious texts and the United States Constitution, thus indicting both for enabling racism.

The book creates and perpetuates a three-tiered identity because it describes the past, rules the present, and predicts the future—all with an eye toward bolstering the institutions that have and will continue to oppress and fragment black identity. Aretha's visitation with her kin/strangers is prophesied there, as is her expiration on 19–6–65 (Juneteenth), and her dental extractions (43, 47, 46). When Aretha protests the latter, Miss Faith retorts that the teeth must be removed so they can be photographed and "entered in the book"; she explains, "think of it as getting yourself chronicled, Mrs. Saxon. You are becoming a full part of the great chronicle! Say that, Mrs. Saxon. You don't want to be forgotten, do you?" (46). In order to be remembered, in Miss Faith's and the book's model of history, Aretha must be disembodied, her mouth left full of holes, spaces that "the book has promised" it will fill with new teeth.

The book also advocates a specific interpretation of memory. Charles, Arthea's former owner, describes this vision of memory in the next scene. He says, while taking Aretha's picture, "Memory is a very important thing, don't you know. It keeps us in line. It reminds us of who we are, memory. Without it we could be anybody. We would be running about here with no identities. . . . There would be chaos, chaos it would be without knowledge from whence we came" (48). Memory in this model relies on linear and hierarchical narratives to define identity. Thus it "privileges white identity" and "upholds white, not black, history and values."[25] Black identity exists here, but only in relation and in service to the white self and its power structures. Ironically, then, Charles's memory model is thoroughly ahistorical because it does not acknowledge the contributions and complexities of African American experience. This type of memory model therefore bifurcates the past into white/black power and history, a binary that divides the world and creates a Third Kingdom, a triple-consciousness.

Memory and remembering are also key themes in part 4: "Greeks (or the Slugs)." In this section Mr. Sergeant Smith waits anxiously for a "Distinction" from the army. His wife, Mrs. Sergeant Smith, and their children, Buffy, Muffy, and Duffy, systematically survey his letters for information about the distinction and his homecoming. Yet Mr. Sergeant Smith earns this distinction and returns to his family only after a mine severs both of his legs. This is an ironic injury since part 4 makes puns of *mine* (explosive), *mine* (claiming, especially relationship—in this case, paternity), and *mine* (dig, as if to excavate) and of *dismembers* (stricken from memory, an opposite of remembers) and *dismembers* (divided).

Mines appear first in the martial sense but are nonetheless linked to Sergeant Smith's relationship to his daughter Muffy. In an effort to reassure Muffy of her father's love when he does not mention her in his letters, Buffy and Mrs. Smith try to explain that the letters might be heavily censored, dismembered by a nebulous authority. Buffy offers, "Sergeant Smith, Muff, deals in a language of codes—secret signs and signals. Certain ways with words that are plain to us could, for Sergeant Smith, spell the ways of betrayal, right, Mrs. Smith? Notice he only says 'Commander.' He isn't allowed to mention his Commander by name. We say Muffy every day but for Sergeant Smith saying your name would be gravely dangerous" (64). Muffy doubts this explanation and begins the following exchange:

MUFFY. Muffy's not gravely dangerous.
MRS. SMITH. Muffy—Muffy—Muffy sounds like minefield. What uh mine, Mufficent?
MUFFY. A mine is a thing that dismembers. Too many mines lose the war.
MRS. SMITH. Good girl.
MUFFY. Remember the Effort. (64)

Sergeant Smith's forgetting to mention Muffy's name and Muffy's name connected, albeit in an aural stretch, to mines thereby creates the dismembered/

dismembered (forgotten) pun. Insofar as forgetting Muffy—especially in contrast to her call to "remember the Effort," that is, Sergeant Smith's devotion to the army—also equates to a disownership, the *mine* (explosive) and *mine* (claiming) also starts here.

As with the kin/can pun introduced in the "Third Kingdom" section, the evolution of meaning from one element of the pun to the other and back again creates an in-between space evocative of that which has formed the Third Kingdom, the play's dominate metaphor for triple-consciousness. In these particular puns, the space conjures memories of slavery as well as lynching and offers a "multi-layered view of how black memory and bodies have been tragically liked—semantically and anatomically—for dis-memberment, destruction in white America."[26]

After Sergeant Smith returns near the end section, though, Muffy revises her initial line to "You stepped on a mine. I read it in the paper. A mine is a thing that remembers. Too many mines lose the war. Remember the Effort. The mine blew his legs off" (70). Sergeant Smith responds only with "You one uh mines?," which he then repeats twice, demonstrating his attempt to "mine" his memory for recollections that will allow him to recognize his children (70). The failure of this mining means that Sergeant Smith's forgetting, the dismemberment/dis-memberment is complete; the fragmentation is physical, subconscious, and linguistic.

Sergeant Smith attempts to explain this fragmentation in the play's closing soliloquy. He laments, "Time for noble seems past. Time for somthin noble was yesterday. There usedta be uh overlap of four hours. Hours in four when I'd say 'today' and today it'd be. Them four house usta happen together, now, they scatters theirselves all throughout the day" (71). Indicative of the triple-consciousness that evolves in the Third Kingdom, this fragmentation is fundamentally temporal. Sergeant Smith remembers a time when the boundaries between his present self and past self were clearer and more linear; his "today" self and his "yesterday" self overlapped, allowing a myriad of possibilities for his future and his potential to do "somethin noble" therein. Now that his "four hours" are disembodied and fluid, he can see only the unfulfilled desire of the past and the inevitable and irreconcilable striving of the future. He, like most of the players in the play, is stuck in "the space in between"—in between fragmented and timeless selves and in between language and that which it tries to express.

Therefore, Garrett has suggested, "The play itself becomes a Third Kingdom, where meanings converge and mutate in a language of codes, signs, and symbols that always remain half-secret."[27] As such the text both describes and enacts each player's triple-consciousness. The secrecy Garrett describes, however is not a death sentence; triple-consciousness, like its Du Boisian ancestor, is at once a "peculiar sensation," a vision with which one is "gifted," and a struggle against constant change, but it is nevertheless still consciousness. Awareness triumphs in this kingdom, even if that triumph remains—at least initially—almost imperceptible.

The Death of the Last Black Man in the Whole Entire World

Parks's second major play, *The Death of the Last Black Man in the Whole Entire World,* premiered in 1990, also at the BACA,[28] and, according to Robert Brustein, it "is too densely written for one mind to absorb at a single sitting."[29] The play follows Black Man with Watermelon, Black Woman with Drumstick, and a chorus of other carefully named "figures," including "Lots of Grease and Lots of Pork," "Before Columbus," and "And Bigger and Bigger and Bigger." Black Man with Watermelon faces a series of executions and resurrections over the course of the play while the figure called "Voice on Thuh Tee V" reports the death of "the absolutely last living Negro man in the whole entire known world" (110).[30]

The three-tiered model of identity formation, triple-consciousness, informs this play as well. In fact the form of the play as a whole underscores the paradigm's applicability. As Alice Rayner and Harry J. Elam explained, "Parks's interest in the 'space in between' is evident in the structure of *Death of the Last Black Man.* Parks divides the play into three panels—'Thuh Holy Ghost,' 'Thuh Lonesome 3some,' and 'In Thuh Garden of HooDoo It'—which are transacted by two choruses; a 'final chorus' follows the last panel. The Choruses attempt to refigure the gaps or spaces in between the three panels"[31]—just as the chorus in *Imperceptible Mutabilites* gives voice to the Third Kingdom as a metaphor for understanding identity in that play.

In panel 1, "Thuh Holy Ghost," Black Woman with Fried Drumstick (henceforth "Black Woman") and Black Man with Watermelon (henceforth "Black Man") discuss Black Man's return from repeated executions. Meanwhile Black Woman keeps offering him hen to eat. This panel revisits two central identity-based themes, linked to triple-consciousness, from *Imperceptible Mutabilities:* temporal fragmentation and wordplay with the word "mine."

Panel 1's title, "Thuh Holy Ghost," symbolizes a part of a triune whole, and the scene supports this three-ness with Black Woman's description of Black Man's Christ-like capture and resurrection—a description that closely parallels both Kin-Seer's and Molly's descriptions of their own divided selves in *Imperceptible Mutabilities.* She recounts, "They comed from you and tooked you. That was yesterday. Today you sit in your chair where you sat yesterday and thuh day afore yesterday afore they comed and took you. Things today is just as they are yesterday cept nothing is familiar cause it was such a long time uhgoh" (107). Black Woman's yesterday, today, and "long time uhgoh" coexist, but in a jumbled and fragmented state. Thus Black Woman's ability to see herself at alternate points in time, like Molly's, allows her to express and explore the crucial temporal element of her triple-consciousness. Black Woman's combination of verb tenses in her reflections underscores this temporal element's impact on identity. Like Molly, she sees from three perspective: "you," "they," and the implied first person. Thus Black Woman's reflection also incorporates the relational and communal elements of triple-consciousness; she shares this history/memory with both Black Man ("you") and the "they" that both formed from him and took him away to his death.

As in *Imperceptible Mutabilities,* this death—here an execution by electric chair and later a lynching—represents the violent history mapped by the space that is in between these three identities. It parallels the disembodied abstract self with the literal physical disembodiment of racialized punishment. "The chair" in Black Woman's memory in fact becomes the electric chair that "they" used to kill Black Man. When there is not "enough electric" to execute him on the porch, they "put the Chair in the thuh middle of thuh City. Outdoors. In thuh square. Folks come tuh watch with picnic baskets" (107); he is then buried in "uh mass gravesite" (109). This move from the Black Man's individual execution to the long and brutal history of lynching, which—as shown in studies such as *Without Sanctuary*[32]—often attracted crowds of enthusiastic white spectators, not only equates lynching and the modern capital punishment, but also highlights the history of both as shared, persistent, and destructive.

This destruction shapes Black Man's language, specifically his engagement with the word *mine.* But while *Imperceptible Mutabilities* uses the *mine* (explosive)/*mine* (ownership)/*mine* (digging) pun, this play contrasts mine with the plural *mines.* Plurality alone signals a connection to multiple selves, but the mine/mines relationship's implications extend far past grammar. In the opening lines of the panel, for example, Black Man says, "Saint mines. Saint mines. Iduhnt it. Nope: iduhnt. Saint mines cause everythin I call mines got uh print uh me someway on it in it dont got uh print uh me someway on it so saint mines. Duhduhnt so saint: huh" (105). He repeats "saint mines" throughout the scene while also wondering first "who gived birth tuh this I wonder who," then "who gived birth tuh me I wonder" (105). Later lines in the scenes clarify that "it" and "this" are the watermelon that names him. In this opening declaration, Black Man asserts that he can claim only that which he recognizes as being or bearing some kind of a reflection of himself. This reflection is a "print," a mark that suggests written text, so the accompanying questions of origins connect this assertion to identity and its relationship with written language. Black Man's inability to see himself in the watermelon that names him, though, shows his initial disconnection with stereotypes that define him in written history.

Black Man does, however, see himself in his own physical body—or parts of it. *Mine* first appears when Black Man claims his feet. He explains, "I kin tell whats mines by whats got my looks. Ssmymethod. Try it by testing it and it turns out true. Fool proofly. Look down at my foot and wonder it its mine. Foot mine? I kin ask it and foot answers back with uh "yes Sir"—not like you and me say "yes Sir" but uh "yes sir" peculiar to thuh foot. Foot mine? I kin as it and through uh look that looks like my looks thuh foot gives me back uh 'yes Sir.' Ssmymethod. Try by thuh test tuh pass for true. Move on tuh thuh other foot. Foot mine? And uh nother 'yes Sir' so feets mine is understood. Got uh forearm thats up for question check myself out teeth by tooth. Melon mines?—. Dont look like me" (107). Black Man confidently claims his foot, so the singular *mine* signals a level of certainly about his identity and physicality; his body is an embodiment of himself insomuch as it looks like him, and he feels he can confirm its identity as part of himself. But this claiming is not without complications. The foot has its own way of speaking that is peculiar, different than Black Man's; thus language separates the man from this body, and since he also has "uh forearm thats up for question," he remains significantly disembodied.

The self conversing with its parts also links this scene back to Kin-Seer's vision of his three selves trying to communicate across the ocean and from the space in between, as well as to Molly's conversation with her temporally disconnected selves in *Imperceptible Mutabilities*. These connections strengthen as Black Man's identity fragments further. A few lines after claiming his feet and disowning the watermelon, Black Man is asking the question again, "Later comes now: melon mine?," and then, "Later ought to now by now huh?: melon mine?"—this time with the "s" missing (107). But the "s" returns for the final two questions, which stand alone in their own lines as simply "melon mines?" (107–8).

The difference between these sets of question is time frame; the former look ahead to the future and its collision with the present. Here Black Man's "third self" is revealed: in the space that is created between Black Man's present self and future self, there is a moment in which Black Man can see himself in the watermelon—and therefore the historical stereotyping of African Americans that this watermelon represents. As in Kin-Seer's vision, this fluid in-between space of identity is communal and radicalized. Stereotypes sanctioned by white hegemonic historiography perpetuate destructive misrepresentations of black culture that reenact a pseudo-slavery, and through the figures in this play, "Parks challenges and satirizes these stereotypes and questions their origins."[33]

In the two choruses in between panels, other stereotypes find voice through the figures that name them, and familiar elements of triple-consciousness—namely temporal disconnection and racialized historical spaces—emerge. In the First Chorus, for example, we meet Voice on Thuh Tee V, who along with the ultraliterary Prunes and Prisms, represents "language media figures."[34] Voice on Thuh Tee V gives evokes the play's title. The voice reports, "Good evening. I'm Broad Caster. Headlining tonight: the news: is Gamble Major, the absolutely last living Negro man in the whole entire known world—is dead. Major, Gamble, born a slave, taught himself the rudiments of education to become a spearhead in the Civil Rights Movement. He was 38 years old. News of Majors death sparked displays of controlled jubilation in all corners of the world" (110).

A few lines later, the voice repeats the news with slight revisions: "Good evening. Broad Caster. Headline tonight: Gamble Major, the absolutely last living Negro man in the whole known entire world is dead. Gamble Major born a slave rose to become a spearhead in the Civil Rights Movement. He was 38 years old. The Civil Rights Movement. He was 38 years old" (110).

The changes, classic Parks "Rep & Rev" (her method for "working to create a dramatic text that departs from the linear narrative style to look and sound like a musical score",)[35] emphasize the temporal disconnect involving Gamble Major's birth, death, and his accomplishments. The repetition of "thirty-eight years old" and "Civil Rights Movement" emphasizes the anachronism. In order to have been this reported age, Gamble Major would have lived simultaneously in past, present (the setting of the play), and future—a three-tiered identity. The missing elements—omitted action and detail—not only enact the space between these identities but also reveal the incompleteness and inaccuracy of black images in the media, thereby offering a "critique of dominant language and media as they disempower black identity.[36] Like the photographs of *Imperceptible Mutabilities,* these images, with their limited perspective, distort the self and its history.

The Second Chorus also takes issue with history, specifically written histories such as the Bible. Here Ham—a character with heavy literary and cultural baggage including, but not limited to, Noah's cursed son, a cured meat, a Zora Neale Hurston play, an August Wilson play, and an African juba[37]—recites his "Begotten Tree," a "densely linguistic" parody of biblical lineage.[38] He begins, "NOW: She goned begotten One who in turn begotten Ours. Ours laughed one day uhloud in from tuh sound hittin thuh air smakity sprung up I, you, n He, She, It" (121), and eventually concludes, "Me-Mines gived out 2 offspring one she called Mines after herself thuh other she called Themuhuns named after all them who comed before. Themuns married outside the tribe joinin herself with uh man they called WhoDatDere. Mines joined with Wasshisname and from that union come AllYall" (122).

The choice of text on which to signify reflects the play's interest in the evolution of identity and African American cultural expression; the Bible in general, and Genesis in particular, describes not only the origins of the body but of the soul, the self. According to Heidi J. Holder, "The Biblical model here provided one of history's great (if somewhat mind numbing) representations of the distant past: a coherent sequence, a neat line of descent. Parks's first revision is to substitute for the names words of stereotypical African-American dialect (with a distinct minstrel-show flavor). The inserted words call to mind the breaking of neat lines of descent, of family coherence, by the institution of slavery; the form and the content here begin to go to war."[39] The space between form and content, between linear and fragmented narratives of descent and development, again inscribes the tragic and shared past. The passage's use of first, second, and third person underscores this three-sided perspective on identity and the origins of triple-consciousness in text and language.

Origins—and endings—are also at issue in the play's final panel, "In Thuh Garden of HooDoo It." Here Black Woman is still trying to get Black Man to eat, but the conversation quickly devolves into a deeply metaphorical discussion of relational identity and then into a series of repeating phrases in which the figures appear, for a time, to be stuck. Near the middle of the scene, Black Man offers an extended examination of his place in time and space. He muses: "We sittin on this porch right now aint we. Uh huhn. Aaah. Yes. Sittin right here right now on it in it aint the first time either iduhnt it. Yep. Nope. Once we was here once wuhduhnt we. Yep. Yep. Once we being here. Uh huhn. Huh. There is a Now and There is a Then. Ssall there is" (126). In this initial observation, there is present, a past, and a semiforgotten past; yet Black Man tries to simplify this binary into "Now" and "Then."

The written text of the play itself, however, resists this binary and elaborates on Black Man's observations with a lengthy parenthetical addendum. Parentheses signal that the words therein are afterthoughts or, as the "Author's Notes: From 'The Elements of Style'" preceding *Venus* indicates, asides to be "softly spoken."[40] This addendum, though, illustrates nuances of Black Man's vision of identity and abandons the binary he first offered: "(I bein in uh Now: uh Now bein in uh Then: I bein, in Now, in Then, in I will be. I was be too but that's uh Then thats past. That me that was-be is uh me-has-been. Thuh Then that was-be is uh has-been-Then too. Thuh me-has-been sits in thuh be-me; we sit on this porch. Same porch. Same me. Thuh Then thats been somehow sits in thuh Then that will be: same Thens. I swing from uh tree. You cut me down and bring me back. Home. Here. I fly over the yard. I fly over the yard in all over. Them thens stay fixed. Fixed Thens. The Thems stays fixed too. Thuh Thems that come and take me and thuh Thems that greet me and then them Thems that send me back here. Home. Stays fixed, them do)" (126).

Here we see Black Man, like Kin-Seer, working his way—through language—into a fuller understanding of identity. His awareness is tripled on multiple levels: he sees the Then/Now/"will be," the I/me/we, as well as the I/me/Them. In the latter, "Them" and their corresponding "Then" are fixed, a contrast to the fluidity generally found in the spaces between the selves. "Them," suggestive of a ubiquitous white racism—the entity responsible for Black Man's continual capture, death, and resurrection, keep him "in a liminal space between the living and the dead. He is dislocated, caught in a continual 'Middle Passage.'"[41] But "Them" is also stuck. Their narrow view of history and humanity keeps them from advancing, evolving, or growing, and, unlike Black Man's situation, here there is no hope for freedom from this stasis.

Black Man's repeating narrative ends with his final burial; yet the play implies that he will continue to exist, not through resurrection, but through memory. He asks his wife (and she asks him back), "Re-member me," and his final words to her are "Call on me sometime." Memory in this play functions as a site for healing; it is a place, Black Woman's closing line suggests, where Black Man can complete his evolution "From one tuh 3 tuh many" (128). He joins the collective consciousness of those who have passed, and she may still call on his spirit and the spirits of all who came before as she continues her own journey. Although he now rests in relative peace, Black Man is not dead as long as he lives in Black Woman's—and the audience's—memories.

CHAPTER 3

"Deliberate Calculation" in Money, Sex, and Black Plays

Venus

A discussion of complicity appears in nearly every critical and scholarly examination of Suzan-Lori Parks's *Venus* (1996), the fictionalized life story of Saartjie Baartman, the Venus Hottentot, who performed in England and France in the early nineteenth century. *Venus* follows a young South African woman (The Girl) who agrees to go to England to make "a mint" as an "exotic dancer" who shows off her ample buttocks and perhaps her genitals (20).[1] Not long after her arrival in England, however, The Girl's "business partner" leaves her with the greedy Mother-Showman, who transforms The Girl into The Venus and puts her on display in a cage and charges admission to see her. The Venus is "rescued" by The Baron Docteur, a rich man with whom she has a love affair, but who eventually abandons her to die so that he can dissect her corpse and become a famous anatomist.

Most interpretive questions about the play and Parks's motive for creating it center on whether Parks and her version of the Venus Hottentot contribute to black female exploitation as well as whether Parks and her Venus are working for or against what critics generally describe as some kind of oppressor, exploiter, colonizer, or white sexist and racist hegemony (and to what degree). These critics generally engage this question of complicity in the play with an eye toward either completely indicting Parks and her Venus or completely exonerating them. Yet the play actually supports both interpretations simultaneously.

In her essay "new black math" (2005) Parks presented a poetic manifesto on the nature of African American theater. She wrote, "A black play is simple. / A black play is COMPLICATED."[2] These lines—one of many paradoxical descriptions in the essay—indicate that for Parks theatrical work is inherently contradictory and messy. So, in *Venus,* she and her Venus can be working within, as well as against, the forces that oppress them. The seemingly illogical nature of this paradox does not destabilize the linear narrative of the play or its revolutionary implications, because, as Parks has suggested, "A black play is double voiced but rarely confused."[3]

So, in *Venus,* what appears to be complicity may be simultaneously read as subversive agency. The play's protagonist, The Venus,[4] acts with what Harriet A. Jacobs called "deliberate calculation" (83),[5] opting for a life based on personal choice rather than external force. Parks's protagonist chooses potential fame and fortune in a form of exploitation that she hopes she can live with over certain slavery as well as unknown and potentially unbearable exploitation. The play makes economics a central factor in this decision and, significantly, in many of the meta-performative aspects of the play—including the greed that eventually leads to The Venus's death and "scientific" display. As such, *Venus* parallels the plight of The Venus, as well as other characters in the play, with that of the modern African American playwright. The modern playwright must choose between catering to the paying public—white and black—and thus allowing her plays to be seen (and read); or the playwright can hope to be miraculously discovered but will more likely face obscurity. At the same time, however, by writing Baartman's story for the stage, the original site of her exploitation, and by profiting from the presentation of this story, Parks maps the theater as a productive and profitable, though still problematic, healing space for African American playwrights. *Venus* as a whole, then, reinforces Parks's descriptions of the paradoxical nature of black plays.

The Venus's agency on stage also reasserts and depathologizes the black female claim to sexual autonomy, a move that channels Jacobs's similar assertions in her 1861 narrative. Jacobs's description of her "deliberate calculation" came after she had decided to choose a lover—one whom she does not love—rather than be raped by her master. Similarly The Venus still faces sexual exploitation in private and public, but her influence over The Baron Docteur and other men in the play does allow her some power and economic advantage that she ordinarily would not have. When their sexual deviance and greed become too potent even for her shameless sexuality to overcome, her agency—as well as her life—are lost.

Parks comes under heavy fire from critics such as Jean Young, who objected to what she saw as *Venus*'s ahistorical portrayal of "Baartman's complicity in her own exploitation;" Young argued that Parks's Venus "reifies the perverse imperialist mind set, and her mythic historical reconstruction subverts the voice of Saartjie Baartman."[6] *New York Times* theater critic Ben Brantley agreed that Parks "doesn't present Baartman as just an uncomprehending victim," but he applauded this decision and the play's accessibility to a broad audience.[7] Anne Davis Basting, on the other hand—citing Parks's repetition of the phrase "Do I have a choice?" and the presence of a flashing NO sign in the Public Theatre's staging of the play—saw the characters in *Venus* as caught up in "physical and economic threats and the weighty momentum of colonialism and sexism."[8] The Venus certainly engages the imperial/hegemonic/white power with innovative and creative tactics, but these tactics are not historically unique.

Jacobs provided a model of a nineteenth-century woman who claimed agency through what some might call complicity—choosing a relationship with a white man. Complicity implies not only consent, but also, in this specific instance, cooperation or collaboration in a completely malignant enterprise. Agency, on the other hand, most simply implies embracing the potential for action—with no moral judgment implied—that serves as an instrument to an end, especially a subversive end. So, in both Jacobs's and The Venus's case, their decisions do not definitively make them complicit in their oppression, for both the morality and the extent of their shares (monetary and otherwise) in the endeavor are questionable. Even if they were equal partners with their oppressors in an endeavor that might be judged evil, accepting this alliance could still be called agency and still be subversive if it brought them some measure of freedom.

The play addresses this agency/complicity at its opening and its closing. Near the beginning and the end of *Venus,* there are lines that can be read as the "bottom line," or the moral of the story. At the beginning of the play, The Mans Brother, later The Mother-Showman, later The Grade School Chum—a conglomeration of three of the play's most despicable characters—speaks the lines. This conglomeration asserts, "Tail end of r tale for there must be an end / is that Venus, Black Goddess, was shameless, she sinned or else / completely unknowing of r godfearin ways she stood / totally naked in her iron cage" (5). But later, in her penultimate utterance of the play, The Venus herself delivers a slightly revised and expanded version of the same lines. She offers: "Tail end of the tale for there must be uh end / is that Venus, Black Goddess, was shameless, she sinned or else / completely unknowing thuh Godfearin ways she stood / showing off her ass in her iron cage. / When Death met Love Death deathd Love / and left Love tuh rot / *au naturel* end for thuh Miss Hottentot. / Loves soul, which was tidy, hides in heaven, yes, thats it / Loves corpse stands on show in museum. Please / visit" (161). Both lines portray The Venus as an unrepentant sinner, standing before her spectators. Yet both lines also highlight her captivity. She does not cower or hide, but she is, after all, in an "iron cage."

Considering the repetition and revision (Parks's "Rep and Rev") between the two passages, however, reveals much more complexity. The Venus asserts her individuality by changing the "r" to "thuh," making it individual, rather than collective. At the same time, she resists letting the story define her, for she does not call it "my" tale. She makes a similar article change before "godfearin," which she also revises with capitalization to "Godfearin." This move not only channels The Venus's conversion to Christianity earlier in the play, but also moves the locus of moral power away from The Mother-Showman and the spectators to a higher, more holy moral arbiter.

Also both passages contain the word *shameless,* evoking other occurrences of "shame" throughout the play. The Mother-Showman, for example, tells one of her customers that The Venus's "heathen shame is real" and immediately turns to Venus to say, "Lets give these folks their moneys worth" (46). The Mother-Showman assumes that the exposed Venus, who refuses to remove the small cloth covering her genitals because "its custom" (29) and whose "face was streamed with tears" (47) as she stood in her cage, expresses shame through her modesty and sadness. The use of "shameless," voiced by The Mans Brother, later The Mother-Showman, and later The Grade School Chum, then, asserts that The Venus has grown so accustomed to her shame, to being locked in a cage and stared at—or touched—by strangers, that she is numb to it. However, according to Harry J. Elam, Jr., and Alice Rayner, "There is no moment, in fact, when Saartjie really does seem to accept her circumstances or her treatment as shameful. Terrible, filthy, miserable, brutal, but never shameful. In the refusal of shame, she maintains an innocence that is not complicity; if it is still within the systems of oppression, it is nevertheless resistant."[9] "Shame" implies that The Venus has complete control over the situation that puts her on stage and makes her a spectacle.[10] Although she comes to find agency *within* her situation, she never has power *over* it. Like Jacobs, who regretted the actions to which the "demon slavery" drove her, The Venus, or at least the authorial voice behind her, also seems to claim—in the words of her contemporary—that those "whose homes are protected by law" and "whose purity has been sheltered from childhood," should not "judge the poor desolate slave girl too severely!" (83–84).

For The Venus, what would be truly disgraceful would be "to go home penniless," and she finds her agency in the promise of economic prosperity (75). When The Man and The Brother present their scheme for an exotic exhibition in England to The Venus, then The Girl, and tell her of her central role and her supposed share in the profits, she dreams, "I would have a house. / I would hire help. / I would be rich. Very rich. / Big bags of money!," but she then asks, "Do I have a choice? Id like to think on it." The Brother, like The Baron Docteur later in the play, answers her question only with a question: "Whats there to think on? Think of it as a vacation! / 2 years of work take half the take. / Come back here rich. Its settled then" (17). From The Girl he demands another answer and thus clearly establishes himself as master of the conversation and indeed the entire situation. Even The Brother's comment that follows, "Think it over, Girl. Go on. / Think it all over," is phrased more like an order than a reassurance of actual choice (17). This is relevant, of course, because while The Girl does indeed have a choice, it is, like Jacobs's choice, the choice between one evil and a lesser evil.

According to Young, one of the play's harshest critics, "Parks frames the scenario around Baartman (The Girl) in this regard: She is a liberated and sovereign individual, capable, willing, and with the authority to control her circumstances and make choices," and this is problematic because it minimizes The Girl's oppression and makes her appear fully complicit in this oppression.[11] But again, agency, or choice, and complicity need not be equated. The Girl's choices only include denying The Man and The Brother, which would likely have resulted either in her kidnapping or in her remaining a slave in Africa, or willingly going with the men. If she signs their contract, she may get the fame and money (or at least a portion of it) they have promised in a country that might be more sympathetic to her oppression, for there, the men tell her, she could be "a Princess" and there will be "a whole street full" of women just like her (16). This ultimately is choice—but not complete freedom. When The Chorus of the Court asks, "Are you here of yr own free will / or are you under some restraint?," The Venus evades the question and responds only with "Im here to make a mint" (75). She has embraced what little agency she has and is using it to move toward the more hopeful and potentially more economically viable option, but she will not call this "free will."

A look at Jacobs's history shows that such an unattractive choice was sometimes the only option available to a black woman in the nineteenth century; thus Parks's depiction of The Venus might not be as ahistorical as Young has alleged. Jacobs described how she knew her situation was dire, for "The influences of slavery had had the same effect on me that they had on other young girls; they had made me prematurely knowing, concerning the evil ways of the world"; so, she writes, "I know what I did, and I did it with deliberate calculation" (83). She goes on to hail the minor liberation, "something akin to freedom" that comes from choice, in that "it seems less degrading to give one's self, than to submit to compulsion" (84–85). Jacobs also admits to an economic element of her agency: "Of a man who was not my master I could ask to have my children well supported; and in this case, I felt confident I should obtain the boon" (85–86). Jacobs—who knew she was destined for sexual oppression—found in her white lover a way to use her agency to secure her children's security and perhaps even their freedom. Thus Jacobs provided a model of nineteenth-century black womanhood that can help make sense of *Venus*'s assertion of agency as subversive. In her version of "the bottom line," The Venus revises the earlier description of her standing "totally naked" to one of herself "showing off her ass," evoking the slang phrase for challenging authority with blatant defiance.[12]

Elizabeth Brown-Guillory has examined this moment in conjunction with The Venus's earlier "Do I have a choice?" line, which "speaks volumes in identifying a woman, as figured in Parks's imagination, who conceivably could have chosen between subjugation by the Dutch colonizers in her native South Africa and exploitation with the possibility of some monetary reward in England and France. One way to read Venus—alias Saartjie—is as an insurgent female character who understands that though she remains an object of patronymic exchange, she also remains capable of resistance. Interestingly, borrowing from the black vernacular, Venus chooses to 'show her ass' as a strategy of resistance."[13]

As the play goes on, it becomes clearer that The Girl/The Venus knows the limits of her choices. For example, when The Brother declares his desire for her after they arrive in England, The Girl responds, "Home? / Love? / You outta take me shopping. I need a new dress. / I cant be presented to society in this old thing" (23). Here The Girl questions or problematizes the options that seem to be available to her—but ultimately are not—and speaks declaratively of the only certainties she has known: greed and economic or sexual exploitation.[14] She uses her seduction for material gain, knowing that The Brother and The Baron Docteur will eventually abandon her. Problematizing the options also suggests that this material gain is not The Venus's ideal choice. "Scene 22: Counting the Take/The Deal That Was" is one of the most obviously money-focused in the play as The Venus and The Mother-Showman count the money—The Venus in multiples of ten, The Mother-Showman in hundreds. In this scene The Venus mentions she could "spruce up" her performance by reading poetry. Stephen Lucasi has asserted, "The audience that The Mother-Showman desires would pay only for a non-reciprocal, *visual* interaction with their object, and this performance must remain visual at the exclusion of speech."[15] So the Mother-Showman responds to The Venus only with "Count!," indicating that The Venus's desire to express herself through poetry and art will remain unfulfilled because, unlike her, the oppressor does not see it as economically viable (51).

Venus also ends her "bottom line" with a poetic addition: "When Death met Love Death deathd Love / and left Love tuh rot / *au naturel* end for thuh Miss Hottentot. / Loves soul, which was tidy, hides in heaven, yes, thats it / Loves corpse stands on show in a museum. Please / visit" (161). Parks returned to the issue of being tidy in "new black math" when she reflected on the changes that have shaped her understanding of black theater since the publication of a previous essay on the subject, "An Equation for Black People on Stage" (1994). She wrote that although there are some similarities in the conversations about the trajectory of the art and of her own aesthetic, there are also key differences: "I was tidy back then. And now Im tidier. Tidier today like a tidal wave."[16] What appears simple at first glance, this suggests, is actually overwhelming and potentially destructive or iconoclastic. The end of The Venus's bottom line, then, is just another paradox. Even as The Venus dies, a victim of the exploitation of her spectators, she still craves more viewers.

Herein lies one of the most compelling connections between The Venus and the African American playwright: the playwright needs, perhaps even craves, an audience. But as with The Venus, questions arise about the lengths to which a black playwright must go to attract this audience, to fill the theater seats with paying customers. Ultimately the black playwright must sell black life, black history, and the black experience to a predominantly white audience, and so, like The Venus, the playwright straddles the line between complicity and agency. Again Parks has explained the situation in terms of a paradox: "A black play knows that racerelations sell./ A black play know that racerelations are a holding cell."[17] The very spectacle that makes "a mint" may be the spectacle that puts the writer and the audience in a metaphorical "iron cage."

In creating these parallels between The Venus and the playwright, it is difficult to make distinctions between Parks's agency, the historical Baartman's agency, and the fictionalized Baartman's agency. Young is one of the few critics who has attempted to do so by drawing on court documents and other records. Other critics rely on Parks's intent, but her comments on the play are ambiguous; they vary widely by interview and therefore ultimately shed little light on interpretive issues as they both discount and support nearly every possible critical perspective. Ironically, in the context of discussing *Venus,* Parks also has denied her individual aesthetic. She wrote, "someone once told me, '*Venus* isn't really a Suzan-Lori Parks play.' To which I responded:

'There isn't any such thing as a Suzan-Lori Parks play.'"[18] Parks's answer becomes more significant when reading *Venus* as a commentary on the theater audience's expectations, for here Parks has seemingly denied her aesthetic culpability in not meeting these expectations. Parks went on to criticize such aesthetic fidelity in economic terms. She claimed that "once Miss X buys into the existence of an Xian style of writing and once that purchase keeps her simply and stupidly repeating her last best hit, well, then Miss X gets really stinky—no matter in what genre she writes or in what camp she parks, naturalists, realists, avant-gardists, or experimentalists."[19]

So why forsake avoiding intentional fallacy and look so much to the author and her intent in *Venus*? Aja Marneweck asserted that "In contemporary African American theatre, there is a strong link between feminist critical intention in the work of playwright Suzan-Lori Parks and issues of race and stereotype." Ultimately Marneweck has maintained that "the play was criticized as racist because there was no authorial voice challenging the stereotypes presented in the play."[20] In *Venus* audiences want to hear the voice of Parks, one of the most celebrated, most visible, and most challenging modern African American writers. Yet this desire proves ultimately insatiable, for to do so would undermine the more creative, subtly subversive elements of the play and let the audience off the hook: "in many ways, the story makes the racism and sexism seem too obvious; the circus sideshow aspect more subtly demonstrates our inevitable complicity in viewing the body."[21] The plays and shows within the play make it impossible to deny that *Venus,* at least in part, is about the nature of spectacle and by extension the creation of that spectacle—that is, about Parks and her contemporaries and the audiences they seek/need.

Yet Parks clearly and willingly has surrendered control of her text to the reader, actor, and director in her *(Rest)*s and Spells, which "directors should fill . . . as they best see fit,"[22] as well as the text she brackets for omission; at the same time, *Venus*'s form often feels very imposing. Her unique language, which Kimberly D. Dixon described as "perfectly suited to act as a force on actor or audience,"[23] evokes the politics of black vernacular—written and spoken—but Parks repeatedly has denied that she is attempting to represent vernacular speech or the vernacular tradition. Brown-Guillory attributed this use of alternate word forms to Parks's thwarting of hegemonic models of discourse. She stated that Parks "rejects any attempt at representing the unrepresentable in European-based discourse," and "much of what her characters speak supplies a performative rendition of their splintered selves occupying a liminal space."[24] Through her unconventional language and her ambiguous *(Rest)*s and Spells then, Parks actively rejected complicity with dominant power structures by rejecting those structures' linguistic and dramatic forms.

Economics becomes a factor in these formal concerns because, in order for Parks's rejection to be its most potent, her art must find a wide audience and readership. And since in publishing, as Lyman has pointed out, "cost, not nuance is of necessity a principal concern,"[25] Parks's very specific formatting stylistics may someday be edited out to trim the price of her volumes. In the meantime, though, these differences draw attention to her work and situate her in a position of ultimate textual authority—she is the only one who can edit her manuscripts. From a nineteenth-century perspective, as Jacobs's and other narrators' histories reiterate, this particular agency is precious. But, from a Broadway perspective, a playwright who wants success must consider how to create a play that appeals to the widest theatergoing audience. Parks wrote that young and old writers are "both trying to write the next Broadway hit while not listening to the voice that wants to write that small, challenging downtown play" and that these compromises signify the "horrid dead ends of writing."[26]

But most of Parks's recent plays *have* been Broadway hits, and she has moved on to the other, perhaps even more insidious box office, the Hollywood box office, by writing screenplays—which met with mixed popular and critical reception—for Oprah Winfrey and Spike Lee. She may be aiming for challenging, but she is certainly not aiming for small. Plus Broadway audiences, polls show, are predominately white and wealthy, and, according to the most recent research sponsored by the National Endowment for the Arts, the percentage of the African American population that attends nonmusical plays has actually declined since 1992.[27] According to the 1992 NEA data, "Participation rates for African Americans more than doubled from 5.8 percent in 1982 to 12.0 percent in 1992," with most of the increase from nonprofit theater. However, according to the 2002 report, this participation rate had declined to 7.1 percent of the African American population. African Americans in 2002 constituted 6.6 percent of the nonmusical play audience, on and off Broadway. In contrast, white viewers constituted 84.1 percent of the nonmusical play audience in 2002.[28] Parks acknowledged the audience issues raised by such surveys, but she subtly mocked the impact: "A black play takes into account that pollsters have found that black folks dont attend the theatres in numbers large enough to influence the selection of plays produced."[29]

In his 1937 *Negro Poetry and Drama,* Sterling Brown wrote of the fundamental importance of the black audience to a black playwright. "Without their own audience," he claimed, "they are doubly handicapped."[30] In an interview with *Crisis* before the Broadway opening of *Topdog/Underdog* in 2002, neither Parks nor George C. Wolfe specifically mentioned the need to bring in black audiences, although both spoke of a need for "new audiences." Wolfe pointed to the stars of the production, Mos Def and Jeffrey Wright, "both artists who have had success with popular culture," as the main draw.[31] In so doing, however, Wolfe seemed to be banking on an audience that comes to the theater not because of an interest in the art on stage but because of an interest in the movie stars on stage. The audience that values "popular culture" will likely expect to see the stereotypes and distorted images of African Americans that popular culture perpetuates. This is exactly the kind of audience that Sterling Brown despised, the kind that "frequently wants flattery instead of representation, plaster saints instead of human beings, drawing rooms instead of the homes of the people."[32]

And this is just the type of audience, black and white, that *Venus* criticizes. *Venus* portrays them as a sex-crazed chorus who want their money's worth, fueling The Mother-Showman's greed and demanding "Gimmie gimmie back my buck!" when The Venus dies (5, 161). But rather than only indict the audience—though they do often transgress beyond the gaze—the play places blame on those who put The Venus on stage: The Mother-Showman and The Baron Docteur. Thus the play seems to indict Parks, as she puts *Venus* on stage, and thus puts The Venus "onstage, to be seen/scened."[33] Elam and Rayner questioned "Parks's own use and display of Baartman's story: for she too is making money from a repetition and spectacle of Baartman, exploiting her even as she tries to help."[34] As part of her work, Parks made The Venus and her own art the spectacle, and the success of the work can be measured, at least to some degree, by box office returns. The chosen degree determines the degree to which Parks and The Venus are complicit in their own exploitations.

Anne Davis Basting also paralleled The Venus or Parks with The Negro Resurrectionist. She wrote, "The Negro Resurrectionist/Watchman faces a decision similar to Venus' before him. Forced to promise delivery of her body for the autopsy, he ponders his limited choices: loss of his job and the certain ensuing poverty, or honoring the bones of the dead."[35] This decision is also reminiscent of the choices the black playwright faces, and indeed many black artists face, when choosing whether to write what will sell or what pays homage to what Parks called "the numerous hard times" past and present.[36] More specifically, Christopher Innes has noted that "like her own character, the Negro Resurrectionist, [Parks] brings dead figures back to life on her stage in new configurations to liberate and re-appropriate history."[37] Neither

Basting nor Innes, however, examined this relationship's more problematic aspects. The Negro Resurrectionist, after all, sells The Venus's body, damming her to an afterlife of forced exhibition. To equate Parks and The Negro Resurrectionist, then, indicts Parks as one of Venus's oppressors, damning her—through the written and performed word—to still more involuntary display.

However, Parks was also granting The Venus the fame she desired, and The Negro Resurrectionist can be read as a signification on Negro *Insurrectionist,* and therefore the character's name may point to Parks "bringing back" a call for a revolution against conventional views of The Venus and the theater. Parks obviously has thwarted the standard form of the play both through her unconventional language and pauses as well as by having the play run through intermission.[38] Elam and Rayner aligned themselves with this more favorable perspective on Parks and suggested that "Her position as a playwright echoes the positions of her characters in the sense that any kind of representation or category, performative or otherwise, will tend to imprison the truth of experience, or history, or resurrection by the very act of representation. Those who look for strictly realistic 'accuracy' are unaware that such accuracy conceals the imaginary dimension of the story. It is easer to jail the truth than to resurrect it."[39]

They also read the intermission scene and The Baron Docteur's call to the audience as "reminiscent of the audience participation initiative enacted by black revolutionary theatre of the 1960s and early 1970s."[40] Parks conjured this tradition in "new black math," her manifesto on the state of African American theater, by including a section entitled "The Intermission," in which a militant character named Black Playwright tries to convince a "Brother on the Corner" and "Sister on the Street" to participate in her call to action, first by giving her money to make a literal call, on a pay phone, to John Brown, Nat Turner, and Sojourner Truth. The brother and sister listen, but again there is an implied paradox, for the section ends with Brother on the Corner asking "Whats she talking about now?"[41] And *Venus* is participatory in that it "engages in a political act of re-memberment" by asking "the spectators to become active participants in the performance of re-membering."[42]

At the same time, Parks quickly indicated her desire to separate herself from the "holding cell" of "racerelations"; such a dependence, *Venus* suggests, is actually the burden of the oppressor, not the oppressed. Aaron Bryant highlighted "Parks' belief that 'Blackness' can be explored on its own—that African Americans' existence is not defined by the presence of 'Whiteness,' that Black people's lives and concerns can extend beyond issues of race."[43] In Parks's words, "The Klan does not always have to be outside the door for Black people to have lives worthy of dramatic literature."[44] Yet *Venus*—in an argument similar to Toni Morrison's in *Playing in the Dark: Whiteness and the Literary Imagination* (1992)—makes it clear that for the oppressor the spectator-spectacle relationship is parasitic, with the spectators feeding off the spectacle's otherness. For example, when trying to draw in audiences for The Venus's show, The Mother-Showman shouts, "Ladies and Gents are you feeling lowly? / Down in the dumps? / Perhaps yr feelin that yr life is all for naught? Ive felt that way myself at times. / Come on inside and get yr spirits lifted. / One look at thisll make you feel like a King!" (45). Since this audience is a paying audience, The Venus's otherness and the disparity between her and her viewers is the source of the show's income, and it would have been the source of her fame and fortune if either The Mother-Showman or The Brother had honored her contract. According to Parks, "A black play knows that when audiences read it primarily through the rubric of 'race relations,' that those audiences are suffering from an acute attack of white narcissism."[45] If this audience's needs parallel Broadway audiences' needs, then Parks's income also depends on giving the predominantly white audience the otherness they need for self-definition.

In *Venus* a main component of this otherness is sexual, for the British and French audience—scientists and non—are fascinated by what they perceive as The Venus's aberrant sexual organs. Yet the play writes against this aberration, instead using The Venus's sexuality to pathologize male sexuality. The Baron Docteur in particular becomes "a metaphorical reflection and literal embodiment of the ambivalent nature of white desire."[46] Both The Baron Docteur and The Chorus of 8 Anatomists expose themselves and masturbate publicly after looking at The Venus, and, earlier in the play, The Brother reveals that his sexual fulfillment is tied to her exploitation. He admits, "I wanted you then and I want you now / Thats partly why we've come here. / So I can love you properly. / Not like at home" (23). After promising her that he will buy her "the town" the next day, he begins groping her. She tries to protest but is cut off by his reassurances, which are couched in promises of fame.

The Venus thus uses her sexuality to achieve some degree of agency over The Brother and The Baron Docteur, but this agency also clearly has limits. Near the middle of the play, The Mother-Showman, especially remarkable because of her mixed-gender name, links money and sexual protection. When The Venus questions The Mother-Showman's accounting and threatens to "be [her] own Boss make [her] own mint" (55), The Mother-Showman convinces her that there is nowhere for her to go where people will accept her and her way of life and that she needs protection from drunken white men. Later, however, these men still rape her—regardless of The Mother-Showman's protection. In the end it is The Venus's sexuality—or, rather, a sexually transmitted disease—that kills her. The Baron Docteur gives her chlamydia, and seeing that her death is probable, he abandons her to imprisonment to hasten this death—and his own fame, since he will dissect her. Male sexuality and greed render her only power impotent.

Sexuality, of course, is an important tool for the playwright because sex sells. The problem in Parks's case is that the sexuality on which she capitalizes has traditionally been misrepresented. Sander Gilman called representations such as the Venus Hottentot "icons." The problem with using these icons in literature, Gilman explained, is that "when individuals are shown within a work of art (no matter how broadly defined), the ideologically charged iconographic nature of the representation dominates." The Venus Hottentot icon is so potent that "Sarah Bartmann's [*sic*] sexual parts, her genitalia and her buttocks, serve as the central image of the black female throughout the nineteenth century."[47] In the play the anatomists' postmortem emphasis on The Venus's sexual organs "reflects the general nineteenth-century understanding of female sexuality as pathological: the female genitalia were of interest partly as examples of the various pathologies which could befall them but also because the female genitalia came to define the female for the nineteenth century."[48] This emphasis is so intense, however, that it becomes pathological itself.

In the play The Venus suggests that staging her sexuality is the best way to remove perceptions of its malignancy, although with complicated implications. She asks, "If I bear thuh bad mark what better way to cleanse it off? / Showing my sinful person as a caution to you all could, / in the Lords eyes, be a sort of repentance" (76). According to S. E. Wilmer, Parks's restaging of the Venus Hottentot icon is ethical, and through it she is "paying respect to those who have disappeared by re/making and staging their histories."[49] As such, she, like The Venus, has found agency in a situation that traditionally denied agency to African American women. Again, however, this subversion is not simple, for immediately following the assertion of her desire to be on display, The Venus denies not only her shame, but also her blackness. She says, "I could wash off my dark mark. / I came here black. / Give me the chance to leave here white" (76). This denial shows Venus engaging the white audience's desire to find self-definition in her, for she establishes herself as the opposite of whiteness and portrays racial definition as something that must be given by authority—in this case, the court. This denial also resonates with Parks's rejection of her aesthetic vis-à-vis *Venus*. By denying her individual role in the art, she has put The Venus and her body on stage alone, potentially reducing the play to only a spectacle with "genitals that people think about long after the curtain comes down."[50]

As a kind of crystal ball for the future of black playwriting, *Venus*'s vision is cloudy. In her dying words, The Venus says, "dont look," but in the final chorus she begs, "please visit" and screams, "kiss me!"—a cry for adoration and affection (159). She both shuns audience participation and embraces it, cooperates and subverts. Parks herself has offered a similar paradoxical forecast: "A black play is on broadway, the great white way. / A black play is not on broadway, and furthermore, aint studying no broadway. / A black play is coming soon to a theatre near you."[51] The pitfall of the paradox is that in each of Parks's scenarios the play is either unseen or seen by the wrong audience, so the black playwright—like The Venus—has no home, no love, and no "mint," but there are plenty of critics, white and black, waiting to dissect her work.

CHAPTER 4

What "Able" and "Angel" Mean to a Welfare Mother

In the Blood

In 1999, the year that *In the Blood* premiered at the Joseph Papp Public Theatre's New York Shakespeare Festival, the United States Census Bureau reported that 39 percent of single black mothers (and thus nearly 1.5 million families) were living below the federally established poverty line.[1] The bureau also reported that while the poverty rate for African Americans as a group dropped to a record low that year, "the poverty rate for Blacks in 1999 [23.6 percent] was still about three times the poverty rate for White non-Hispanics (7.7 percent)."[2] To explore the causes and effects of this harsh reality, Suzan-Lori Parks blended this bleak backstory with another, Nathaniel Hawthorne's dark romance *The Scarlet Letter* (1850), for her first "Red Letter Play," *In the Blood.*

The "Red Letter Plays" are the two plays in Parks's corpus that feature scarlet-hued letter A's: *In the Blood*'s sequel, *Fucking A* (2000), focuses on an abortionist named Hester Smith, who has an A branded above her left breast, and that brand will not heal. Her A "weeps as a fresh wound would" and thus remains red with infection (125).[3] *In the Blood* tells the story of Hester La Negrita, a poor, black, mostly illiterate, single mother of five children—all of whom are doubled with an adult character in the play. Each of these adult characters, male and female, confesses to a sexual fascination for Hester as well as to sexually exploiting her in some way. The Doctor (the middle son) and the welfare lady (also known as "Welfare" and the oldest daughter) are also trying to sterilize Hester, while her white "friend" Amiga Gringa (the youngest daughter) steals from her. Reverend D (the youngest son), her most recent lover, refuses to acknowledge her out of fear that it will damage his ministry and his status in the community, and her first lover, Chili (doubled with the oldest son Jabber), finally returns after years of absence only to reject Hester when he discovers the children she conceived with others during their separation. Throughout the play Hester's health deteriorates, and she eventually has visions of Armageddon. Hester's circumstances, coupled with the trauma of hearing Jabber call her a slut, drive her to beat Jabber to death, and she uses the blood of her murdered son to write an "A"—scarlet by nature—on the ground next to his body.

In the Blood's main signification on *The Scarlet Letter* seems to be the parallel ambiguous meaning of the letter A. Hawthorne scholars have noted the novel's "refusal to articulate that word for which the novel's title presumably stands" and have pointed out that the word *adultery* is referenced only once in his novel and that is in the related form *unadulterated* (47),[4] referring to the sun that shines on Hester as she leaves her prison with Pearl.[5] Over the course of the story, the text suggests multiple redefinitions of the scarlet letter as Hester Prynne and her community come to understand the A and its significance. While in *Fucking A,* the branded letter distinctly signifies "abortionist," *In the Blood* follows *The Scarlet Letter*'s example more closely and makes its A multivalent. At the same time, these layers of meaning can all be linked to the two A's that Hawthorne does explicitly offer in *The Scarlet Letter*—Able and Angel. *In the Blood*'s A thus speaks back to a literary and social history that is fraught with oppression while also wholly innovative and timely.

Hawthorne's clear emphasis on Able and Angel mandates that Parks's readers consider both as possible interpretations/significations for Hester La Negrita's scrawled A.[6] Both possibilities reveal elements of Hester La Negrita's fragile and fragmented identity—wearied by systematic attacks and her own shortsighted choices—as well the play's indictment of the forces that seek to undermine this identity.

While understanding Hester Prynne's A is indeed challenging, the quest is ultimately just a puzzle—not a matter of life and death—for Hester emerges from the text redeemed and strong. On the other hand, the near whirlwind of possible meanings for Hester La Negrita's A and for the play leaves viewers/readers to feel disembodied and disillusioned, because ultimately the world of the play leaves Hester La Negrita similarly disembodied and disillusioned. Understanding Hester La Negrita's A *is* a matter of life and death. Jailed for infanticide and likely dying of AIDS, she bears the burden of an amalgam of sins, identities, and interpretations of her self placed on her by her oppressors; she emerges from her text unredeemed and broken.

The play thus shows how history, revealed by *The Scarlet Letter* to be a tragically haunting force, has retained its potency. The same ambiguous signifiers define Hester Prynne and Hester La Negrita, but the nuances of the significations are different, indicating how time and circumstances have made it impossible for Hester La Negrita's story to end with anything other than her destruction. Parks's repetition of Hawthorne's themes thus shows reverence and relevance. As she did in *Venus,* Parks has presented us with a woman "who has been famously romanticized and mystified," asking us to "consider her again through the lens of our cruel and continuing histories of oppression."[7] Yet Parks's substantial revision of Hester Prynne and *The Scarlet Letter* also shows that time, and thus history, have become only more malignant for America's present-day Hesters, especially if they are black and poor. Indeed time and history have only complicated Hester's plight. New oppressions, related, yet different, compound the old and ultimately leave her without hope or escape.

"A" Is for Able

In *The Scarlet Letter,* Hester and those around her eventually "refused to interpret the scarlet A by its original signification" (110). Instead, "the letter was a symbol of her calling," and "they said that it meant Able; so strong was Hester Prynne with a woman's strength" (110). Most obviously Hester is an able seamstress, "so skilled that even the community leaders call upon her to embroider their robes."[8] Hester's expertise as a seamstress allows her both artistic expression, as she adorns her mark, and financial freedom. Parks's Hester La Negrita, by contrast, cannot even thread a needle and appears to be illiterate. Hester Prynne is also "Able" because she is an effective philanthropist whose "nature showed itself warm and rich; a well-spring of human tenderness, unfailing to every real demand, and inexhaustible by the largest. Her breast, with its badge of shame, was but the softer pillow for the head that needed one" (110). Hester La Negrita, although she does bring sexual satisfaction to some of the play's characters and does attempt to feed and comfort her children, cannot respond to her oppression with compassion, and she turns to violence against her own child.

All these differences serve to separate Hester La Negrita from her seventeenth-century counterpart and the nineteenth-century feminism that Hawthorne knew, proving again the difficulty of equating white and black women's oppressions. According to Leland S. Person, Hawthorne's Hester sits "on the dividing line between black and white feminism—the line that some white nineteenth-century feminists either ignored or erased. Objectified in a way that associates her with slave mothers, Hester retains some privileges of her status as a white feminist who, like [Margaret] Fuller and [Elizabeth] Peabody, presumed to occupy the subject position of women."[9]

For *In the Blood,* Parks made this dividing line even more distinct. While Hester Prynne's oppression is certainly real and relevant, Hester La Negrita's, two centuries later, is not only deeper, but also more pervasive. One of the first times the later Hester writes the letter A, her son Jabber—who seems to be acting as her teacher—says simply "Almost" in response to her creation. Hester is almost happy, almost married, almost able to support her children, almost literate. But Hester does not move beyond "almost" because of the selfish opportunism of those around her—black and white, male and female. When A means Able, then, Hester La Negrita is left only with a negative identity—what she is unable to do and unable to achieve. The play does not emphasize what Hester La Negrita *is,* rather only what she *is not.*

To reinforce the growing modern separation between black and white women, *In the Blood* gives us Amiga Gringa, the poor white woman who claims to share in Hester's oppression but actually participates in it. Amiga, who will make money by selling "the fruit of [her] white womb" without guilt, steals food and money from Hester and sets her up to be raped (71). Amiga also cannot thread a needle, but she criticizes sewing as a profession, implying that it is beneath her, even though she is also poor.

After refusing Hester's offer to find her sewing work, Amiga explains, "Thats not for me. If I work Hester, I would want to be paid a living wage. You have agreed to work for less than a living wage. May as well be a slave. Or an animal. . . . Wouldnt catch me doing that. Chump work. No no no. But its a good thing you are. Example to the kids" (66). Amiga's whiteness—doubly inscribed by her name, a racial marker that opposes Hester's—allows her the privilege to reject unjust labor demands. Having sold her white children, Amiga does not have the stigma of being a begging unwed mother like Hester, who admits: "no ones gonna give money to me with me carrying Baby around" (27). As such, Amiga will either find legitimate work with a living wage or will make more money from her illegal/illicit activities than Hester, allowing for at least the possibility that Amiga's poverty is not permanent or systematic. Also, by praising Hester for being an "example to the kids," Amiga implies that Hester will pass her economic dependence on to her children, who should accept this position in the social hierarchy.

The sewing scene also evokes a comparison of Hester La Negrita and Harriet Wilson. Wilson's autobiographical heroine Frado in *Our Nig* (1859) is an "expert with the needle" and "soon equaled her instructress" (124).[10] Frado, like Hester Prynne, can then use sewing as a means of support. This connection shows that the situation is perhaps even more dire for Hester La

Negrita than for a nineteenth-century black woman, for Hester La Negrita has no substantive means of survival. Parks, like Wilson, also links her protagonist's domestic skill with written text; self-supporting labor and personal expression through literacy become parallel needs.

Frado's sewing instructor "sought also to teach her the value of useful books; and while one read aloud to the other of historic deeds and names renowned, Frado experienced a new impulse. She felt herself capable of elevation; she felt that this book information supplied an undefined dissatisfaction she has long felt, but could not express" (124). Similarly, when Welfare gives Hester La Negrita fabric to sew, she asks, "Can I express myself?" (59), and at the beginning of the next scene, there are "Lots of A's written in Hester's practice place," but she still cannot thread the needle (64). One key difference, of course, is that Frado discovers the expressive elements of literacy through reading—specifically reading history—while Hester looks to writing. Hester's multiple attempts at writing combined with her frustrated sewing efforts show that she has not yet found the outlet for expression that Frado discovers, and literacy stands out as the most important skill Hester is unable to master.

Women's writing, and literary mastery especially, also has a complicated history vis-à-vis Nathaniel Hawthorne. In an infamous January 19, 1885, letter to publisher William D. Ticknor, Hawthorne complained that the country was "wholly given over to a damned mob of scribbling women." One cannot help but recall these words along with Hawthorne's most famous novel as Parks's Hester scribbles the letter A—the only letter she writes over the course of the play—on the wall of her house and eventually "in the blood" of her murdered son. Reading this red A as a final and futile assertion of literacy invites a closer look at Hawthorne's "scribbling women" comment in his letter to Ticknor. According to Michael Winship, this comment "has resonated through recent discussions of American literary history" for it begs us to consider issues such as "the relationship between popular success and literary quality," the impact of "gender politics" in literary evaluation, and how "the economic factors facing authors and publishers fostered or discouraged authorship in the United States."[11] Applied to *In the Blood,* the comparison encourages readers to challenge assumptions about women's writing as well to as examine the boundaries of Hester La Negrita's perceived illiteracy, especially as these boundaries may be informed by her social and economic influences.

For example, there is evidence in the play that suggests Hester is not illiterate, or at least not so illiterate as first impression and most critics suggest she is. Only the chorus that mocks Hester at the beginning and end of the play explicitly calls her illiterate, as it shouts on both occasions, "CANT READ CANT WRITE" (5, 108). The stage directions comment only that the letters of the word *slut* are "mysterious to her" (12), a description that potentially complicates the play's definitions of language and literacy rather than excludes Hester from engaging them.

First and foremost it is difficult to accept that Hester can write only one letter, just as readers would certainly not believe that Hester Prynne could embroider only one letter. Most obviously, the letter A is itself composed of another letter, "V," and a V very easily becomes a "W." Hester La Negrita's oldest son Jabber describes the letter A's shape as—"legs apart hands crost the chest" (11). And Deborah Geis has asserted that this sexualized description of how to make the featured letter "reveals the extent to which for [Hester], too, it has become a kind of bodily marking."[12] So, why not V? Would not V, as the enormous popularity of Eve Ensler's *The Vagina Monologues* (1996) has taught us, have actually been more sexual (just "legs apart") and easier to make (fewer lines)? And why not W, the first letter of most interrogative pronouns as well as of words that could all be loci for Hester's oppression—*woman, whiteness, Welfare*? Furthermore Hester herself never admits to her illiteracy, and the play gives us no reason to distrust her. On the contrary, she adamantly declares to Amiga Gringa, "I can write my damn name. Im not such a fool that I cant write my own goddamn name. I can write my goddamn name" (32). Also, when the Doctor asks her to read the eye chart, on which the letters spell SPAY, she claims that she needs glasses—wholly probable considering her poor diet—and likely makes out the A because it is the letter to which she is most emotionally attached and because its outline is one of the most distinct in the alphabet (42). These assertions meet with no contradiction from the stage directions, as seen when Jabber tells his literacy-related lies by saying he cannot read the SLUT written in Hester's practice place.

Meanwhile other parts of the play also suggest that Hester may have a better grasp of language than the chorus acknowledges. In some instances readers encounter surprisingly elevated diction in the midst of dialect, such as when Hester tells Jabber, "You gonna disparage me I aint gonna practice" (10). And at times, the depths of Hester's literary creativity is striking. Geis has suggested that "Hester has a gifted imagination" seen especially when "she helps the children to enjoy the meager soup that she feeds them for dinner by telling them that it has everything they love in it" as well as in the fairytale she creates about their fathers (83). These stories, asserted *New York Times* theater critic Margo Jefferson, are important because they help audiences "realize that those folk tales we love so would be narratives of misery and woe if poor and powerless storytellers hadn't invented supernatural forces to save the day."[13] Ultimately, however, Hester's "fables," almost entirely fabricated, are happy only for a time and eventually end in war and death, thereby poignantly implying that the ability to write happy endings—and even to write history—belongs almost exclusively to the rich and powerful.

If Hester can indeed read and write, then the obvious limits on her literacy—the forces that make some letters mysterious—must come from circumstance. Hester's longing for self-expression compels her to demonstrate this literacy in particular ways to fit particular situations and leads her to focus on the letter *A* because of its relevance to her. For instance, when she writes the A for Welfare, Hester does so in response to the woman's insistence that Hester reveal the name of Baby's father:

WELFARE. You dont have to say it out loud. Write it down.
She gives Hester a pencil and paper. Hester writes. Welfare looks at the paper
WELFARE. "A."
(Rest)
Adam, Andrew, Archie, Arthur, Aloysius, "A" what?
HESTER. Looks good dont it? (58)

Although he is not given a first name in *In the Blood,* in *The Scarlet Letter,* "good Master Dimmesdale['s]" full name is, of course, Arthur Dimmesdale (79). The A simultaneously names the delinquent father and sexual abuser, allowing Hester to express her emotional angst, and protects his anonymity as prescribed by the patriarchal power structure, so that she might still hope to receive financial support from him.

This discretion links Hester La Negrita not only to Hester Prynne but also to another nineteenth-century African American writer and mother, Harriet A. Jacobs. Person explains of *The Scarlet Letter's* Hester, "Refusing to name her child's father, resisting the efforts of the good masters to take her away, planning an escape to freedom—Hester resembles slave mothers like Harriet Jacobs" who were forced to do the same (44). The connection to Jacobs has threefold significance in Hester La Negrita's case. In addition to both women's forced adherence to patriarchal norms, Jacobs's narrative, *Incidents in the Life of a Slave Girl* (1861), clearly withholds information from the reader both out of modesty and because it "is not 'a narrative of the life of a slave' but a presentation of 'incidents,' carefully selected and shaped."[14] In addition Jacobs, who was literate even while enslaved, withheld her literacy from her tormentor, Dr. Flint, who wanted her to read the foul notes he wrote in his attempts to seduce her.

Withholding literacy is also not unprecedented in *In the Blood.* In the play's opening scene, Jabber does just this to spare his mother's feelings. He is capable of reading the text of the word *slut* that someone has "scrawled on a wall" near their home (9), but he cannot bring himself to do so. When he tells Hester he "cant" read it, the stage directions call his bluff and counter that "he knows what the word says, but he won't say it" (11–12). With Hester the play does not completely clarify whether she cannot or will not read the mysterious scrawl, just as there is ambiguity regarding whether she cannot or will not read the Doctor's SPAY eye chart later in the play. Harry J. Elam, Jr., asserted that the *slut* on the wall "marks a public branding and abasement, just as from the outset of Hawthorne's novel, Hester Prynne is humiliated and exorcized from the community as she exits from prison."[15] And Jon Dietrick posited that "Jabber clearly understands the slipperiness of the talk/action distinction, understands, that is, that talk *is* action, that symbols are involved in the creation of the real and vice versa."[16] In refusing to read the word, both Hester and Jabber reject the stigma and create a clear distinction between written and spoken language.

The text of the play reinforces this distinction. The stage directions, which would go unspoken in performance, cannot go unread. Because these stage directions never explicitly affirm or deny Hester La Negrita's illiteracy, the ambiguous personified voice of the stage directions—a quasi-narrator—most prominently inspires incredulity about Hester's inability to read and write. Again, this may be a trope that Parks borrowed from her literary ancestor Hawthorne. According to Leslie Ginsberg, "the Janus-faced narrator of the novel—who is simultaneously reliable and unreliable, is a revealer and a concealer—is a narrative voice that ultimately invites us to read *The Scarlet Letter* as a primer for grownups, whose subject, like all primers, is the process of reading itself."[17] In the case of *In the Blood,* doubts raised by the quasi-narrator of the stage directions highlight issues not only about reading (and writing, as explored above), but also what Elam called "another form of literacy, a cultural literacy that [Hester La Negrita] must learn to appreciate through the course of the play."[18] Both the audience and Hester must learn to accurately "read" situational subtleties for personal and social significance as well as "read" people for key verbal and nonverbal communication. Just as Hester La Negrita should not blindly trust the former lovers who promise to help her and claim to have only her best interests at heart, the theater audience should not trust the dialogue of the play. Cultural literacy, then, is the ability to see and understand the value of the subtext inherent in every text, written and spoken.

Audience members at a production of *In the Blood,* hearing only the spoken words, would come away with a wholly different understanding of Hester La Negrita than that of the play's readers. Viewers, for example, would not know until the end of the play that Jabber was lying about not reading the word *slut,* nor would they see how the stage directions sympathize with Hester as she "continues trying to thread that damn needle" (67). More important, only readers see the textual clues leading up to Hester's final breakdown and Jabber's violent death. As Jabber confesses that he withheld his literacy, he explains, "I was reading it but I was only reading it in my head I wasnt reading it with my mouth I was reading it with my mouth but not with my tongue I was reading it only with my lips and I could hear the word outloud but only outloud in my head" (103). He tells Hester, "I didnt wanna say the word outloud in your head" because "it was a bad word" (103). He does not want his voice to be the voice in his mother's consciousness that calls her a slut, but his naïveté and the desire to play "a child's joke" are stronger than this impulse (106). When he finally does say it "outloud," it is in quotation marks: "I read 'slut'" (104). The first four times he says the word it appears this way, but when he says, "You said if I read it youd say what it means. Slut. Whassit mean?," the quotation marks disappear (104).

And at this moment readers and viewers are audience to two different plays and two different Hesters. The viewing audience, when hearing this line read aloud—no matter the inflection the actor puts on each word—cannot help but hear Jabber call his mother a slut, and his murder, while still senseless, seems justified as this epithet links Jabber with all the other exploitive men in the play. Hester then kills her son to prevent him becoming yet another misogynistic patriarch like his father or Reverend D.

Readers, on the other hand, see that he is not calling her a slut, but simply saying the word. Still, the lost quotation marks on Jabber's fifth utterance of the word *slut* indicate a key linguistic shift that harkens back to an oddly mimetic conversation between Hester and Reverend D near the beginning of the play. Both scenes draw a clear distinction between mere repetition and Parks's "Rep & Rev"[19]—repetition with a hint of personal revision—thereby also reinforcing that Parks was making *The Scarlet Letter* her own.

In her first exchange with Reverend D, Hester repeats all of the minister's scripted words back to him as he tells her how to confront the father of her child:

REVEREND D. You must go to him and say, "Mister, here is your child!"
HESTER. Mister, here is your child!

REVEREND D. "You are wrong to deny what God has made!"
HESTER. You are wrong to deny what God has made!
REVEREND D. "He has nothing but love for you and reaches out his hands everyday crying wheres daddy?"
HESTER. Wheres daddy?
REVEREND D. "Wont you answer those cries?"
HESTER. Wont you answer those cries? (48)

The quotation marks here serve as a source of abstraction, a potential versus an actual speech. Outside of the quotation marks, the words are real, weighty, and demanding of action. In her unquoted repetition, Hester not only leaves out assurance of love but changes Reverend D's meaning by delivering the words to an unexpected audience, himself.

The same is true in the closing scene with Jabber. "Slut" in quotation marks is simply an abstraction. Hester barely reacts when Jabber says it. Taken out of the quotation marks, however, the word changes for Hester. Jabber's voice now says it "outloud in [her] head," joining a chorus of others who have already done so. Like Hester's earlier words to Reverend D, this word—outside of the abstracting quotation marks—now demands action and justice, and she beats him to death with a club that was "stolen by one of her children from a policeman and thus a symbol of the authorities with whom Hester does battle every day of her life."[20] For the reader, then, Hester is more like Euripides's Medea, killing out of spite and vengeance against a world that has unfairly branded her a slut.

Regardless of the motivation, Hester's punishment for Jabber's murder is the inevitable loss of her "womans parts," the source of her "treasures" and the only ability granted her by the unsympathetic chorus who asserts, "SHE DONT GOT NO SKILLS / CEPT ONE" (43, 5, 7). Hester's sexuality is her only significant source of money and sympathy, but unfortunately, as theater critic Sarah Wilkinson has explained, her "sexual acts are paradoxically both Hester's saving grace and her downfall, her only way to acquire money and the reason why she has none."[21] Still, as in *Venus,* sexuality is ultimately a site of agency for Hester. In choosing her partners, just as in choosing when to reveal or withhold her literacy, Hester asserts the small amount of control over her life that she can. Hester, unfortunately, tends to waste her agency on bad decisions, but she takes responsibility for this shortsightedness ("My lifes my own fault. I know that" [59]). Thus Elam has suggested that Hester La Negrita "is a victim, but also tragically complicit in her own oppression. Her tale offers a poignant, contradictory conjunction of suffering and survival, institutional neglect, and individual abuse."[22] She ends the play unable to express herself and also likely unable to bear more children and create the "whole army" of "Bad Bastards" that may have protected her from an antagonistic world (107). As in *Topdog/Underdog*, the curtain closes on a sorrowful murder with bloody hands and no hope.

"A" Is for Angel

Hester La Negrita's heavenward gaze, especially during her visions of Armageddon, evokes the second explicit meaning of A in *The Scarlet Letter.* The novel equates A with angel in one of its most dramatic and memorable chapters, "The Minister's Vigil." In this chapter Hester Prynne, Dimmesdale, Pearl, and Roger Chillingworth converge on the scaffold on which "evildoers are set up to public shame" (108). Pearl chastises the Reverend, her father, for refusing to acknowledge her and her mother, shouting: "Thou was not bold!—thou was not true!" (108). Dimmesdale proceeds to preach one of his "richest and powerful" Sabbath sermons the following day, and he is approached by a sexton who hands him a glove found on the scaffold: "'Satan dropped it there, I take it, intending a scurrilous jest against your reverence. But indeed, he was blind and foolish, as he ever and always is. A pure hand needs no glove to cover it. . . . And since Satan saw fit to steal it, your reverence must needs handle him without gloves, henceforward,' remarked the old sexton, grimly smiling. 'But did your reverence hear of the portent that was seen last night. A great red letter in the sky,—the letter A,—which we interpret to stand for Angel. For, as our good Governor Winthrop was made an angel this past night, it was doubtless held fit that there should be some notice thereof'" (108–9). The sexton, in spite of his clearly erroneous reading of the event's meaning, subtly links Dimmesdale's sin and his guilty struggle with an intriguing sign in the heavens that undoubtedly points to Hester Prynne, the novel's best candidate to be an angel, the agent of God.

Parks's characters also struggle with sin, and Hester La Negrita, like Hester Prynne, is an unlikely angel but nevertheless acts as an agent of God. She becomes the avenue for the manifestation of the other characters' innermost sinful desires and exploitative tendencies. Indeed the play describes Hester's exploitation predominantly through each character's (including her own) "Confession" at the end of scenes. These confessions indict government and religion, as well as sexual dishonesty and double standards, as culprits in Hester's continued subjugation. Since the play's opening list of characters pairs each of her children with one of these sinful adults, it is clear that Hester must literally bear the burden of their sins, just as she bears the child who is the result of them. But unlike Hester Prynne, Hester La Negrita bears five symbolic children, rather than just one, so the sins and the penance are much more intense and pervasive—crossing race, gender, and class lines—than those in Hawthorne's text.

The first confession is the Doctor's. Parks's Doctor, like Hawthorne's physician Chillingworth, seems to care for Hester on some level, but he is ultimately self-serving and collaborates with the bisexual Welfare in Hester La Negrita's sterilization. Welfare's confession comes next in the play. Both the Doctor and Welfare "confess" to a breakdown or erosion of their philanthropic spirit and a need to separate themselves physically and emotionally from those they are committed to serve. Welfare says simply, "The balance of the system depends on a well-drawn boundary line/and all parties respecting that boundary" (61), but the doctor explains: "When I see a woman begging on the streets I guess I could / bring her in my house / sit her at my table / make her a member of my family, sure. / But there are hundreds and thousands of them / and my house cant hold them all. / Maybe we should all take in just one. / Except they wouldnt really fit. / They wouldnt really fit in with us. Theres such a gulf between us. What can we do?" (44).

Elam posited that both the Doctor and Welfare can justify their exploitation of Hester because "sexual desire enables boundaries of class and propriety to be crossed, and therefore complicates constructions of identities and hierarchies of difference. Still, while sex complicates these relations, the existent power dynamics and boundaries of identity remain intact."[23] Ironically, while Welfare and the Doctor seek an emotional and physical distance from Hester, they do not seek sexual distance from her.

This seemingly paradoxical distinction suggests that Hester's sexuality is not, for these characters, in any way connected to her physical or emotional self, that is, to her individual identity. Hester "finds no sense of self, no freedom in these acts. Sex does not liberate her from but only imprisons her more in the system."[24] She is simply an agent through which the Doctor and Welfare discover or express their own sexuality. The Doctor remembers that while having sex with Hester it was as if "she was giving me something that was not hers to give me but something that was mine / that I'd lent her / and she was returning it to me" (44–45). When Welfare finally works her way through half-truths and hedges to admitting her "sexual interest" in Hester, she claims merely to have been "swept away" by the moment (62).

Indeed these confessions are devoid of the repentant spirit the ritual implies. Hawthorne, in both *The Scarlet Letter* and *The Marble Faun* (1859), was clearly skeptical of both confession and even private penitence as adequate penance for sins. Even though Dimmesdale whips himself out of guilt related to his continuing silence about his affair with Hester, for example, he still has great "dread of public exposure" (105). Denis Donoghue stated, "To Hawthorne, it appears that sin is an act, a condition, a state of consciousness, such that I will not reveal to my community—or indeed to anyone. The sin consists in my refusal to come clean and to tell the neighbors what I have done."[25] By exposing each character's exploitation of Hester La Negrita, Parks figuratively put them on the scaffold to which *The Scarlet Letter*'s sexton refers. Thereby the "evil-doers are set up to public shame." However, this shame is revealed only to the play's theater audience, not to the "onstage" public, so the penance is essentially meaningless.

Also Parks's sinners seem anything but sorry and certainly show no desire to do penance for their sins. According to *Village Voice* theater critic Michael Feingold, the confessions are not so much about characters repenting, or accepting shame, but speaking "in their own defense."[26] It is ultimately Hester who must literally bear the burden for each sin, by bearing a child that represents that sin. The Doctor gives her Trouble; Welfare gives her Bully. Philip C. Kolin has suggested that "for Hester, 'in the blood' symbolizes her offspring, whom she has physically and spiritually conceived."[27] As such Hester is a potent agent of God—a reverse Christ figure. Hester does not die for these sins but gives birth to them, turning these sins into "her treasures," her children that she nurtures and, again, for whom she sacrifices.

Kolin also maintained that Hester "evokes the Blessed Virgin Mary cast as a welfare mother pushed beyond the limits of pain."[28] Indeed Chilli—Chillingworth's more obvious double—imagines Hester La Negrita as a Virgin Mary figure. When Chilli takes back his proposal to marry her after meeting all her children, he explains: "I carried around this picture of you. Sad and lonely with our child on yr hip. Struggling to make do. Struggling against all odds. And triumphant. Triumphant against everything. Like—hell, like Jesus and Mary. And if they could do it so could my Hester. My dear Hester. Or so I thought. / *(Rest)* / But I dont think so" (96). Chilli, who deeply fears that marriage will lead to his emasculation, wants to feel omnipotent. This becomes clearer each time Chilli takes out his watch to test whether or not he knows the time. His obsession with guessing the time reveals his desire to control it, to be the master to even the most minute details of his reality, to be God-like.

In imagining Hester as Mary and their child as Jesus, the miraculous Son of God, Chilli lives his God fantasy. His confession reveals that he "ultimately decides to find fault with her for being true to the same qualities that he once admired in her (passion and unbridled sexual freedom)."[29] As in the miracle of immaculate conception, when young Hester and Chilli are together, they defy natural laws and "float weightless" because "gravity was a law that did not apply to those persons under the age of 18" (97). Hester is an agent of God here because she is the avenue through which God reminds Chilli that he is a mere mortal, powerless against time and circumstance. Her "fall" serves to prove that "times change" (97).

Hester is also a humbling force for Reverend D, who believes that God has sent Hester to punish him. He confesses, "And now the hate I have for her / and her hunger /and the *hate* I have for her hunger. / God made me. / God pulled me up. / Now God, through her, wants to drag me down/and sit me at the table / at the head of the table of her fatherless house" (79). Reverend D, a modern Booker T. Washington, takes ultimate pride in telling his audiences how he is "a man who has crawled out of the quicksand of despair" and "has pulled himself out of that never ending gutter" to become "the man on the soapbox, telling you of a better life thats available to you" (46–47). A man of God, Reverend D should be a philanthropist, but Hester La Negrita reveals, "his heart is real hard. Like a rock." (30). Just as the women Gwendolyn Brooks described in "The Lovers of the Poor" (1960) want "The very very worthy / And beautiful poor,"[30] Reverend D "enjoys having the tired and the depraved come knocking on his door. Come gathering around his soapbox," but they must be "famous poor, not miscellaneous poor" (47, 73).

Reverend D's failed philanthropy is especially obvious in Hester's case, not just because it includes sexual exploitation, but also because it is so easily juxtaposed with the successful philanthropy of Hester Prynne. As stated above, the people of *The Scarlet Letter* come to admire Hester Prynne for her philanthropy, dubbing her "Able," as there is "none so ready as she to give of her little substance to every demand of poverty" and "none so self-devoted as Hester when pestilence stalked through the town" (110). This description comes in the chapter entitled "Another View of Hester," which immediately follows the sexton's equation of A with angel. The text subtly suggests that this angel label fits Hester as well as or perhaps better than able, for she has become "a self-ordained Sister of Mercy; or, we may rather say, the world's heavy hand had so ordained her, when neither the world nor she looked forward to this result" (110). Hester La Negrita similarly has become an agent of God, also ordained by circumstance, but instead of giving benevolence, she desperately needs it.

And this is just the type of mercy that Reverend D, as a man of God who fashions himself as a Christ figure,[31] should give. But instead of helping Hester, he, Welfare, and the Doctor "use Hester for masturbatory, self-gratification, and self-indulgent fulfillment of their missionary desires. They justify their exploitation of Hester through the narcissistic celebration of their own charity towards her, the erotics of benevolence."[32] Yet, in his last appearance, the Reverend—like his double in *The Scarlet Letter*—has no fear of exposure. He dares Hester, "Tell on me! Go on! Tell the world! I'll crush you underfoot" (103). But Reverend D, unlike Arthur Dimmesdale, is not repentant. He is ready to confront his sins, but he fears no wrath from God or the world. Therefore, according to Geis, "Parks seems much more willing than Hawthorne to deny any sympathy for the Reverend; her vision of this character is an implicit critique of the way Hawthorne, by having Dimmesdale die at the end, leaves us with a somewhat more ambiguous set of feelings for his character."[33] Hawthorne even gives his reader evidence that Dimmesdale physically punished himself, through whipping, and may have even been marked by God with stigmata, in the form of "a SCARLET LETTER—the very semblance of that worn by Hester Prynne—imprinted in the flesh" (174). Hawthorne's Dimmesdale also pays for his sin with his life, whereas in the cruel modern world of *In the Blood,* it is an innocent child—not even Reverend D's own—who must perish.

The modern world of *In the Blood* also presents an interpretation of angel that Hawthorne could never have imagined. Both Amiga Gringa and Welfare's confessions suggest a homosexual aspect of Hester's identity, thereby linking Parks's *In the Blood* to Tony Kushner's *Angels in America: A Gay Fantasia on National Themes* (1991/1993).[34] Kushner's two-part play follows a handful of characters as they confront AIDS and homosexuality in the late 1980s. The protagonist, Prior Walter, is dying of AIDS. An angel visits the ailing Prior and tells him that he is a prophet sent to make the world "stop moving," because the uninhibited progress of humanity has driven God away from heaven (179). Prior eventually ascends to heaven and confronts the angels, rejecting his mandate because he wants to keep moving, keep living, for it is human nature to "live past hope" (267).

Not only does Parks dedicate *In the Blood* to Kushner (and others), but her play suggests that Hester herself has been infected with "the ultimate disaster of modern times," which is not the single motherhood that Reverend D indicates when he speaks the line, but AIDS, a disease that travels "in the blood" of its victims (47). Welfare explains in her confession, "I was so afraid I'd catch something" (63), and in his the Doctor admits to having unprotected sex with Hester. Since he is also a drug abuser, he may have even given her the disease. As early as the prologue, the chorus tells us Hester has "bad news in her blood" and that "what she gots catchy" (7). They also claim that they can see this, "plain as day" (7), just by looking at her, perhaps indicating that she already has the telltale Kaposi's sarcoma lesions, which Kushner's Prior Walter describes as another kind of "scarlet" branding: "The wine-dark kiss of the angel of death" (27). The failing eyesight Hester describes to the doctor as well as her paralyzing intestinal discomfort are also possible symptoms. And she is, after all, based on a "Prior" Hester.

In the Blood, then, unlike *The Scarlet Letter* and *Fucking A,* places importance not only on what the A *means,* but also on where the A *is.* This focus on location begins at the play's opening when Hester La Negrita refuses to write her A's in the practice place where someone has scrawled the word *slut.* Instead, Hester La Negrita tells Jabber, "I practiced. In my head. In the air. In the dirt underfoot" (10). The A can be both internal and external. Hester Prynne can, and at one point does, cast off her A in *The Scarlet Letter,* and Hester Smith's brand, in theory, could be surgically removed or altered—or at least covered. When the A is "in the blood," however, it is permanent and deadly. Parks depicts Hester La Negrita's A as "catchy": inheritable, communicable, and like a virus, invisible while still highly potent.

More important than whether or not Hester actually has AIDS are the characteristics she shares with AIDS patients. Kolin points out that "blood symbolizes Hester's sexual sins and shame," and because she is "a sexual outcast" her "polluted blood is her biological scarlet letter."[35] So it is with those diagnosed with HIV/AIDS, especially in the late 1980s and early 1990s. HIV/AIDS, regardless of the source of infection, is often linked in people's minds with sexual promiscuity. African American women, who like gay men are often stereotyped as promiscuous, have been and still are particularly at risk of HIV infection, especially from men who they believe to be their monogamous heterosexual partners. According to the Centers for Disease Control and Prevention (CDC), "In a study of HIV-infected persons, 34% of African American men who have sex with men (MSM) reported having had sex with women, even though only 6% of African American women reported having had sex with a bisexual man."[36] The effects of this trend are obvious and devastating: the CDC estimates that in 2004 African American women represented 64 percent of the 123,405 women with HIV/AIDS and were "approximately 23 times" more likely to be diagnosed with the disease than white women (48.2 out of 100,000 black women versus 2.1 out of 100,000 white women).[37] These statistics point to yet another way that men, especially black men, have failed Hester La Negrita and her contemporaries.

Connecting *In the Blood* with *Angels in America* helps demonstrate how an angel might be a useful symbol for understanding Hester and her modern world. According to Amy Schindler, "Angelic symbolism has been appropriated from traditional religious systems in order to shape new strategies of individual and collective behavior in a period of social transformation," and additionally "an Angel represents a spiritual but nonjudgmental sign of intervention to help people deal with the AIDS crisis."[38] Examining Hester as a "spiritual but nonjudgmental" angel sent to encourage "new strategies of individual and collective behavior" shows that she does not harshly criticize her oppressors; she simply expects "the worldll take care of the women and children," not judge them and abandon them (32). She embodies a persistent yet embattled cry for health care and welfare reform as well as more honest sexual relationships and friendships. And finally she asks, "Having made it next to impossible for the poor to survive, how do we expect them to do it?"[39]

Angels in America links "a literal language of the diseased body and a metaphoric language of the body politic" as Prior's "physical symptoms, particularly repeated references to blood and bleeding (fluid vehicles of transmission and infection) are intended to function as a metonymy of the devastation wreaked upon the entire American homosexual community by AIDS."[40] Hester's symptoms function the same way vis-à-vis black motherhood and the welfare system, and thus *In the Blood* creates the same parallel. Hester is America—the new Republican mother—"treasures," lesions, and all.

Hester La Negrita's confession, the last of the play, reveals that she, like Prior, is a prophet. While Feingold argues that this final confession indicts Hester as "her own worst exploiter," portraying "her devotion to her offspring as a kind of bipolar disorder, violently repudiated and the megalomaniacally embraced,"[41] a more redemptive reading has Hester realizing that her inter-racial children were the army she needed to fight the great battle for her survival. Her visions of Armageddon—complete with eclipse, trumpets, and "the hand of fate with its 5 fingers"—foreshadow an epic holy war in which Hester will finally have the opportunity to vindicate herself after hundreds of years of misplaced judgment and oppression. The play also closes with this image as Hester repeats, three times, "Big hand coming down on me," while "she looks up with outstretched arms" (109–10). Her link to Prior Walter would suggest that she is appealing to Heaven for another chance to prepare her army.

Prophets, of course, are not angels, but like angels they are agents and messengers of God. Biblically the prophetic and angelic are often paired. In *Angels in America,* for example, when Prior asks the Mormon mother Hannah Pitt what he should do to "reject the vision" the angel brings, she replies, "Grab her, say 'I will not let thee go except thou bless me!' Then wrestle her till she gives in" (250). So too does Parks's prophet Hester La Negrita seem to say to her intertextual angel and ancestor Hester Prynne. The Prior Hester has left her namesake a legacy that her circumstances will not let her fulfill. Hester La Negrita cannot be a "self-ordained Angel of Mercy" because she needs mercy too badly herself, just as she cannot be Able in a world that allows her no opportunities, no "leg up." The reader too must wrestle with the Prior Hester and her scarlet letter because they both still haunt literary and cultural history with their persistent warnings about sin, sexuality, and patriarchy. Yet the Prior Hester and her letter are simultaneously inadequate, barely a beginning for expressing the hardships of our twentieth- and twenty-first-century Hesters.

According to Feingold, *In the Blood* reminds audiences, "The Judas kiss of ambiguity is the only one that theatre knows how to give. If we go home tormented by the questions it raises in us, it's done its social duty."[42] But what of the play that leaves its own characters tormented? And what of the audience's social duty as its members turn from the stage or put down the book and leave Hester behind looking up at the sky? Perhaps they should follow her gaze and look for a blazing letter in the sky or the five-fingered hand of fate darkening out the sun like an eclipse. Or perhaps they need simply look around at the real Hesters, prior and present, that tend to slip beyond and outside the gaze—the women living in poverty, dying of AIDS—since much of the world, *In the Blood* subtly asserts, wears a bloody A that signifies "apathy."

CHAPTER 5

Folding and Unfolding History, or Identity Fabrication

The Lincoln Plays

In *The America Play* (1995), a suit, a hat, a set of beards, and a fake wart help "The Lesser Known" feel connected to Abraham Lincoln both ideologically and temporally. In *Topdog/Underdog* (2002), brothers Lincoln and Booth believe that switching identities involves merely taking off old or putting on new clothes, just as an actor puts on a costume to get into character for a performance and then leaves that costume behind to return to his offstage life. In both plays, clothes and costumes highlight the fluidity, exteriority, and superficiality of identity, especially in its relationship to history and memory because as Lincoln and Booth and the characters in *The America Play* recall national history and even their own pasts, costumes dominate their discussions.

These costumes distract audiences' or characters' gazes from the interiors of themselves or the other characters and take these gazes to the exterior, the superficial. However, the superficial becomes so prominent in the characters' lives that eventually mask and wearer become hard to separate and the costumes they wear and engage actually come to irrevocably define them.

The America Play tells the story of a gravedigger called The Foundling Father, or The Lesser Known, a man who has—or at least believes he has—a resemblance to The Great Man, Lincoln. The Lesser Known ends up working as a Lincoln impersonator, first giving speeches, and then pretending to get shot at an amusement park called The Great Hole of History. He leaves his family and heads West to build a replica of the Great Hole of History, in which most of the action of the play transpires. The second half of the play takes place thirty years after he leaves with his wife Lucy and son Brazil digging in the "exact replica of The Great Hole of History," for artifacts to show in their Hall of Wonders as well as for The Foundling Father's body. He returns on his own, however, and tries to reconnect with his family before his death at the end of the play.

Topdog/Underdog follows two unfortunately named brothers, Lincoln and Booth, as they negotiate poverty, familial responsibility, and racial/historical determinism. The brothers share an apartment in which all the play's action takes place. Lincoln, who used to be a successful 3-Card Monty hustler, now works as a Lincoln impersonator at an arcade. He wears a top hat and whiteface, and spectators pay to "assassinate" him. Booth, a kleptomaniac, wants to become a 3-Card Monty player, and he pesters Lincoln to teach him the trade. When Lincoln finally submits and the two play against each other, Booth loses his "inheritance," a knotted stocking that may be filled with money that his mother gave him before she left the family. Outraged, Booth kills Lincoln.

Topdog/Underdog is longer and more linear than its predecessor, but Verna A. Foster, who has examined both plays together in her analysis of "The Lincoln Myth," argued, "The historical themes of the later play can best be understood in light of their more explicit articulation in the earlier one," such that "*The America Play* and *Topdog/Underdog* illuminate one another."[1] The Foundling Father is a literary "faux-father" to Lincoln, and in order to best understand Lincoln, a reader needs to understand his origins. *The America Play* provides a kind of theoretical framework for examining the intersections of history and identity, and *Topdog/Underdog* puts that theory into practice.

The main character in both plays is a Lincoln impersonator who spends much of the play talking about his outfit. In a play, of course, clothes are not just clothes, but costumes—with all the implications that come with that label. Costumes are more complicated than mere clothes because they must both reveal and hide an identity. In any play the costume designer's role "is not to give the actors 'something to wear,' not to 'make them look pretty,' not even to 'dress the stage'; rather, it is to aid in the interpretation of the play as a whole and of each character in the play. A good costume becomes part of the actor's characterization; it clothes the character properly, so that the audience is never aware of the dress as separate from the character."[2] A writer may use a costume to highlight elements of a character, and a character may put on that costume within the play to hide or highlight elements of him- or herself. The Lincoln costumes in both plays epitomize this hiding and highlighting. As with many costumes, the pieces include both a clothing and a makeup component and possibly a mask. Although makeup and beards can function as a mask—a covering of the face—a costume as a whole is also a mask, covering an actor's identity with another in order to obscure wholly.

The Lincoln costumes move beyond mere characterization to come alive with virulent or parasitic sentience, possessing or infecting the characters with which they come into contact. This life grows both from the significance and meaning with which history has imbued the suits and top hats, as well as from the life that they usurp from their wearers, The Foundling Father and Lincoln. The plays suggest that it matters not if a Lincoln impersonator is white or black (or in blackface or whiteface), so long as he wears the right clothes: the Lincoln costume. This costume becomes an all-inclusive signifier of Lincoln-the-President and has a hypnotic effect on those who come into contact with it, charming them into believing that whoever wears the costume is actually Lincoln-the-President. For The Foundling Father and Lincoln, the costume's effect is internal; it distracts and disrupts their perceptions of their true interior selves. For others the costume shifts the gaze away from the man in the costume and onto the merely superficial, the Lincoln costume itself.

In *The America Play,* the importance of costume is underscored by the physical text of the play since, as Katy Ryan pointed out, "The front cover of *The America Play* displays a picture of Lincoln's top hat, beard, and dark suit against an American flag. There is no body, no color—only the outline of a president."[3] The Foundling Father is identified in act 1 as "The Foundling Father as Abraham Lincoln," indicating that he is wearing his Lincoln outfit and is in character throughout. At the beginning of the play, he describes, in third person (he calls himself "The Lesser Known"), his "strong resemblance" to Lincoln (whom he calls "The Great Man"): "There was once a man who was told that he bore a strong resemblance to Abraham Lincoln. He was tall and thinly built just like The Great Man. His legs were the long part just like the Great Mans legs. His hands and feet were large as the Great Mans were large" (160).[4] The Foundling Father complements this slight physical resemblance with what he clearly believes to be a central element of his costume, beards. He explains, "The Lesser Known had several beards which he carried around in a box. The beards were his although he himself had not grown them on his face but since he'd secretly bought the hairs from his barber and arranged their beard shapes and since procurement and upkeep of his beards took so much work he figured that the beards were completely his. Were as authentic as he was, so to speak. His beard box was of cherry wood and lined with purple velvet. He had the initials 'A.L.' tooled in gold on the lid" (160). The Lesser Known fabricates the authenticity of his manufactured beards by labeling them with Lincoln's initials and associating effort, even desire, with ownership.

He then goes on to imagine an alternate history in which The Great Man's and the Lesser Known's paths cross: what would have happened if the men had met in the afterlife or even if Mary Todd Lincoln had called The Lesser Known to dig her husband's grave (160). And if he had been summoned, The Foundling Father as Abraham Lincoln reports, he would have "boarded a train in his look-alike black frock coat bought on time and already exhausted" (161). But his dreams of temporal overlap—of somehow coming into contact with The Great Man with whose identity his own identity is so invested—remain unrealized because "none of this was meant to be. For the Great Man had been murdered long before the Lesser Known had been born" (161).

Still, everywhere The Lesser Known went, The Foundling Father reports, "people remarked on his likeness to Lincoln. How, in a limited sort of way, taking into account of course his natural God-given limitations, how he was identical to the Great Man in gait and manner how his legs were long and torso short. The Lesser Known had by this time taken to wearing a false wart on his cheek in remembrance of the Great Man's wart." With the addition of the wart, the audiences "pronounced the 2 men in virtual twinship" (164). The spectators knowingly overlook obvious physical differences in favor of declaring identity based on a few minor congruities. These "physical differences" become more historically significant when—as is the case in most productions—The Foundling Father is black.

In *Topdog/Underdog,* Lincoln has a similar experience with the schoolboy he meets on the bus. Although Lincoln consistently asserts that he does not like to wear his costume outside of work, he decides to forego this preference in favor of not missing the bus home. On the bus he meets a boy who asks him for his autograph. Lincoln explains, "I pretended I didn't hear him at first. I'd had a long day. But he kept asking. Theyd just done Lincoln in history class and he knew all about him, he'd been to the arcade but, I dunno, for some reason he was tripping cause there was Honest Abe right beside him on the bus" (11).[5] The boy asks for Lincoln's autograph without realizing the superficiality of the situation or noting the obvious paradox of a black man in whiteface dressed as Lincoln.

The kid has "done Lincoln" in his class so he "knew all about him." He had even been to the arcade earlier that day to shoot the man he knew so well. Yet, he cannot separate Lincoln-the-President from a Lincoln impersonator—he does not know actual history from a disparate facsimile. The play thus problematizes conventional historical knowledge and the modes of imparting it to or sharing it with others, especially youth. Through the deceptive effects of the Lincoln costume and elements thereof, *The America Play* and *Topdog/Underdog* show history to be fluid and unstable because it allows itself to be so easily transferred onto an unrealistic paradigm that borders on the absurd—a black man in white face dressed up as Lincoln-the-President. As both plays later explore through their arcade shooters, the sole way to make this paradigm viable rests on the boy's ability to focus exclusively on the Lincoln costume—time, place, and race must fade away. Subsequently this boy's fluid and unstable version of historical knowledge, sanctioned by his whiteness, renders Lincoln's blackness—and thus a defining element of his identity—insignificant, or rather, invisible.

A key difference between The Foundling Father/The Lesser Known and Lincoln in *Topdog/Underdog,* though, is that "The Foundling Father identified with Lincoln. But Linc asserts his own separate and equally significant identity."[6] With the exception of the offstage interaction with the schoolboy, *Topdog/Underdog* does not enact or recall any moments in which Lincoln speaks as Lincoln-the-President.

The Foundling Father, however, speaks the whole of act 1 "As Abraham Lincoln." In the course of the act 1 performance, The Foundling Father interjects the occasional "wink to Mr. Lincoln's pasteboard cutout" (160) or "nod to the bust of Mr. Lincoln" (160), after which The Foundling Father performs the wink/nod he just described to a cutout/bust on stage. These gestures, Deborah Geis has argued, point to "the play itself as a nod or wink toward history, with the reminder that Lincoln himself is at this point primarily an icon, a statue or a cardboard cutout. For the character of The Foundling Father, the nod and wink are engagements with the character he is playing, as if he is both playing homage to Lincoln and upstaging him."[7] The Foundling Father seeks to embody Lincoln and enact his legacy for the viewing audience.

Yet, throughout *Topdog/Underdog,* Lincoln himself struggles with this distinction between his own identity and that of Lincoln-the-President. At the beginning Lincoln seems anxious to separate himself from the character that he plays. Like *Invisible Man*'s jaded Vet, who advises the naive protagonist to "play the game, but don't believe in it,"[8] Lincoln believes that he can be Lincoln and Lincoln-the-President because he thinks the costume simply to be part of a con. When he realizes that he can make money off the boy on the bus, he considers asking for five dollars "cause of the Lincoln connection" but, he says, "something in me made me ask for 10" (11). That something is the player or trickster Lincoln that is—at least at this point in the play—totally distinct from Lincoln-the-President.

This early separation between Lincoln-himself and Lincoln-the-President becomes even more evident as Lincoln continues his story: "All he had was a 20. So I took the 20 and told him to meet me on the bus tomorrow and Honest Abe would give him the change" (12). Lincoln knows that he is not honest nor is he Abe (Lincoln-the-President). Aware that the next day he would ride the bus without his costume, invisible as Lincoln-himself (just a black man on a city bus), he completes his con of the rich boy to his own financial gain. Lincoln is making money from this scheme facilitated by the Lincoln costume, but the implications for black identity are grim. He is in danger of falling into the trap that Houston A. Baker, Jr., believes characterizes Ellison's Trueblood. In *Invisible Man,* Trueblood becomes a kind of minstrel whose masking leads him to be ostracized by his own community and embraced by the white one because he "has indeed accepted the profit motive that gave birth to the mask in the first place."[9]

Yet Lincoln imagines that, like his predecessor, he will leave his Lincoln costume behind one day and walk off the job. He says, "I said to myself thats exactly what I would do: wear it out and then leave it hanging there and not come back. But until then, I would make a living at it. But it dont make me. Worn suit coat, not even worn by the fool that Im supposed to be playing, but making fools out of all those folks who come crowding in for they chance to play at something great. Fake beard. Top hat. Dont make me into no Lincoln. I was Lincoln on my own before any of that" (30).

This early Lincoln provides a marked contrast to the Lincoln at the end of the play who does not, or perhaps cannot, remove the Lincoln costume. Here, at the beginning of the play, Lincoln asserts his personal identity clearly and distinctly. He also points out the historical inaccuracies and paradoxes inherent in the suit and emphasizes that for him, the Lincoln gig is just another hustle. He mocks his shooters' notions of historical transference.

Of course, Lincoln is not wearing the Lincoln costume when he speaks these lines in scene 1. He is not under its spell. He realizes here that the clothes alone are insignificant. The clothes are "fake" and "not even worn by the fool that Im supposed to be playing." These lines—alongside The Foundling Father's discussion of his own fake beard and "look-alike black frock coat bought on time and already exhausted"—suggest that the characters inscribe the clothes and costumes with the meaning, weight, and power that they take on in the plays. Even if The Foundling Father or Lincoln wore Lincoln-the-President's actual suit, the suit itself would not carry meaning: the clothes themselves did not witness history; the wearer did. The clothes themselves are just empty signifiers; they are just cloth. Like its perception of a word, a name, or a mask, the audience brings the meaning to the clothes and imbues them with significance based on experience. Historicized and racialized memory give the Lincoln costume both meaning and life.

Other African American writers, most notably Jamaica Kincaid (in her novels *Annie John* [1985], *Lucy* [1990], and *Autobiography of My Mother* [1995]), have exposed "clothing's ability to preserve within itself a sort of memory and to transmit that memory to successive wearers."[10] But, in *The America Play* and *Topdog/Underdog,* the significance does not transfer from wearer to wearer—it is not the former impersonator that affects Lincoln. Rather significance transfers exclusively from clothes to character based on the meaning put into the clothes by that specific character. The character need not even put on the clothes, just interact with them. This transference applies to the Lincoln costume as well as all other articles of clothing in the plays. None of the men in either play wears his father's suits (Booth only imagines that he does), and the suits that Booth steals are new; previous wearers may have tried them on, but their influence on the imbued meaning of the boosted suits could only be fleeting.

The first time Lincoln appears on stage, he has just come home from work wearing his Lincoln costume. The stage directions tell us that even though Lincoln sneaks up on Booth, "the presence of Lincoln doesnt surprise him, the Lincoln costume does" (9). In the lines that follow, Booth continues to express his revulsion, without explaining the root cause of it. Yet Booth clearly, at least at this moment, does not express revulsion for Lincoln-himself—his past or present actions—but for the effects of the Lincoln costume, with all of its racial and historical baggage.

In addition to calling his brother a "shiteating motherfucking pathetic limpdick uncle tom" (21), signaling not only emasculation but also racial assimilation, Booth calls Lincoln "all spooked out and shit" (9) and tells him, "take off that damn coat, man, you make me nervous standing there looking like a spook, and damn that face paint, take it off" (11). In African American culture and literature, the term *spook*—evoked most famously by Sam Greenlee's 1972 novel *The Spook Who Sat by the Door*—can signify spy as well as a more pejorative, racialized insult. It also implies ghostlike spectrality, the ghosts of Lincoln-the-President as well as the brothers' familial past. So, when Booth repeats the term *spook,* he layers these various meanings onto Lincoln. Although Lincoln is wearing only a costume and seems himself oblivious to its effects at this point in the play, Booth perceives that the costume completely demeans his brother. At best Lincoln is a ghost, a shadow of himself who has given up his chosen profession as a card dealer and become reduced to the haunting image of a dead president and a dark era in American history. At worst he is completely stripped of his identity, unrecognizable and undesirable even to his own brother, or he is a spy, a white man's pawn infiltrating his people. This conversation also foreshadows the merging of Lincoln and Lincoln-the-President later in the play as well as Lincoln's death at Booth's hand. Thus the play indicates early on the inevitability of the brothers' fates, fates anticipated by superficial, external elements—their names and Lincoln's costume.

Booth also expresses concern that seeing Lincoln in the costume will cause Grace to leave him. He explains, "She sees you in that getup its gonna reflect bad on me. She coulda seen you coming down the street. Shit. Could be standing outside right now taking her ring off and throwing it on the sidewalk" (10). The effects of the Lincoln costume are not limited to Lincoln and Booth. The clothes emanate an unpleasant aura, so powerful it can, theoretically, even negate the love of a woman. And in fact Grace never appears. Like the mother and the angry shooting housewives, she is always off-stage or remembered—a ghost or specter essentially invisible herself. If she indeed does not exist beyond Booth's imagination, then she can be read to represent the slippage of Booth's identity into insanity as well as his hope—for love, happiness, and, as her name implies, salvation. Indeed Sandy Alexander has observed, "Grace is evoked whenever Booth needs a 'saving grace' to save face in front of his big, topdog brother Lincoln."[11] By claiming that the Lincoln costume has the power to negate Grace's love and her presence, Booth is essentially claiming that the costume—with all of its negative connotations about the past and the present—chases away any hope that he might have for the future.

Lincoln himself alludes to the negative aura of the Lincoln costume when he awakens in scene 4 still in his costume after sleeping in it. Although the previous scene begins the same way with no mention from Lincoln, he is upset this time. After relieving himself, "He claws at his Lincoln getup, removing it and tearing it in the process. He strips down to his t-shirt and shorts" (54). He explains, "Hate falling asleep in this damn shit," and launches into an extended soliloquy in which he imagines killing his employer and reminisces fondly of his days as a hustler (54). Remarkably, in this soliloquy Lincoln oscillates among the first, second, and third person, even within individual paragraphs, indicating that he is struggling with self-definition and perspective: "Got yrself a good job. And when the arcade lets you go yll get another good job. I dont gotta spend my whole life hustling. Theres more to Link than that. More to me than some cheap hustle. More to life than cheating some idiot out of his paycheck or his life savings" (55). The shift in reactions to the Lincoln costume between the beginning of scene 3 and the beginning of scene 4 can be read as part of this struggle. The opening stage directions of scene 3 tell us only that Lincoln "is horrific, bleary eyed and hungover, in his full Lincoln regalia" (38). In this early moment, just one scene previous, Lincoln shows no fear or revulsion for the costume. The events in the remainder of scene 3 thus catalyze a change in Lincoln that brings him to the revulsion he expresses at the beginning of scene 4 and the identity crisis that follows it.

Structurally scene 3 is the center of the play. After Booth details his date with Grace, the action turns to Lincoln's description of his daily assassination at the arcade, and *(Rest)*s fill this description. Parks explained in "From *Elements of Style*," excerpted at the front of the play, that *(Rest)*s indicate "where the figures experience their pure true simple state."[12] Thus Lincoln's description of his daily assassination reveals the "real deal" about his job as a Lincoln impersonator. He says, "Its pretty dark. To keep the illusion of the whole thing / *(Rest)*" (49). Lincoln's job takes an emotional toll. Dressed as Lincoln-the-President, he dies countless times a day, and he witnesses this assassination—his own assassination. However, he is a disembodied witness: "But on thuh wall opposite where I sit theres a little electrical box, like a fuse box. Silver metal. Its got uh dent in it like somebody hit it with they fist. Big old dent so everything in it gets reflected upside down. Like yr looking in uh spoon. And thats where I can see um. The assassins. / *(Rest)* / . . . Me looking at him upside down and him looking at me looking like Lincoln. Then he shoots. / *(Rest)*" (49–50).

He sees his murder, but in reverse, upside down, and in a costume. Lincoln's gaze is on the reflection of his would-be assassin, but the assassin's gaze is on Lincoln "looking like Lincoln" in the Lincoln costume. And even though he is dressed as Lincoln-the-President, the murder is real to him because it is he, Lincoln, who is alive, not Lincoln-the-President: "And there he is. Standing behind me. Standing in position. Standing upside down. Theres some feet shapes on the floor so he knows just where he oughta stand. So he wont miss. Thuh gun is always cold. Winter or summer the gun is always cold. And when thuh gun touches me he can feel that Im warm and he knows Im alive. And if Im alive then he can shoot me dead. And for a minute, with him hanging back there behind me, its real. / *(Rest)*" (50).

The assassins rely on sensing Lincoln's life—the softness of live tissue, the reaction of warm flesh to the cold metal barrel of the gun—to re-create Lincoln-the-President's death for sport; they resurrect Lincoln-the-President, through Lincoln, just to kill him again. However, Lincoln's black body only appears to bring Lincoln-the-President back to life for the assassins, for, as Lincoln intuits in this scene, the historical incongruities—again time, place, and race—can suggest only that they are shooting Lincoln-himself.

To make the imaginative leap to Lincoln-the-President, the arcade shooters in both *The America Play* and *Topdog/Underdog* must rely on Lincoln's invisibility as well as a completely constructed and superficial historical reality. The Lincoln costume rationalizes this construction and their shooting. It also allows them to believe that Lincoln-the-President is not dead and that they can remake history or place themselves within it by shooting a live version of him, even if that version is a black man in white face. Based on Lincoln's description, the dummy replacement of him *will* likely fail because the assassins will not be able to feel its life. The Lincoln costume truly functions here as a kind of possession or parasite; the suit feeds off the "historical" shooters, but it needs a live host to thrive.

In *The America Play,* assassination scenes are repeatedly enacted throughout the play with a variety of assassins interrupting the action to shoot The Foundling Father. Each shooter, identified as Booth in the stage directions, shouts a different line after firing the gun: a man—a weekly regular—yells, "The South is Avenged!" (165); a woman screams, "LIES" (168). These lines, Ilka Saal has suggested, "reflect the fantasies and anxieties the *faux* assassins project into their imitations,"[13] and, by extension, on to The Foundling Father.

Topdog/Underdog does put Lincoln's repeated assassination on stage, but in his descriptions of these shooters, Lincoln provides significant details about what his shooters are wearing. The aggregate of these descriptions implies that a wide variety of Americans, young and old, male and female, comes to the arcade to shoot Lincoln, to participate in historical re-creation. Thus the play explores a variety of motivations for shooting a black man dressed as Lincoln-the-President. The businessmen come in "dress shoes," implying wealth and formality or power; killing Lincoln, for them, kills competition from African American businesses or businesspeople (49). This wealth, formality, and power also highlight the disparity between Lincoln's socio-economic status and their own. Children come as well, but in "school uniforms"—implying education as well as conformity (50). Their presence not only reaffirms that children learn a skewed and corrupting view of history in school, as suggested earlier in the play by the boy on the bus, but also that white hegemonic views of race—indeed even the desire to kill a black man—are systematically instilled in American youth. The tourists in "theme park t-shirts" (50) add a disturbing performative entertainment element, reminiscent of *The America Play's* Great Hole of History, the theme park that The Foundling Father and Lucy visit on their honeymoon and of which The Foundling Father makes "an exact replica"—that becomes the play's setting.

The Foundling Father as Abraham Lincoln explains that the Great Hole of History was, "A Big Hole. A theme park. With historical parades. The size of the hole itself was enough to impress any Digger but it was the Historicity of the place the order and beauty of the pageants which marched by them the Greats on parade in front of them" (162). Later in the play, Lucy paints a much more substantive picture of what they saw there and its impact: "At the Great Hole where we honeymooned—son, at thuh Original Great Hole—you could see the whole world without goin too far. You could look intuh that whole and see your entire life pass before you. Not your own life but someones life from history, you know, [someone who'd done something of note, got theirselves known somehow, uh President or] somebody who killed somebody important, uh face on a postal stamp, you know, someone from History. *Like* you, but *not* you. You know: *known*" (196).[14] The hole allows its visitor to be someone else: someone greater. That someone is in a way a projection of the visitor, but the hole conflates the projection and the actual as the visitor craves a closer connection with greatness.

The Foundling Father/The Lesser Known feels compelled to build "an exact replica of the Great Hole of History" because he tried performing selections from Lincoln's speeches, but he "was a curiosity at best. None of those who spoke of his virtual twinship with greatness would actually pay money to watch him be that greatness" (164). So he tried letting people "come and throw old food at him," and this met with some success: he began a profitable traveling show and "people began to save their old food 'for Mr. Lincoln'" (164). But when a spectator "remarked that he played Lincoln so well that he ought to be shot, it was as if the Great Man's footsteps has been suddenly revealed;" shooters started paying a penny to "kill" him, and "The Lesser Known became famous overnight" (164). Haike Frank has maintained that, in *The America Play,* "The fact that the public shows greater interest in Lincoln's murder than in his political speeches and, by implication, his political deeds, points to the dominance of fragmentation and the power of sensationalism in society."[15] The shooters come to the replica of The Great Hole of History to find a connection to the past, and they find this connection by embracing a limited, violent view of history.

In both plays these shooters sanction their desire to kill a black man by disguising it as the desire to participate in historical re-creation and by shifting Lincoln-the-President's identity onto The Foundling Father and Lincoln-himself. The costume transforms the men and allows the re-creation of history in addition to the rewriting of it with a new black victim. Even though their victim's blackness removes the authenticity of re-creating Lincoln-the-President, the assassins indeed still participate in historical re-creation because, by writing in this black victim, they are essentially becoming members of a lynch mob, lining up to kill a black man. Day after day they lynch him, killing him by rendering him each day more invisible to himself because of his invisibility to them; with each shot they slowly kill him by contributing to his transition into the real assassinated.

In *Topdog/Underdog,* Lincoln wears whiteface, but the assassins come from behind him, in full view of his black neck. It is Lincoln's blackness, however, that renders his identity invisible and allows the assassin's gaze to shift exclusively to the superficial, embodied by his costume, to define their actions. As Ellison's narrator explains with the "tall blond man" he fights in the street, there are two types of seeing—one superficial, that allows a white stranger to insult a black man who bumps into him, another more meaningful, that cannot *see* the same rage-filled black man kicking and punching him. Invisible Man remembers, "One night I accidentally bumped into a man, and perhaps because of the near darkness he saw me and called me an insulting name." But as Invisible Man holds the stranger and starts "to slit his throat," he explains, "it occurred to me that the man had not *seen* me, actually."[16] Similarly, Lincoln's assassins see him, but they don't *see* him. They see that he is a black man, and thus they reduce him to a set of superficial and pejorative stereotypes—a laborer or a minstrel—and render him expendable. They do not *see* that he is Lincoln, a brother, a poor man who is struggling to survive and who is allowing himself to be killed to do so.

But there is also a black man who comes to Lincoln's arcade, a man who sees beyond the costume. The brothers' brief exchange about this man oozes with ambiguity. For example, Booth asks Lincoln if the man is "a brother" and if the man knows that Lincoln is "a brother" (34). Lincoln answers both questions indecisively, highlighting the ultimate permeability of racial lines. Booth also calls this man Lincoln's "Best Customer" and is careful to ask Lincoln whether this black customer actually shoots. "He shoot you?" Booth inquires; Lincoln replies, "He shot Honest Abe, yeah" (33–34). In his answer to this inquiry, complicated by the threat of intraracial violence, Lincoln again seeks to draw a clear line between himself and Lincoln-the-President. He evokes the "Honest Abe" moniker he used when hustling the schoolboy on the bus, indicating a desire to inscribe his Lincoln arcade gig as just another con.

In his whispers to Lincoln, the black shooter captures the same essence of superficiality implied by the play's use of clothing up to this point. He asks, reminiscent of Molly's key lines in *Imperceptible Mutabilities in the Third Kingdom,* "Does thuh show stop when no ones watching or does thuh show go on?" and tells Lincoln, "Yr only yrself . . . when no ones watching" (34).

These whispered utterances highlight the performative nature of identity in *Topdog/Underdog*—who the brothers are changes based on who their audiences want and/or expect them to be. Under the white gaze, wearing the Lincoln mask, Lincoln is invisible. When he is with Booth, he is the Topdog, and he must perform the guarded big brother role that the volatile Underdog expects. The only time Lincoln is onstage when "when no ones watching" is scene 4. Here Booth is onstage, but he is "fast asleep, dead to the world" (54). Scene 4 consists entirely of Lincoln's monologue—or dialogue with himself—and, as previously described, proves to be the most tumultuous scene in terms of Lincoln's identity.

Immediately before this scene, at the end of scene 3 Booth and Lincoln practice adding "spicy shit" to Lincoln's death scene (50). This practice at first amuses the brothers, but the mood changes significantly when Booth yells, "I am the assassin! *I am Booth!!* Come on man this is life and death! Go all out!" (52). Although he has only just shot Lincoln, dressed as Lincoln-the-President, with a pretend gun, Booth has internalized his role as Booth-the-actor, the assassin. The brothers could have just as easily practiced this scene without the Lincoln costume. The action is not physically contingent upon it. Yet, Lincoln puts on his costume expressly for this practice, waits for Booth, and then continues to wear it for a full scene, indicating that the action must be at least emotionally contingent upon it. Booth screaming "I am the assassin!" breaks down a psychological barrier between Lincoln's life and Lincoln-the-President's life and makes the superficial costume very real. At this point, Lincoln cannot separate himself from Lincoln-the-President because of the overwhelming superficial historical similarities. Booth's taking up of the Booth-the-actor role for the first time in the play compounds the effects of the Lincoln costume; the dominating superficiality, inspired by the Lincoln costume itself, has completely obscured both brothers' identities—both for themselves and for each other. In essence the costume creates a new Booth that is Booth-the-actor. By the end of the play, Booth, having slowly made his full transition to assassin, is completely unable to separate himself from the legacy of Booth-the-actor, the assassin after whom he is named.

The last line of Lincoln's scene 1 "Emancipation" proclamation—"I was Lincoln on my own before any of that"—although intended to assert independence from his costume, does leave room for this type of complication between the brothers. The grammar of this line suggests no difference between the first Lincoln and the second, and it creates a kind of equation between Lincoln and Lincoln-the-President. As Lincoln has been working at his job for some time, the equation could describe the cumulative effects of impersonating Lincoln-the-President; or it could suggest something more historical. Simply by naming the brothers Lincoln and Booth, although the father meant it to be "a joke" (24), the play suggests interconnectivity within history and identity. Lincoln—as an American and especially as an African American—must have a set of cultural assumptions, though likely superficial or apocryphal, about Lincoln-the-President, "The Great Emancipator." The Lincoln costume takes Lincoln further into the interconnectivity between himself and the historically loaded, yet still superficial, signifier "Lincoln," and the assassinations take him even further.

Similarly The Foundling Father's name "suggests that he is both linked to one of the *Founding* Fathers, and that he himself is a 'foundling,' or orphan" (99). Abandoned by history, his character challenges the audience to consider the origins of the historical symbols that define him and his show, and he does so most pointedly through his costume choices. He explains in act 1, "I think I'll wear the yellow beard. Variety. Works like a tonic. / *(Rest)* / Some inaccuracies are good for business. Take the stovepipe hat! Never really worn indoors but people dont like their Lincoln hatless" (168). This descriptions of the famous hat and the yellow Lincoln beard—which Brazil unearths at the end of the plays in his search for his father's bones—show The Foundling Father's understanding "that the historical persona is a constructed image, accuracy is less important than reinforcing a persona" (105). The Foundling Father works within the blurred boundaries between real and fabricated history because he understands the value of playing into his audience's historical expectations, even when the audience expects inaccuracy.

Yet it is also possible to go too far with these historical changes. Earlier in the play, for example, The Foundling Father explains of the same yellow beard, "This is my fancy beard. Yellow. Mr. Lincolns hair was dark so I dont wear it much. If you deviate too much they wont get their pleasure. Thats my experience" (163). He also talks about a beard that he often takes out "on the holidays. I got shoes to match. Rarely wear em together. It's a little *much*." (161). When the images become too fake, audiences cannot help but confront the truth behind their construction.

Topdog/Underdog also explores this confrontation point when both brothers are disturbed by the reaction that Lincoln's "spicy shit" evokes for them. After this gruesome death scene, Lincoln delivers one of the play's most poignant and memorable sets of lines: "People are funny about they Lincoln shit. Its historical. People like they historical shit in a certain way. They like it to unfold the way they folded it up. Neatly like a book. Not raggedy and bloody and screaming" (52). Although Lincoln is framing this metaphor with the image of a book, the language and the image do not match. Books are opened and closed, not folded and unfolded. The point nonetheless conveys clearly: the history in books is sanitized and superficial. But Lincoln's folding and unfolding apply more aptly to fabric, specifically clothing and especially his Lincoln costume. The Lincoln costume highlights that audiences will believe in, if not wholly prefer, an unbelievable Lincoln impersonator, a black man in whiteface dressed as Lincoln-the-President who dies quietly, only to come back to life again for the next customer to kill. When Booth becomes the assassin at the end of scene 3, Lincoln can no longer fold history, or the Lincoln costume, back up and put it away as he found it; he cannot leave the suit behind. He claws desperately at the costume in scene 4 because the history is no longer superficial; it is deeply personal.

The play itself nearly immediately implies the application of this "folding and unfolding" metaphor to costume. The next set of lines pertains explicitly to the Lincoln costume and Lincoln's personal struggles with it. After a *(Rest),* Lincoln continues, "I am uh brother playing Lincoln. Its uh stretch for anyones imagination. And it aint easy for me neither. Every day I put on that shit, I leave my own shit at the door and I put on that shit and I go out there and make it work. I make it look easy but its hard. That shit is hard. But it works. Cause I work it" (52). Here Lincoln more clearly acknowledges the personal identity sacrifice and self-displacement needed to put on the costume. He realizes here that in leaving his "own shit at the door" to put on the Lincoln costume, part of his own identity is being usurped by Lincoln-the-President. He attempts to position himself as a master of masking, a skill—at least in the form *Invisible Man*'s grandfather describes—that can be very powerful and subversive if used correctly, but the subversive elements and the fulfillment that comes therewith are missing from Lincoln's mask. Rather he again points only to the detrimental effects. He acknowledges the toll that the Lincoln costume takes on him when he must leave himself behind in order to put it on, thereby rendering himself invisible. Also, in admitting that "a brother playing Lincoln" would be "uh stretch" for his audience, he shows he has recognized that the assassins cannot logically believe that they are killing Lincoln-the-President; they are there to kill him. Lincoln thus identifies the role he plays in his own assassination. He has willingly accepted the superficiality that defines his invisibility—a superficiality that only works because he plays it like a 3-Card Monty game. Having achieved this realization, the next time Lincoln wakes up in his costume, at the beginning of scene 4, he tears it off—but not for long.

And although The Foundling Father yearns to feel an identity connection with Lincoln-the-President, the superficial identity he creates for himself out of this desire is ultimately destructive. Physically, because of the constant exposure to gunfire, he is partially deaf, which, according to Geis, "reflects the sense in which the decision to create his character involves both an awareness of the past and a willingness to turn a deaf ear on certain aspects of it."[17] More important, though, the persistent longing, combined with the suppression of his true identity, has fragmented him and prevented him from knowing both his family and himself. The Foundling Father as Abraham Lincoln details these effects when he says, "They both had such long legs. Such big feet. And the Greater Man had such a lead although of course somehow still 'back there.' If the Lesser Known had slowed down stopped moving completely gone in reverse died maybe the Greater Man would have caught up. Woulda had a chance. Woulda sneaked up behind the Lesser Known unbeknownst and wrestled him to the ground. Stabbed him in the back. In revenge. 'Thus to tyrants!' Shot him maybe. The Lesser Known forgets who he is and just crumples. His bones cannot be found. The Greater Man continues on" (172–73). In this passage The Greater Man represents the self that The Lesser Known would have been if he had not spent his time trying to make himself into just The Great Man, Lincoln. But since he never allows himself to realize his potential as The Greater Man, he leaves no enduring legacy.

The Foundling Father's fragmentation also manifests itself in the form of the play. In act 1, he appears as a three-part self, similar to that seen in the characters of *Imperceptible Mutabilities in the Third Kingdom* and *The Death of the Last Black Man in the Whole Entire World.* He speaks in the third person and is at once The Lesser Known, The Foundling Father, and The Foundling Father as Abraham Lincoln. He is separated from his family, and he tells a disjointed story of death and impossibilities. When The Foundling Father reappears in act 2, the text identifies him as just The Foundling Father. There is no mention of The Lesser Known, and he does speak some lines in first person. While the stage directions do not specifically say what The Foundling Father wears in act 1 or 2, the text suggests that he may not be wearing his full Lincoln costume in act 2 since Brazil already has the box marked A.L. and at least one beard. Without the full costume, he is more himself; he reaches out to his family and tries to explain his past. Yet there is no reconciliation: his lines generally consist of pasted-together Lincoln quotes or other famous one-liners, his family will not hug him, and ultimately he dies, the victim of an assassin's bullet.

In *Topdog/Underdog,* Lincoln's dualistic relationship with the Lincoln costume only deepens as the play draws to its close. When the arcade fires him, Lincoln comes home wearing part of the costume—the frock coat—and carrying the rest in a bag (60). He soon puts the entire suit back on so that Booth can take a picture of him in it, and he remains in the costume for the rest of his play and, as such, for the rest of his life (90). His dependence on the Lincoln costume shows when he ponders going back to beg for his job. To this, Booth responds, "Link. Yr free. Dont go crawling back. Yr free at last!" (62). By evoking the words of Martin Luther King Jr., the play makes Lincoln's struggle timeless and equates his struggle with the Lincoln costume to a struggle for civil rights and personal freedom. But, as in King's speech, these rights and freedoms, at least for Lincoln and Booth, are still just a dream. The brothers are bound by all the costume signifies: revisionist history, slavery, racism, double-consciousness, poverty, and even their own personalities.

Lincoln's coming home, fired, with his suit is especially significant because at the beginning of the play, as mentioned above, he insists he will leave it behind when he leaves his job. This gesture of leaving the clothes behind parallels both his father's and his mother's abandonments, both of which are memorialized in the play by the clothes each parent left behind. The play links the father especially almost directly to the Lincoln costume in Lincoln's mind. After talking about his "fake old" work costume, Lincoln—following a *(Rest)*—makes the connection to his father: "Remember how Dads clothes used to hang in the closet?" (29). Booth then adds, "Until you took em outside and burned em. / *(Rest)* / He had some nice stuff. What he didnt spend on booze he spent on women. What he didnt spend on them two he spent on clothes. He had some nice stuff. I would look at his stuff and calculate thuh how long it would take till I was big enough to fit it. Then you went and burned it all up." Lincoln responds, "I got tired of looking at em without him in em" and, after another *(Rest)*, returns to the Lincoln suit: "They said the fella before me—he took off the getup one day, hung it up real nice, and never came back" (29).

This connection between the father and Lincoln-the-President shows the formative role that both have played in Lincoln's identity as well as Booth's. Booth thinks that he can grow into being a man like his father simply by growing into his clothes—thus transferring his father's identity onto himself. Lincoln, on the other hand, complicates the father's legacy. In other words, as Nicole Matos has explained in her essay on the role of clothing in Jamaica Kincaid's novels, "The generic rebellion of destroying clothing often becomes paired with another, more specific rebellion, something absolutely, expressly forbidden."[18]

Topdog/Underdog adopts a similar paradigm but revises it subtly. Instead of exclusively signaling rebellion, Lincoln's motives are more paradoxical. In burning the Father's clothes, Lincoln both affirms and denies clothing's ability to imbue identity. For example, when Booth asks, "Whyd he leave his clothes though? Even drunks gotta wear clothes," Lincoln responds, "Whyd he leave his clothes whyd he leave us? He was uh drunk bro. He—whatever, right? I mean, you aint gonna figure it out by thinking about it. Just call it one of thuh great unsolved mysteries of existence" (89). Lincoln's response takes the emphasis away from the father's clothes and transfers it back to where it belongs, the father's actions. The clothes cannot stand for the father because they are just a shell. "Without him in em," they are just an empty signifier. Yet the clothes hold some significance, for they still can signal his absence and the pain associated therewith. If the clothes were truly meaningless, Lincoln would not need to burn them or allow them to hang around for so long before burning them.

This paradoxical relationship with his father's clothes mirrors the duality Lincoln fights when putting on the Lincoln costume. Indeed, in turning immediately from the father's empty suit to the empty Lincoln costume, the play equates the two absences, suggesting that "The Great Emancipator" is also missing or has left the brothers specifically and black America in general. Rather than reject and burn Lincoln's clothes, as he does with his father's, Lincoln, like The Foundling Father, steps into them and attempts to play the role of Lincoln-the-President. In *The America Play,* Lucy explains that her husband "knew only that he wanted to grow and have others think of him and remove their hats and touch their hearts and look up into the heavens and say something about the freeing of the slaves. That is, he wanted to make a great impression as he understood Mr. Lincoln to have made" (166).

This more politically and socially minded motivation resurfaces again at the end of *Topdog/Underdog* when Lincoln puts on his costume and mask for the last time. In this final scene, Lincoln's whiteface mask signals impending civil war. He applies the white paint for Booth's photo in "two thin smears" that look "more like war paint than whiteface" (91). Although the play leaves his motives for this somewhat ambiguous, Lincoln *will* battle his brother for power in an epic clash of ideologies. This historical resonance suggests that even more than a domestic father, Lincoln needs a political leader. He cannot leave the Lincoln suit empty because to do so has social as well as personal implications—it leaves America without an emancipator, and more immediately it leaves him and Booth without the money to survive and liberate themselves from poverty.

At the same time that Lincoln discusses leaving his costume behind and the father's leaving his clothes behind, the men are dressing up in Booth's boosted suits. Booth steals predominantly clothes and accessories, superficial items that can easily be exchanged for others. Booth is essentially shopping (or shoplifting) for new identities, and his true identity remains mysterious. The play identifies him, on the Dramatis Personae, as the Underdog to his brother and tells us very little else about him outside of his relationship to Lincoln. He tries to steal Lincoln's wife, and the first time Booth is on stage alone—at the play's opening—he is playing Lincoln's game, 3-Card Monty. The only other time is at the beginning of scene 2, when he "comes in looking like he is bundled up against the cold" in layers of boosted clothes (25). Booth proceeds to peel off the layers of clothing, and although the audience would expect to see Booth himself in this scene since there is "no one watching," the play shows only layer upon layer of stolen clothes. Furthermore his actions evoke humor, which "hides" him even more. As he peels off each layer of stolen identity, the true Booth is never revealed, only more clothes. Under his coat "he wears a very nice new suit. He removes the jacket and pants revealing another new suit underneath. The suits still have the price tags on them" (25). It is clear that Booth does remove the second suit at some point, since he later "lays one suit out on Lincolns easy chair" and another "on his own bed" (25). But, the stage directions do not tell us what Booth should be wearing under the second suit with the price tag—what he was wearing underneath all the layers, what he was wearing before he put on the first item he stole—nor do they express how or when he should remove the second suit with the price tag still on it. Thus the written text of the play leaves Booth's final identity ambiguous, fluid—and essentially up to the audience or director to assign. Under the layers of superficial stolen identity, there is no deeper identity for Booth.

Also, since these actions are represented only in stage directions, this moment is a purely visual experience. Booth does not represent himself through language but only acts. His identity, then, can be read as strictly performative. This performance, however, reveals nothing beyond Booth's deliberate and artistic shoplifting skills, for the stage directions' disrobing description ends abruptly and without resolution when Lincoln enters the scene with his payload and they begin to role-play a Ma and Pa scene. The previous stage directions, then, serve only to highlight the superficiality of Booth's identity: it is entirely stolen.

Booth also steals His and Hers dressing gowns for himself and Grace to wear on their romantic date. Again, whether Grace even exists or still has a relationship with Booth fundamentally does not matter. In either case his fascination with her and his linking of her with an article of clothing indicates further slippage of his identity; he is either faking wealth and privilege or falling further into insanity. When Grace fails to show up to the party that Booth has planned for them and to put on the costume that he has set out for her, Booth's fairy tale fails; Booth dresses up for the ball, but his princess never shows up. His vision of a perfect marriage to the woman of his dreams (whether she is make-believe or not) is thwarted. This fairy tale parallel allows us to situate *Topdog/Underdog* more firmly in the critical conversation about clothing's relevance in literature. Most scholars explore clothing's relationship to female characters exclusively, and, the "Cinderella Complex," as Mary Jane Lupton described it, is a helpful paradigm through which to examine clothing's influence on women. Lupton defines the "Cinderella Complex" as "a dangerous cultural attitude towards women, digested early and constantly reinforced: By looking right, and dressing right, and attending the right dances, a woman can get out of working and be financially supported by, if not a prince, then at least a young male executive."[19] Clothes then not only define identity, but also determine potential for success and marriage. In Booth's case Grace signifies this success, and in failing to put on the identity he steals for her—thereby allowing him to put on the matching wardrobe—she thwarts his success.

So, although women are absent from the stage in *Topdog/Underdog,* women's impact, influence, and valuation are not. Since clothing and the obsession therewith is typically socially defined as a women's concern, by making clothes a central concern for Lincoln and Booth, Parks not only challenges a stereotype, but also broadens—to include men—the scope of investigation into the effects of society's image consciousness on identity. Parks has mentioned in interviews that some people think that the play is written by a man and that others question her credibility as a female artist writing about men.[20] Through clothes Parks proves that audience expectations and overreliance on the importance of image can take its toll on any actor, male or female.

Women are not absent from the stage, however, in *The America Play.* Lucy, The Foundling Father's wife, dominates act 2. Lucy, who lives a as single mother for more than thirty years, supports her son by working as a "Confidence," or secret keeper.

In act 1 The Foundling Father as Abraham Lincoln explains that, as The Lesser Known "had assumed the superiority of his own blood and hadnt really expected the mother to exert any influence" over their son Brazil's appearance (162). However, the text suggests that Lucy in fact is the stronger as well as the more generous partner in the marriage. While Brazil digs for artifacts to display in the Hall of Wonders, Lucy lists everything that she gave to her husband, repeating, "Thuh apron from uhround my waist. / Thuh hair from my head" (193). The apron, a clothinglike accessory, symbolizes an idyllic domesticity, a world in which Lucy was allowed a complete family—a partner for herself, a father for son—and a home outside of a hole in the ground. The hair recalls The Foundling Father's earlier discussion of his beards, which are made from collected human hair. As such, the hair Lucy gave him likely went to construct a beard that he then used in a historically inaccurate Lincoln costume, now rendered more complex and symbolic since it is composed—at least in part—by the physical and emotional sacrifice of a black woman.

Lucy also maintains her ability, or at least her desire, to see through historical fabrications and to understand their impact. When Brazil gets caught up in his exaggerated stories about the "original" Great Hole of History, Lucy corrects him, "That Hole back East was uh theme park son. Keep your story to scale" (180). She also sees that while Brazil looks more physically similar to his father as he matures, the more important transformation is in the clothes he has inherited (or not) and the roles he chooses to accept. She observes:

LUCY. I swanee you look more and more and more like him ever-y day.
BRAZIL. His chin?
LUCY. You got his chin.
BRAZIL. His lips.
LUCY. You got his lips.
BRAZIL. His teeths?
LUCY. Top and bottom. In his youth. He had some. Just like yours. His frock coat. Was just like that. He had hisself uh stovetop hat which you lack. His medals—yours are for weepin his of course were for diggin. (190)

For Lucy the extent to which Brazil has put on (or has yet to put on) copies of his father's clothes represents the extent of his transformation into a celebrated faker. She knows that the clothes do not represent a transition into greatness, but rather a transition away from reality. Lucy thus abides by her manifesto, declared at the beginning of act 2, to seek "tuh know thuh real thing from thuh echo. Thuh truth from thuh hersay" (175).

According to Foster, this issue "of distinguishing the 'truth' of history from the 'hearsay,' that pertains in *The America Play*" also creates "the uncertainty of Booth's inheritance."[21] In *Topdog/Underdog,* this inheritance—an undergarment, the mother's money-filled (perhaps) stocking—shows that "Booth exists in a kind of sexual and economic limbo,"[22] and it becomes the fragile thread by which Booth's sanity, and perhaps his entire identity, hangs.

In the Ma and Pa play, Booth plays the mother role, as he obviously identifies more with the mother in his family since she leaves him the inheritance despite the fact that he is the younger brother. Even at the beginning of the play, Booth threatens to gamble with this inheritance. However, Lincoln knows—at least at this point—that his brother is joking, and he tells him, "Thats like saying you dont got no money cause you aint never gonna do nothing with it so its like you dont got it"—to which Booth retorts, "At least I still gots mines. You blew yrs" (17). Though on the surface the brothers are speaking of economic responsibility, they are also more subtly speaking of family ties. Lincoln, in spending his paternal inheritance, has at least started the process of dissociating himself from his father's legacy. Booth, in keeping the mother's money-filled(?) stocking, unsure of the monetary value of its contents, still defines himself in connection with this inheritance and, subsequently, his mother's abandonment.

Therefore, when the brothers return to the subject a few pages later, Booth is again on the defensive as he describes the day his mother left and gave him the stocking: "She was putting her stuff in bags. She had all them nice suitcases but she was putting her stuff in bags. /*(Rest)* / Packing up her shit. She told me to look out for you. I told her I was the little brother and the big brother should look out after the little brother. She just said it again. That I should look out for you. Yeah" (21). Thus Booth's bequest from the mother is not exclusively economic. This maternal inheritance also gives him license to feel superior to Lincoln, for despite the fact that he is "the little brother," the mother designates him as the Topdog. Also, in the lines immediately following this description, Booth attempts to emasculate Lincoln by calling him a "shiteating motherfucking pathetic limpdick uncle tom," and he screams, "Here I am trying to earn a living and you standing in my way. YOU STANDING IN MY WAY, LINK!" (21). Contrary to any hopes that Lincoln might have of being a black "Great Emancipator," the mother's mandate, symbolized by the possibly money-filled stocking that accompanies it, binds Booth to Lincoln. Even though Lincoln actually supports his brother emotionally and financially, Booth makes his life and his identity contingent on his brother's, an action seemingly based on the mother's final charge. The stocking makes Lincoln a link, unseverable—save by death—that ties Booth to his brother.

Indeed, when that tie is severed, Lincoln dies. After Lincoln wins the money, the stage directions read simply, "Lincoln brings the knife down to cut the stocking" (107). Booth, previously laughing, stops the action with "I popped her" and goes on to describe Grace's murder (107). Again Grace's existence, already established as questionable, is irrelevant here. In killing his "grace," Booth has killed his hope and his capacity to forgive. Thus he redefines himself again, telling his brother, "That Booth shit is over. 3-Cards thuh man now" (108). By equating this murder and shift in personal definition with the threat of the stocking's destruction, the play links elements of

Booth's personality—most obviously his sanity and familial responsibility—to the article of clothing.

Seemingly sensing Booth's break with sanity, Lincoln tries to return stocking. But Booth insists his brother keep it, and again the stage directions read, "Lincoln brings the knife down to cut the stocking." But this time, "In a flash, Booth grabs Lincoln from behind. He pulls his gun and thrusts it into the left side of Lincolns neck. They stop there poised" (109). Lincoln then only utters one more word—"Dont"—before Booth kills him. Booth's impulsive murder of his brother in reaction to the threat of, or actual destruction of, the mother's stocking imbues this article of clothing with multivalent meaning vis-à-vis the brothers' identities. First, the play questions the brother's common paternity through its focus on the mother's affairs. Lincoln gives voice to this suspicion earlier in this scene when he asks Booth, "I know we *brothers,* but is we really brothers, you know blood brothers or not" (103). By severing, or threatening to sever, the maternal tie, Lincoln removes any definitive familial tie to Booth. They are now just two *brothers* arguing over money and a con; there is no link connecting Booth to Lincoln or "standing in the way" of Booth getting his score. When Lincoln takes possession of and possibly destroys the stocking, he simultaneously invalidates and destroys the mother's mandate to Booth to watch over Lincoln. Booth is now the self-appointed Topdog with no sense of responsibility to the one he views as Underdog; thus his vengeance is swift and bloody.

Ironically it is at this point in the play, when Booth most vehemently and ruthlessly asserts his rejection of his name and of Lincoln, that he fulfills the elements of his identity that are most historically linked to Booth-the-actor. John Wilkes Booth-the-actor's supposed declaration "sic semper tyrannis" (thus to the tyrants), channeled by *The America Play*'s regular shooter, suggests a power play; Booth now sees his brother just as Booth-the-actor saw Lincoln-the-President—as a ruthless demagogue poised and determined to destroy his identity and way of life. So now he is Booth, killer of Lincoln. He is the assassin. Simply renaming himself does not secure 3-Card the separation he had envisioned. In the penultimate paragraph of the play, he shows that he finally understands this and expresses a still-unfulfilled desire to break free: "Watch me close watch me close now: Ima go out there and make a name for mysself that dont have nothing to do with you" (110). Yet again he is determined to do so with Lincoln's game: 3-Card Monty.

With these lines Booth also brings attention to another set of important suits in *Topdog/Underdog,* the suits of cards in the brothers' 3-Card Monty game. Three-Card Monty play not only opens and nearly closes the play, but also provides the narrative backdrop for Lincoln's pivotal soliloquy in scene 4. Card suits are divided into two groups, the red and black—clubs and spades versus hearts and diamonds. For the play's confidence men, Booth and Lincoln, these categories more precisely separate the winners from the losers. When Booth plays 3-Card Monty, the black card loses, and when Lincoln plays, the red card loses. These suits can be read as symbolic of each brother's identity. In trying to take on the role of "The Great Emancipator" by putting on the Lincoln suit, Lincoln privileges blackness and racial uplift. Lincoln is also the mouthpiece for the play's most astute observation about racial dynamics, expressed in terms of a card game: "You was in such a hurry to learn thuh last move that you didnt bother learning thuh first one. That was yr mistake. Cause its thuh first move that separates thuh Player from thuh Played. And thuh first move is to know that there aint no winning. Taadaa! It may look like you got a chance but the only time you pick right is when thuh man lets you. And when its thuh real deal, when its thuh real fucking deal, bro, and thuh moneys on the line, thats when the man wont want you picking right. He will want you picking wrong so he will make you pick wrong" (105–6).

In 3-Card Monty, Lincoln can win, but in life he cannot. Racial discrimination has reduced him to poverty and lawlessness. White America, the play implies, is playing with a stacked deck, especially economically. Lincoln, then, looks for power wherever he can find it—even if it means playing the game, in Ellison's sense or in his own.

Booth, on the other hand, privileges violence—onstage and off—and looks to bloodshed and anger, both commonly associated with redness, when his brother and Grace do not fulfill the roles he has assigned them, or when, in Lincoln's case, Booth loses to a more worthy opponent. Also in Booth's game it is the heart that wins. The heart signals his dependence on the emotional and perhaps even his complete rejection of the rational. The competition, and its bloody ending, links the 3-Card Monty play to the dozens tradition in which players must demonstrate verbal and intellectual prowess, and the competitor who first resorts to physical violence concedes to inferiority through his lack of self-control.

Parks intersperses game play throughout *Topdog/Underdog,* and Booth loses the endgame, not only because Lincoln is better at 3-Card Monty—especially since he uses emotional distraction to manipulate his brother—but also because Booth escalates the game from mere play, predominantly vocal, to physical violence and ultimately death. Equating 3-Card Monty with the dozens makes the struggle between Lincoln and Booth less personal and more essentially masculine and racial. When throwing the cards, Lincoln and Booth—on the surface just Link-the-stink and 3-Card, two street hustlers—compete to demonstrate their superiority. At the same time, they are also Lincoln and Booth, would-be assassinated and assassin, fighting to survive. When Lincoln dies, Booth claims his dominance through his unique possession of his inheritance, the possibly money-filled stocking—now called the "money-stocking" in the stage direction, but *Topdog/Underdog* closes with screaming, an emotive release, rather than language. Only Booth and this money-stocking remain. There is no language, no card play, and no audience—just an assassin alone with his left-behind article of clothing.

Both *The America Play* and *Topdog/Underdog,* then, end with gunshot wounds, gaping and bloody "holes of history." Through this wound, Brazil, now the emcee in *The America Play*'s Hall of Wonders, presents his father's corpse to the audience and claims his own "inheritance of sorts"—which in act 2 he defines as "the Hole" his father dug (185). Before he leaves the stage, he gestures to his father's coffin and says, "To my right, our newest Wonder: One of thuh greats Hisself! Note: thuh body sitting propped upright in our great Hole. Note the large mouth opened wide. Note the top hat and frock coat, just like the greats. Note the death wound: thuh great black hole—thuh great black hole in the great head.—And how this great head is bleedin.—Note: thuh last words. —And thuh last breaths. —And how thuh nation mourns" (199). Brazil now sees his father as his father saw himself, as a "Reconstructed Historicity" to be paraded in front of eager spectators (163). As such, in Brazil's eyes, his father "is reduced to 'the large mouth,' 'the top hat and frock coat,' and so forth without even a 'his' attached"[23] to inscribe his humanity in general, let along his specific individual identity. The gaping hole just adds another layer of resemblance between The Great Man and The Lesser Known, like a new accessory for his hat, coat, wart, and beard, but now there is no life left for the assassins to take.

CHAPTER 6

As We Advance Living

Getting Mother's Body

In her *New York Times Book Review* evaluation of Parks's first novel, Laura Miller wrote, "Obviously, William Faulkner's 'As I Lay Dying' is tangled up in the unconsciousness of 'Getting Mother's Body,' but it would take an analyst of Dr. Freud's caliber to figure out just what that means."[1] While certainly amusing, Miller's claim is only partially correct. Despite other critics' assertions to the contrary, *Getting Mother's Body* (2003) indeed has an "unconscious"—a deeply provocative set of contexts and subtexts—and *As I Lay Dying* (1930) is, of course, a part of it. But *As I Lay Dying* is not alone in this unconscious mind. After all it takes more than one thread to be truly "tangled up." Faulkner's *Light in August* (1932) primarily and James Baldwin's *Blues for Mister Charlie* (1953) and *Notes of a Native Son* (1955), Ralph Ellison's *The World and the Jug* (1964), August Wilson's *Two Trains Running* (1992) and other plays from his history cycle, and Alice Walker's essay "In Search of Our Mothers' Gardens" (1974) all appear to provide important contexts for *Getting Mother's Body* (2003).

These texts' appearances, though, are often just as conscious as unconscious, and the novel itself attempts to teach its readers how to make sense of both the characters' and the novel's relationships with the haunting past. *Getting Mother's Body* offers these lessons through its reflections of and upon the journey to revise and reimagine history.

The journey of *Getting Mother's Body*'s protagonist Billy Beede is a reflection of the novel's journey to revise the literary past; specifically Billy's process of engaging and revising her mother's legacy parallels *Getting Mother's Body's* process of revising "Billy" Faulkner's novels. In addition

Parks's specific repetitions, revisions, and reversals offer a reflection on the journey's significance for both the one doing the revising and for the subject of her revision. Observations about Billy Beede's journey to revise her past and observations about the novel's journey to revise past texts complete the sentence that begins "On the journey, there is . . ." While not similar enough to be wholly allegorical, both of these parallel journeys nevertheless add to an understanding of what it means to revise, to be revisionary, and to avoid repeating the mistakes of a complicated and emotionally volatile past. When taken together, the outcomes of these journeys help complete the sentence that begins "The journey leads to . . . ," demonstrating how the novel also reflects on, or critically examines, the very journey it represents.

Getting Mother's Body, which opens in late July 1963 in Lincoln, Texas, tells the story of an orphaned, pregnant, and unwed sixteen-year-old Billy Beede, who spends the first third of the novel traveling to Texhoma, Texas, to meet her lover Clifford Snipes (alias Clifton and Snopes), who has promised to marry her. When she arrives there, however, Billy does not find Snipes, but his wife. Billy decides to return to Lincoln, but first stops in Gomez, Texas, for a consultation with an abortionist. Once home, Billy works furiously to raise the money to terminate her now-unwanted pregnancy and exorcise any trace of the treacherous Snipes.

Before leaving for Texhoma, Billy receives a letter from friends in New Mexico explaining that the remains of Willa Mae Beede, Billy's mother, are in danger of being paved over for a new grocery-store parking lot. Billy initially claims to be apathetic about the fate of her mother's bones and the treasure rumored to be buried with them, but when lying and hair styling fail to raise the money she needs, Billy decides that Willa Mae's treasure is her next best option to fund the abortion. Still virtually penniless, Billy steals a truck from the transsexual Dill Smiles (Willa Mae's embittered former lover) and heads toward Willa Mae's grave in LaJunta, New Mexico. Billy's aunt and uncle, June and Roosevelt ("Teddy"), as well as her cousin Homer, end up along for the ride, but Dill pursues them in a hearse driven by Laz Jackson, the undertaker's son, who also happens to be hopelessly in love with Billy.

Laz and Dill arrive in LaJunta ahead of the Beede caravan, and Dill is determined to prevent anyone from disturbing Willa Mae's grave. It is only after a drunken late-night talk with her mother, Even, that Dill relents and helps Billy and the others exhume Willa Mae's remains. When the coffin is opened and there is no treasure to be seen among the bones, most of the diggers leave the graveside in despair, but Billy suddenly remembers one of her mother's old tricks; she asks Laz to check what remains of the hem of Willa Mae's dress, as she often hid her real jewels in the hem, "just in case"

(159).[2] There Laz finds the treasure: a diamond ring. Billy decides to bring her mother's body back to Lincoln for a proper burial, complete with angel headstone, near the other Beedes. On the way home, Billy feels a new connection with her baby and does not to use the treasure to pay for an abortion.

The two journeys in the novel, the first to Texhoma and the second to LaJunta, parallel two of Faulkner's most famous fictional quests. Based on the form and structure of *Getting Mother's Body,* the LaJunta journey's parallel is the more obvious: the Bundren family's quest to bury their matriarch, Addie, in *As I Lay Dying.* Meanwhile Billy's journey to Texhoma in search of the father of her child is more reminiscent of Lena's search for Lucas in *Light in August.*[3] *Getting Mother's Body* revises both novels by rejecting some elements of their legacies and re-creating others. As in Parks's other literary and historical revisions, the resulting text is both innovative and historically aware, urging readers to embrace a new text while simultaneously seeing the old text again with fresh perspective. *Getting Mother's Body* is exceptional among Parks's texts because it a novel. It is more exceptional still because it not only is revisionary in terms of Faulkner's works, but it also provides a reflection of the revisionary process in the novel's main action: Billy Beede's journeys and her desire to signify on her mother's life in order to revise the trajectory of her personal history.

At the same time, the novel reflects on this revision, offering insight into what is at stake in, and inevitably grows out of, the journey. This reflection on the journey comes not only from Billy, but also from the characters that accompany her. All the novel's characters are on journeys of their own, all are haunted by their pasts, and all are looking to discover and understand their inheritances. As they reverse the trajectory of *As I Lay Dying,* they also reverse the wrongs of the past as well as the trajectories of their own lives, from paths of self-destruction or self-repression to paths of self-awareness. Similarly the novel marks an aesthetic reversal for Parks, as it shows her exploring a new genre, engaging her own literary ancestors, and writing a new kind of character—one that can be redeemed and find happiness.

Both the Parks's journey in this novel to revise Faulkner and Billy Beede's journey to revise her mother's inheritance begin by problematizing the legacy or inheritance with which the revisionary must contend. Looking at Billy's journey and the novel's journey side by side not only illuminates this pattern, but also helps underscore the importance of the rejection/questioning in the novel. According to Miller, the "prevailing question of inheritance" in *Getting Mother's Body* "is whether Billy will turn out like her mother," an unmarried, abused hustler with unfulfilled dreams and a child she cannot support.[4] Billy, of course, seems determined that she not end up like Willa

Mae, especially since Billy's relationship with the married Snipes seems to have set her on the path to doing so. When Aunt June suggests that Willa Mae would have stolen the wedding dress she wanted, rather than buy it as Billy is planning to do, Billy flatly asserts, "I ain't no Willa Mae" (18). Later, when June wants "to bring her down a notch," she tells Billy, "The apple don't fall that far from the tree" (19). Billy, adding the emphasis of profanity, again proclaims, "I aint no goddamned apple" (19). Even in the opening postcoital scene with Snipes, as Billy seems as equally free spirited as her legendary mother, she is quick to "disown" Willa Mae when Snipes brings her up. Billy declares, "Willa Mae passed and it didn't bother me none. I was glad to see her go" (9). She calls her mother "a liar and a cheat" who was "getting locked up in jail every time she turned around. Always talking big and never amounting to nothing" (9). Snipes, initially taken aback by Billy's irreverent tone, reminds her that "Willa Mae's pockets of gold ain't nothing to sneeze at," but Billy simply replies that "any jewels she had was fake," and "a good story's all it makes" (9).

In each of these scenes, Billy describes her identity exclusively as antithesis. She does not say anything about who she *is,* but only who she *is not.* Also, as Billy disparages her mother, she recounts, "I feel mad and then I laugh," indicating that under this rejection lives not apathy, or even antipathy, but hurt (9). In short Billy Beede, laughing to keep from crying, has the blues, but unlike her mother, she has not, at this point in the novel, remembered how to sing them.[5] She has no productive release for her pain. Later in the text, Teddy wants "to tell Billy how she's just like her mother" but fears "that would be like picking at a scab" (224), implying that Billy's wounds from her mother's loss are still fresh, so fresh that that are not scars, but scabs, able to be reopened at even the slightest disturbance. The gory circumstances of Willa Mae's death, which Billy witnessed firsthand, are undoubtedly the source of this pain. Attempting to abort an unwanted child, Willa Mae bled to death. The mother's self-destructive, infanticidal hatred for one child would certainly lead that mother's other child to question her mother's love. Teddy's observations about the impact of Willa Mae and her actions on Billy suggest that maternal affection is more than mere sentiment. Billy does not, for example, harbor such strong feelings for Son Walker, her father, who also abandoned her and whom she does resemble physically.

Billy directs her complex feelings toward Willa Mae into a rejection of her treasure. As seen with Booth's stocking in *Topdog/Underdog,* the mother's treasure, or "inheritance," signifies a complicated legacy that the beneficiary often fears or cannot fully understand. When Billy, speaking of the treasure, tells Snipes, "A good story is all it makes," the novel suddenly makes the legacy metadiscursive: finding and realizing the true value of this treasure, both for Billy vis-à-vis her mother and for the novel vis-à-vis Faulkner, is the central element of *Getting Mother's Body*'s story.

Although the novel does come to embrace much of the inheritance Faulkner's legacy bequeaths, the novel's initial rejection of Faulkner's texts is equally as obvious and unilateral as Billy Beede's rejection of Willa Mae. The form of *Getting Mother's Body,* with each chapter told in the present tense from an individual character's point of view, immediately indicates that Parks's novel will engage *As I Lay Dying* through its narrative structure. However, *Getting Mother's Body* begins with Billy Beede's unforgettable question, "Where my panties at?" (3)—a stark contrast to Darl's rather mundane, although equally vernacular, "Jewel and I come up from the field, following the path single file" (3). By beginning with Billy's demanding feminine voice, the novel assertively declares its privileging of the feminine.

Billy Beede does have some thematic parallels with Dewey Dell, her *As I Lay Dying* counterpart—both are pregnant, unwed, and angry—but, as Glenda Dicker/sun has asserted, "Ms. Billy Beede is a good deal more complicated than the ironically named Dewey Dell Bundren."[6] Dewey Dell is also largely silent in Faulkner's novel, her voice limited to only a handful of chapters that portray her as a helpless victim. Even *Light in August* begins not with Lena's words, but her thoughts, and they are told not in her own voice, but the narrator's. And while the also unwed and pregnant Lena certainly plays a more central role in her novel than Dewey plays in hers, her quest is not personal or maternal, but paternal. She is looking not for freedom or for self; she is looking for Lucas, her baby's father. Since all of the women involved in the novel's initial rejections of heritage are mothers or mothers-to-be, Billy's initial feelings about Willa Mae and the novel's initial signification on Faulkner both point to the importance of the feminine in general and the maternal specifically. Thus *Getting Mother's Body* sets in motion a journey that leads to an expanded understanding of—and in many ways a privileging of—the maternal.

As Billy continues on her journey, she moves from rejecting Willa Mae's legacy to embracing it. Yet this acceptance does not mean that Billy becomes Willa Mae. Rather *both* Willa Mae and Billy are transformed. Willa is "resurrected" literally and figuratively: her bones are moved out of the bulldozer's path, and through her songs—which become increasingly pensive over the course of the novel—she comes back into Billy's life. Billy, healed by the catharsis that accompanies seeing her mother's bones and remembering her mother's songs, finds both the individuality and love she needs to allow herself to become a mother. As it charts Billy Beede's journey, the novel subtly revises key moments, characters, and themes from Faulkner's texts. Just as Billy Beede "resurrects" Willa Mae, Parks's revisions "resurrect" Faulkner's text, taking readers back to the original text and asking them to see this text anew, this time with more focus on the mothers.[7] Meanwhile *Getting Mother's Body* fills the space in between these revisions with its own text, thereby creating a story that, like a child, could not have come into being without its mother but, like Billy Beede, can now exist independently of her, a new story.[8]

Billy Beede's first journey in the novel, her trip to Texhoma and Gomez and then home again to Lincoln, is significant because while Lena's journey in *Light in August* is linear, Billy's journey doubles back on itself; she ends up back home. Yet Parks does not include the entire final portion of this journey. The novel portrays only Billy's trip to Texhoma, the heartache she encounters there, and the trip to Gomez to meet with the abortionist. The next time Billy appears, she is back home with no explanation of how she got there. When she arrives, she talks with Teddy "blood-to-blood" in hushed tones and then lays on her pallet for an entire day, not eating or talking, only staring at her name carved in the bottom on the counter (78). This suggests that the journey home was emotionally tumultuous for Billy, one of uncertainty, and questioning. Indeed, even after her return, it is June, not Billy herself, who describes Billy's actions, as if Billy's interior thoughts and feelings here are unspeakable by nature. Although the text later reveals that she takes a bus with the five dollars she did not give the abortionist, the absence of this information from the narrative action at the time is significant because it shifts the emphasis away from the journey itself and on to the effects of that journey. Although the return to Lincoln means that there is no physical advancement for Billy, there is clearly emotional change in Billy after the trip home. Billy's mysterious "blood to blood" conversation with Teddy—also not detailed in the text—combined with her decision to return to Lincoln in the first place, point to an emerging reconnection with family and place.

The return to Lincoln is also a move away from following her mother's path, for unlike Willa Mae (and Lena), Billy does not continue to wander in search of either her baby's father or some kind of escape. Since the first option is immediately dismissed by the burning of the wedding dress, thus severing Billy's connection to Snipes and to Lena, the second remains an option for Billy. In the chapter that immediately follows Alberta Snipes' description of Billy's visit and dress burning, the bus ticket salesman, Fat Junior Lenoir, recounts that the first destination Billy considers is LaJunta, Willa Mae's resting place as well as the place that she chose for her botched abortion (71).

When Billy does travel to LaJunta in the second journey of the novel, she does so with her family—her cousin Homer and her surrogate parents Teddy and June—and along the way they visit every other living member of the Beede family. Like the Bundrens, the Beedes have had their share of bad luck, but, unlike their Faulknerian counterparts, they seek to resurrect a body, not bury one. Anse Bundren travels because he has promised his wife that she will be buried with her people, and Teddy seeks the same for his sister, although he and June also cannot help but think about how resurrecting Willa Mae's treasure might change their lives for the better. Also like the Bundrens, the Beedes are a dysfunctional lot, plagued by insecurities, bitterness, and regret. Teddy, a preacher, can no longer hear the voice of God and has lost his church because of it; June thinks her father left her with Teddy (without saying good-bye) because the family was unwilling to support a handicapped child; Homer wants to be a "race man" but is ashamed of his family's poverty.

Yet rather than be destroyed by these vices, as the Bundrens are in *As I Lay Dying,* each of *Getting Mother's Body's* characters is in some way recreated or renewed by the quest. Teddy, for example, figures out that God speaks only to men who treat women well. He recalls that, "God had been quiet from the moment I turned our borrowed car around, from the moment I put my foot down and reminded June that I was the husband, and the wife would bend to the husband's will because I'm my own man which means I didn't want to go to California and live under her daddy's thumb" (179). The church that Teddy builds is made of wood that is so superficial and weak that the structure, unlike his sister's repossessed furniture, does not even leave a mark on the ground that once held it after it is repossessed and then destroyed in a plane crash. But after they arrive in LaJunta, Teddy apologizes to June, who subsequently tells him they should "chance it" and go back to Lincoln so Teddy can try preaching there (238). Earlier in the novel, June describes feeling as if she "done fell into the river of Beedes and got swept along in they thick brown water" (172), but by acknowledging that the feminine is not subordinate to the masculine, Teddy helps release June from this anger and helps her accept him as her husband, her partner. June soon after finds all that she has ever sought, children and a leg to replace the one she lost as a teenager, for when Billy acknowledges that her child is June's "grandbaby," she installs June as mother and matriarch (257).

The significance of the LaJunta journey becomes clearer when examining how Parks's title departs from Faulkner's. In her *New Leader* review of the novel, Rosellen Brown asserted that *Getting Mother's Body* "could be called

As I Lay Dead."[9] But such a name would do Parks's revisionary aesthetic, as well her novel's story, a grave disservice. The novel is not engaging Faulkner this closely, and no one in Parks's novel is really dead or even dying. Even Willa Mae, like Addie Bundren, actually lives on in the text after her physical death. Addie herself even appears in Parks's text, reinvented as a hair shop client bent on sending Billy to beauty school.

Also, where Faulkner's title suggests passivity, Parks's title denotes movement, a process or a journey. The "I" in *As I Lay Dying* most obviously refers to Addie's state in the initial pages of the novel, but since a title by nature describes the whole work and the novel continues after Addie's death, the title also suggests that each of the characters is approaching a spiritual or emotional destruction or death. *Getting Mother's Body* substitutes "Mother's" for this "I." "Mother's" here names the dead as well as the living because only Billy calls Willa Mae "Mother." At the same time, because Billy explains "I calt her 'Mother' in my head, but not out loud" (173), the title centers itself on Billy and—like Faulkner's title—on both a physical, external journey and an internal, metaphorical journey.[10] So Parks's revision of Faulkner's title not only differentiates her text from his, but also links them by highlighting the simultaneously individual and communal nature of both.

Individually the text marks an aesthetic shift for Parks, a shift away from drama. When Homer and Teddy are arrested after Homer is caught speeding, Homer argues with the racist white sheriff. Homer then comments, "The Negro-College-Going Youth eyes the White-Just-Back-from-Fishing-Sheriff. If we was in a play these would be our parts. There's plenty of times a man has, in a situation just like this, forgot himself and just played his part" (167). This seeming commentary on drama provides some clues as to why Parks may have shifted from playwriting to novel writing. As Booth in *Topdog/Underdog* demonstrates when he tries to change his name to "3-Card," a character in a play cannot choose to change his name or identity in the middle of a scene. In the novel, however, Homer can choose whether he will play this "Negro-College-Going Youth" role. His choice to "remember himself," and indeed the white sheriff's choice to do the same, likely saves his life. Brown suggested in her rather critical review of the novel that *Getting Mother's Body*'s characters are equally as stereotypical as those in Parks's *The Death of the Last Black Man in the Whole Entire World*; they just aren't labeled as obviously. Brown wrote that many of the characters "are so familiar that perhaps they are, in their way, analogs of the characters in Parks' plays after all, who live under the titles of their archetypes as though they wore signs."[11]

Yet in many ways this familiarity stems from a grounding in time, place, and tradition that Parks's previous works do not generally have. *Topdog/Underdog* and *In the Blood*, for example, give their settings as simply "here" and "now." *Venus* has a nineteenth-century context, but this context is quickly complicated by the appearance of anachronisms, such as mention of a television.[12] But *Getting Mother's Body* is set in late July 1963 in Lincoln, Texas; LaJunta, New Mexico; and a few places—all clearly named—in between. The narrative form of the novel allows place to be represented more thoroughly because each place need not be physically represented on the stage. As Faulkner demonstrated with Yoknapatawpha County, in a novel a writer can even create a place that feels quite real, with much of that reality being defined by the characters, even the seemingly stereotypical ones, that pass through that space.

In a novel Parks can also give her characters more freedom, because she can remove herself, the writer, almost completely from the text. This strategy manifests itself most obviously in the lack of authorial narration, which actually is often present in Parks's plays in the form of specific, omniscient stage directions that go far beyond simply telling characters where to stand and include important textual information, impossible to represent on stage, for the play's readers.

Brown has claimed that in giving up this control, Parks has created a novel that is "essentially a series of monologues, 'opened up' the way films are opened up (this is to say, enacted by too many characters in too many places to be staged). There is no authorial voice or binding narrative thread, no conceptual complexity."[13] However, Parks has not given up authorial control completely. In adopting *As I Lay Dying*'s chapter structure, Parks named her characters and their legacies.[14] Also, her revision of *As I Lay Dying* and *Light in August* not only has provided a clear narrative thread on which Parks has layered complexities; it also has allowed for the emergence of authorial voice as Parks has written both alongside of and against Faulkner's stories. If it is not his voice, it must be hers.

The novel also creates a space for the emergence of authorial voice that is distinctly different from the space created by stage directions in Parks's plays. Stage directions, as discussed previously, are only available only to readers of the text, not to those watching the play in performance. In a novel, even a novel such as *As I Lay Dying* or *Getting Mother's Body*, that is a "series of monologues,"[15] every word on the page is available to all readers—even those listening to a reading of the text will miss nothing. Thus the authorial voice in *Getting Mother's Body* does not problematize the disconnect between the seen and the unseen, but rather the disconnect between the novel's historical time and the author's. As Billy gets on the bus to Texhoma, Teddy warns, "This is 1963. . . . It aint safe you going all the way out there by yourself" (121). He later adds, "It's 1963 and a Negro life is cheap. The life of a Negro man is cheap. The life of a Negro woman is cheaper. The price of everything is always going up though, so could be that the price of Negro life too will get high. Maybe the price'll rise to reach the value of the cost we brought in slavery times. Not this year though. Not the next. Maybe by nineteen hundred and seventy. Maybe by nineteen hundred and eighty or nineteen hundred and ninety the price will go up. Maybe by the year two thousand, but surely, the world will end by then" (124).

Usually when a character in a novel mentions a year as a means of comparison he or she does so to show progress. Teddy, however, speaks with disappointment, not hope, seemingly knowing what he could not know unless the author let him know, that "not this year" and "not the next" and indeed not for many years would Teddy see the safety and value of black life for which he wishes.

This temporal disconnect in *Getting Mother's Body* is reminiscent of one of Parks's most famous locations, the "Great Hole of History" from *The America Play.* In this text the mother figure Lucy describes the Great Hole of History (also called the "Great Hole"), the theme park where she honeymooned with her husband, The Foundling Father, the Abraham Lincoln impersonator. At this park, she explains, "you could see the whole world without goin too far. You could look intuh that whole and see your entire life pass before you. Not your own life but someones life from history, you know, [someone who'd done something of note, got theirselves known somehow, uh President or] somebody who killed somebody important, uh face on a postal stamp, you know, someone from History. *Like* you, but *not* you. You know: *known*" (196).

Critic Haike Frank has claimed that through the Great Hole of History "identity is clearly defined as inauthentic" because "if history exists only in a void and our life is represented by the people in that void, do we then exist ourselves? All of history amalgamates in this theme park; difference is erased by the all-comprising myth of greatness."[16] The Great Hole of History is a void in which history's important moments, those that have had the most potent impact on the world, are contained. This void, like a twisted temporal mirror, allows visitors to put themselves into history in an attempt to experience it more immediately and personally.

What *Getting Mother's Body* presents at first seems to be a smaller, more personal version of the Great Hole of History, "The Hole." The Hole is a vulnerability that stems from a person's experiences and circumstances, his or her personal history. The vulnerability can be a virtue or a vice, and nothing can fill The Hole save the exact remedy for its owner's personal pain. The first mention of The Hole in *Getting Mother's Body* is Billy's first time seeing The Hole for herself. Billy is describing what she sees in Mrs. Jackson as she is trying to convince the woman to sell her the "show dress" in the window of Jackson's Formal for the $63 Snipes has provided for wedding apparel: "I see something in her, something I'm not sure of at first. Something my mother might call The Hole. It's like a soft spot and everybody's got one. Mother said she could see The Hole in people and then she'd know how to take them. She could see Holes all the time but I ain't ever seen one. Until now. Words shape themselves in my mouth and I start talking without thinking of what I need say. It's like The Hole shapes the words for me and I don't got to think or nothing" (27).

Later, speaking from the grave in her first chapter, Willa Mae sings a song called "Big Hole Blues" and then describes The Hole in more detail through prose narrative. The song describes a jealous man preparing a grave for his cheating lover. The Hole is "in my dirt" and although it is only "as long as I am tall," it "goes down as deep as the deep blue sea" (30). The man swears he is only kidding, but the singer is wary nevertheless and resolves to "leave this big old holey place" (30). Willa Mae goes on to explain that "to get the best of a situation you gotta know a man's Hole. Everybody's got one, just don't everybody got one in the same place." The Hole is "not just the lack" of something, but also the craving for it: "A Hole-in-the-heart person craves company and kindness, not no book" (31).

The America Play's Great Hole of History and *Getting Mother's Body*'s Hole share, then, an acknowledgement of absence as well as the potential for victimization. In *Getting Mother's Body,* however, the concept becomes more personal and ultimately more maternal. A person's Hole is not linked to the "story" of American history but to their own personal stories, just as in "Big Hole Blues," the beloved's Hole is in dirt that she identifies as her own. Since it is also a grave here, it represents not only the absence of life but also the culmination of a life's events, the end of a journey. Whereas in *The America Play,* the Great Hole of History's spectators see a false reflection—a self that is not really the self—in *Getting Mother's Body,* The Hole seemingly reveals only information about the subject being seen. In fact The Hole, rather than just passively revealing itself to the seer (Billy), actually possesses her. She explains, "The Hole shapes more words in my mouth, all I gotta do is let them out" (27). This possession suggests that The Hole is independent of both players; neither party involved actually has choice, and both are players in a scene masterminded by The Hole itself, implying that The Hole in *Getting Mother's Body* is not a smaller version of its predecessor, but can actually be read as a bigger, more pervasive version of the Great Hole of History. Not just limiting itself to capital-H history, The Hole's effects extend to both seer and seen.

Yet, the new, more general Hole might not be as malignant as its ancestor. Its visual connection posits its potential as a kind of second sight, an opportunistic craftiness, or even a survival/defense skill. The Hole is also always linked in some way to the maternal. In the initial scene with Mrs. Faith Jackson, for example, The Hole prompts Billy to ask who made Mrs. Jackson's wedding dress, which was the model for the dress Billy wants. Mrs. Jackson responds that her mother made the dress, but then "she goes quiet" (27). Billy, following where The Hole leads her, goes on: "'Willa Mae, you know, my uh—'/ 'Your mother,' Mrs. Jackson says, saying 'mother' out loud for me. / 'Yes, ma'am, well, she's passed, but she sure woulda loved to see my wedding day, seeing how she was always jilted and never lucky enough to get married herself.'/ We stand there quiet, both looking at the dress" (27). In forging a connection between her own mother and Mrs. Jackson, solidified by Billy leading Mrs. Jackson to vocalize the word *mother* in both instances, Billy—or The Hole through her—finds Mrs. Jackson's Hole, the yearning to pass on maternal inheritance, the "treasure" her mother gave her.

The next chapter is the one in which Willa Mae sings her first song and describes The Hole. The placement of this chapter suggests that in discovering the nature of The Hole, Billy has also come to a new understanding of her mother. The chapter, however, begins with "The next song I'ma sing," indicating that Willa Mae has been singing all along, but has only just now been resurrected for Billy Beede. As the novel continues and Willa Mae's songs follow Billy's life, Billy begins to hear and sing them herself. Remembering the songs leads to her remembering how to pull the very profitable "ring trick" and eventually, how to find her mother's treasure.

A closer look at the scene with Mrs. Jackson also reveals that finding The Hole can be interpreted as accurately interpreting a person's social and emotional cues. In Mrs. Jackson's case, silences—known as Spells and *(Rest)*s in Parks's plays—reveal the points at which she is most affected by Billy's story, the times at which she is most vulnerable. The Hole, then, is Billy's social and cultural literacy, which allows her to "read" this situation. Billy likely learned most of this skill from Willa Mae, but her surrogate mother, June, also demonstrates high levels of cultural literacy throughout the novel.

It is June who "reads and know things" and who reads the latent dishonesty in "Ms. He-She-It" Dill Smiles's gender masking as indicative of an underlying untruthfulness in Dill's character and in her story of Willa Mae's death (25, 42). Ironically it is these two mother figures, Willa Mae and June, who are equally responsible for Billy's more traditional literacy as well. Willa, very practically, teachers her to read using the signs along the road, but June, known for her "pretty words," teaches Billy to write (41). Teddy, who cannot read and write, erroneously reads Dill as "the most honest person I know" because she "don't open no mail that ain't addressed to her and Dill Smiles don't flout no dying wishes of the dead" (25). He also later misreads that Homer would make a good husband for Billy.

Ultimately Billy rejects the more exploitative version of The Hole by questioning its morality after she and her family pull Willa Mae's "ring trick" and take advantage of the racist Rude's "Hole"-y pockets (that is, greed). This rejection suggests that even though The Hole is initially destructive, a certain degree of self-awareness can lead the seer to overcome its influence, trading The Hole for a wholeness rooted in a truer understanding of maternal inheritance that does not depend on others' insecurities. In finding her wholeness, Billy must confront and work within a complicated and painful past in order to heal.

Most of the action of *Getting Mother's Body* focuses on this familial and individual struggle, but behind this personal narrative is the looming civil rights march of August 1963, which proved to be one of the most important in American history. While the march is of interest only to the secondary characters in the novel, the fact that Parks incorporates the event—even just as a subplot—highlights the absence of similar social and political events in Faulkner's novels. There are certainly racial tensions in *Light in August;* yet Joe Christmas does not ever consider joining the NAACP, and *As I Lay Dying* would be a completely different novel if Jewel Bundren were in the Klan.

Yet, even while it is engaging Faulkner's novels, *Getting Mother's Body* creates space for complementary and/or interconnected individual and communal histories to exist simultaneously, thereby creating a new history that is more accurate than either would be on its own. Parks concludes in "Possession": "Through each line of text I'm rewriting the Time Line—creating history where it is and always was but has not yet been divined."[17] In one of the best examples of such creation in *Getting Mother's Body,* Teddy, emerging from prison, explains, "I've heard men say that free air smells and feels different from the air of bondage. It's true. There is a lightness to it and a crispness and a willingness of the air. In the cell the air is hard like the cell is hard. The first breaths They breathed when They was set Free, back in the day, that musta felt different too" (177). Linking his story with the legacy of slavery makes the past more relevant and visceral while also connecting a personal, modern struggle with an enduring struggle against white racist power. And even the novel's white characters participate in this new historical approach: Myrna—"The Flashy Gal" Billy meets on the bus to Texhoma who has satchel of red, white, and blue Pabst beer-can pancakes—can be read most redemptively as a jaded white feminist who has been betrayed by the very southern patriarchy that claimed to cherish her and who has found her only chance for even the most subtle liberation in exercising reproductive choice (59). Similarly Birdie, who has lost her paternal inheritance through her marriage to Rude, finds her only outlet in promiscuous sex, *National Geographic,* and imagining how cremation "would burn up all evidence of what could be called [her] indiscretions" (207).

Parks has further complicated the socio-racial and aesthetic issues in her novel by taking on yet another topic previously left relatively untouched in her plays: color prejudice. But more so than representing a particular political issue, skin color in the novel contributes to unlocking the complexities of *Getting Mother's Body's* creative inheritance, linking whiteness and blackness to literary "ancestors." According to June, Billy really "don't favor her mother"; "Willa Mae was light and fine featured," whereas "Billy is dark," supposedly like her father, Son Walker (19). When Homer looks at Billy's picture of Willa Mae, he sees "a white woman, or what looks like a white woman" (146). And Billy recounts how the woman at the jail in Santa Anna did not believe that she was Willa Mae's daughter (174). Accepting the whole of Willa Mae's inheritance means accepting her mixed-race legacy.

This choice is reminiscent of the choice that African American writers face when engaging historical material and literary influences. Black writers, especially iconoclastic writers such as Parks, face tremendous pressure to write politically charged works, clearly rooted in and engaged with African American literary and cultural tradition. But Parks wrote in her essay "An Equation for Black People Onstage" that "As there is no single 'Black Experience,' there is no single 'Black Aesthetic' and there is not one way to write or think or feel or dream or interpret or be interpreted. As African Americans we should recognize this insidious essentialism of what it is: a fucked-up trap to reduce us to only one way of being. We should endeavor to show the world and ourselves our beautiful and powerfully infinite variety."[18]

Parks's sentiments here echo Ralph Ellison's words in "The World and The Jug." In this essay, Ellison famously engaged white critic Irving Howe's assertion that Ellison and James Baldwin ungratefully underestimated Richard Wright's influence on their work. Ellison responded, "I respect Wright's work and I knew him, but this is not to say that he 'influenced' me as significantly as you assume. . . . One can do nothing about choosing one's relatives, one can, as an artist choose one's 'ancestors.'" Accordingly Ellison labeled Wright, along with Langston Hughes, a "relative," but included among his "ancestors" T. S. Eliot and William Faulkner.[19]

Herein lie the more communal elements of Parks's text; *Getting Mother's Body* charts the difficulties inherent in revisiting a well-known text and the challenges that African American writers in particular face when evoking both white and black ancestors and a racist past. Although it certainly seems that Parks has embraced Ellison's right to choose his ancestors, she has not exclusively channeled white male "ancestors." Just as the novel subtly engages *Light in August* alongside *As I Lay Dying* in its revision of Faulkner, so too does it engage other texts, specifically African American texts. In the previously mentioned scene with Homer and the sheriff, for example, Homer goes on to explain, "In the middle of the quadrangle at school there's a little stone plaque dedicated to the memory of Randall Clay. I used to think it would be a fine thing to tell men like this Sheriff here just what I think of them and then end up killed and honored by a plaque with my name on it. Until now" (167). This scene recalls Richard's murder in James Baldwin's *Blues for Mister Charlie* (1953). Baldwin, of course, is not only a key figure in African American literature, but he was also Parks's beloved teacher, who once told her that she was destined for literary greatness.[20]

Parks also borrows feminine models from another of her black literary fathers, August Wilson. Specifically Parks's supernatural Willa Mae parallels the supernatural Aunt Ester, who appears in Wilson's *Two Trains Running* (1992), *King Hedley II* (1999), and *Radio Golf* (2005). According to Harry J. Elam, Jr., "By Wilson's own admission, Aunt Ester is far from a static site of remembrance, but rather a living force, actively mediating for spiritual and cultural change. She not only embodies a collective history but a personal one, for she is a woman who has loved and lost, who has been married and given birth. Hers is an embodied knowledge that she shares with others, and her embodiment makes the metaphysical an element of the everyday."[21]

While Willa Mae lives only a fraction of Ester's years, she nevertheless fills these years with similar experiences that blend the personal and collective. She is a single mother, a lover, a fighter, a lesbian, a criminal, a daughter, and a survivor of domestic violence. As with Aunt Ester, "history and memory commingle in her body,"[22] which eventually even appears in the text as brown bones. Elam also has posited that Aunt Ester, "in a riff of aural signifyin', sounds quite similar to 'ancestor.'"[23]

Combining Elam's "aural signifyin'" with Ellison's sentiments that there are ancestors artists choose and relatives they do not allows Willa May to represent the tension between fate (will) and choice (may). In her final chapter, as Billy reflects on her journey to and from LaJunta and the time that has passed since, she concludes: "Folks take after they folks. That's the law of nature. The thing about not watching my mother get old is that I wasn't never sure what I was gonna get, cause if you don't got yr folks to look at, if all you got to look at is a picture of a woman standing beside a cactus, a picture took by a man who weren't ever really your daddy, then you don't got a good idea really of where yr headed. When I seen her bones I knew what we all knew, that we's all gonna end up in a grave someday, but there's stops in between there and now" (257). She has come to see the beginnings and endings as predetermined, but all the points in between as potential choices. She can choose to embrace Willa Mae's memory and to cherish her treasure without following, step by step, in her footsteps to the grave.

By merely suggesting a connection to the mother's legacy, Parks has shown her ties to a black literary mother, Alice Walker. Walker wrote in her 1974 essay "In Search of Our Mothers' Gardens": "Only recently did I fully realize this: that through years of listening to my mother's stories of her life, I have absorbed not only the stories themselves, but something of the manner in which she spoke, something of the urgency that involves the knowledge that her stories—like her life—must be recorded."[24] Similarly Billy Beede sees the urgency in protecting her mother's bones. Immediately after Willa Mae sings of her lineage in a song called "Promise Land," Billy announces to Dill that she will not allow the bulldozers to "dig Willa up and scatter her all which way," because, she asserts with a compelling reversal of language, "*My mother* don't deserve to be scattered to the winds like that" (248, emphasis added). While Billy Beede does not literally want to write her mother's story, like Walker she understands that the bones are the embodiment of her mother's legacy, the real treasure that must be preserved and honored.

Billy comes to understand embodiment through the help of Aunt June, her adopted mother. June, who lost her leg when she was Billy's age, laments that she will never, even in death, be a whole self.[25] The money Laz gives the family for Willa's ring, however, is enough to buy June a new prosthetic leg, and although she must learn how to walk again, the accomplishment becomes doubly significant because "she walked her first steps the same day as her first grandbaby did (257).

This ending, part of a nearly unilaterally happy conclusion, is not only reminiscent of the similarly tidy conclusion to Walker's *The Color Purple,* but it offers a final look at the future of white and black literary inheritance. In this closing chapter, narrated by Billy, predominantly in the past tense, Billy has come to see her child not as a Snipes, but as its own individual self, completely separate from Snipes as well as both independent of and intimately connected to herself. She describes how "Riding back to Lincoln, looking at my ring, I could feel the baby inside me. I hadn't never really thought of a name for it, but riding home I felt like I could. Not pick out a name though, just let one come to me without thinking. Like it had a name already, and if it had a name already then it already was. And if it already was then it was always gonna be" (257).

Since in this novel a name in many ways describes a character's essence, signifying at least part of what he or she is and will become, Billy realizes here that the role of the mother is to help discover this identity and pass it along to the child. The text does not reveal the baby's name or even its gender, because the child—just like the offspring of Parks's and Faulkner's combined aesthetics—can be anything readers want to imagine it to be. The knowledge that informs this imagining comes not just from a single mother, but a continuum of mothers and of journeys those mothers have traveled. Billy represents this continuum as she links her baby, herself, and her mother to the road on the way home. She recalls, "My belly sat in front of me. In front of my belly, beyond the hood of the truck, was the back of Laz's hearse with Mother's body riding inside and the road unrolling out ahead" (257).

In this metaphor, the father—literal and adoptive—is important but secondary. Laz, who by all accounts loves Billy and who was excited about her child even when he thought she was marrying Snipes, has literally resurrected Willa Mae and has given Billy and her family the financial and emotional support they need to heal. Snipes/Snopes, who could arguably represent Faulkner himself, has been rendered nearly irrelevant, save for whatever reflection of him can be found in his child, raised and nurtured according to the mother's choices. Since, however, Snipes's light skin, signaling a mixed-race heritage, matches his "yellow shiny shirt" (16), at least part of this reflection will be of whiteness.

But the child, the repetition as well as the revision of the parents, is also free to reject any part of the inheritance, to make his or her own choices. In her discussion of such repetition and revision in "From *Elements of Style,*" Parks suggested that "Rep & Rev are key in examining something larger than one moment. Rep & Rev create space for metaphor & c."[26] Thus

Getting Mother's Body, the metaphorical child of two literary imaginations, represents this type of Rep & Rev by twisting some of Faulkner's most important metaphors to create space for new ones.

As I Lay Dying offers a metaphorical moment that on first encounter seems insignificant, but later, when reviewed in the context of the narrative as a whole, provides a central interpretative lens for the work as a whole. This narrative key comes from the mysteriously omniscient Darl, who, as the family advances toward a treacherous crossing, foresees that the human heart can be equally treacherous: "Before us the thick dark current runs. It talks up to us in a murmur become ceaseless and myriad, the yellow surface dimpled monstrously into fading swirls traveling along the surface for an instant, silent, impermanent and profoundly significant, as though just beneath the surface something huge and alive waked for a moment of lazy alertness out of and into light slumber again."[27] Parks revised this idea, of course, by giving each of her characters what Laz calls a "subterranean" identity, a true identity that can be seen only when a character is free from emotional bondage to reflect on his or her own interior. The novel also, through June, calls the Beede family a current capable of sweeping her away and subsuming her identity.

Similarly *Light in August,* a novel that considers the consequences of desperate movement as well as stifling stasis, contains the following reflection, offered in an unattributed authorial voice: "Though the mules plod in a steady and unflagging hypnosis, the vehicle does not seem to progress. It seems to hang suspended in the middle distance forever and ever, so infinitesimal is its progress, like a shabby bead upon the mild red string of road."[28] Parks revised this moment as well, both through multiple instances of Billy approaching as "a speck on the road" that gets shaped into her as she gets closer, but also in the novel's nearly constant movement (21). As Willa Mae sings in her final song, "The Great Wheel keep rolling along," Parks's characters indeed progress steadily—by bus (eleven or otherwise), truck, car, and hearse—on their journey to resurrect Willa Mae and their complementary journeys to understand the significance thereof.

In between and also alongside her revision of Faulkner, Parks also created her own new metaphorical moment. Multiple instances of reflection—including Laz's shining the light from his mirror on Billy as he looks at her in reverse and Billy's looking at herself in the car door mirror as she ponders Willa Mae's photograph—culminate in a final observation about reflection narrated by Lazarus.[29] While he waits for Billy's arrival at the Pink Flamingo Auto Court, behind which Willa Mae is buried, he notices the motel's empty pool. He remarks: "It's painted blue, so, from a distance, you would think it had water in it. If you passed the Pink Flamingo quick without stopping, you would, maybe in the heat of the desert, kick yrself for not stopping to take a dip. But there ain't no water in this pool. There's just a wooden diving board that looks full of splinters, sticking out like a dried-up tongue over the big blue-painted cement hole. I always thought the water made a pool blue, not the paint" (214). When Candy, Dill's half sister, tells Laz that "only guests can use the pool," Laz insightfully (and humorously) responds, "They got to bring they own water too" (214).

Water in general, though, is naturally blue when it reflects the color of the sky. In the case of this pool, there is something beneath the surface that alters the reflection. Without any water, the "reflection" is fake. The pool is in effect a "Hole." Guests who want to use the pool "need to bring they own water" and thus their own vehicle for reflection to fill The Hole. But even then, the reflection will be a combination of the sky from above and the color below. This simple blue pool, then, is reflection of and a reflection on identity, just as Parks's novel is a reflection of and on the journey to find that identity.

CHAPTER 7

"This film has been modified from its original version"

Girl 6 and *Their Eyes Were Watching God*

For stage productions of a play the written script must be widely circulated to actors and directors to ensure the survival, let alone the success, of the production. These actors and directors must then re-create the spectacle for viewers, many of whom will have read the play themselves, and these viewers will ultimately judge the merits of the play and its producers within the context of each individual performance. The public, however, rarely has access to the script or screenplay for a film, and even when a text version of a film is available, it is often in prose rather than dramatic form.

In film the finished product, the spectacle itself, is circulated. Since the production elements are permanent, its success and survival depends solely on the audience's judgment of that spectacle alone. This is true even when the film comes from a novel, for the novel and the screenplay, predominantly because of length, cannot be the same text or even exactly the same story. The screenplay, like any text that has been revised, is a new text, related to the old but still wholly original. But, unlike with most revised texts, the new screenplay's new text itself remains hidden, and thus the audience sees only the interpretation of an interpretation.

Suzan-Lori Parks's adaptation of Zora Neale Hurston's beloved *Their Eyes Were Watching God* (1937) is a perfect example of such creative revision. The film *Their Eyes Were Watching God* (2005), produced and presented by Oprah Winfrey, has met harsh criticism for straying too far from Hurston's text. Critics have focused almost exclusively on what the film added or left out but paid little attention to the interpretive effects of this revision. Indeed the changes to the novel are so significant that calling the film by the same name as the novel seems almost inaccurate, not only because Hurston's text deserves accurate representation, but also because the film has its own message, purpose, and, therefore, interpretive value.

Nearly ten years before her work on *Their Eyes Were Watching God,* Parks's first foray into Hollywood, *Girl 6* (1996), produced and directed by Spike Lee, also met with skeptical reviews. This earlier film, rather than engage a previous text, is an original script that looks to film, television, and even Parks's own history. As with *Their Eyes Were Watching God,* this effort was born with weighty cultural inheritance: Parks's Obie Award; Spike Lee's growing popularity and reputation as a black cultural critic and icon; soundtrack writer and performer Prince's undeniable fame and talent; and a well-known cast of Hollywood power players, such as Quentin Tarantino, Isaiah Washington, Theresa Randle, and Lee himself.

Rather than focus on how or why both *Their Eyes* and *Girl 6* fell short of audiences' and critics' perhaps unreasonably high expectations, a more productive examination of these films focuses on what both contribute to African American literary and cultural history. In addition, since both films feature extraordinary female protagonists, both offer innovative examinations of black female sexuality and the stereotypes that have come to define it.

Girl 6

Parks's first major film portrays the trials of a phone-sex operator, Girl #6, as she struggles to find her identity while working in industries that traditionally perpetuate sexual stereotypes about black women, stereotypes she associates most directly with television and film representations of black female characters. The film re-creates scenes from prominent and controversial racialized TV shows and films, with Girl 6 and other characters replacing the original actors. These clips provide a narrative backbone for the action, which is self-consciously metadiscursive, as the film ends with the character Girl 6 walking toward the Chinese Theatre, which is showing the film *Girl 6*. In this film Parks focused on the sexually taboo—the unspoken and the unspeakable elements of fantasy, desire, and longing; *Girl 6* is a visceral film that seeks to unnerve its viewers by making the private very public, forcing the viewer to confront the realities of sexuality. In so doing, the film depathologizes "abnormal" sexuality and sexual fantasy, especially for women, while simultaneously questioning Hollywood's sexualization of black women.

The film opens with Girl 6 (Theresa Randle), whose real name is never confirmed, beginning to recite a monologue for an audition with Q.T., a Hollywood director (Quentin Tarantino). She eventually storms out of this audition, however, after uncomfortably complying with Q.T.'s request that she show her breasts to the camera. Following fights with her manager and her acting coach about her dedication to acting, Girl 6 works as a free agent in a variety of odd jobs. Exhausted, she sees an ad for phone-sex operators that promises great pay, and she begins to pursue such a job.

On her first interview, which she attends dressed as a school girl, complete with pig tails and round glasses, she meets the madam (Madonna). The job requires women to work from home, and Girl 6, finding this prospect intimidating, moves on to a second interview for a job as an "office girl." The office hires her, and the film follows her through her training, her first call, and her quick rise to unparalleled success as the most popular phone-sex operator in the office.

Soon, however, the job becomes too personal. Girl 6, who comes to take on her phone-sex persona "Lovely" almost full time, falls for one of her callers and agrees to meet him. When he does not show, Girl 6 immerses herself in her "career," working both as an office girl and an "at home" girl for the first madam. Girl 6 distances herself from her best friend and neighbor, Jimmy (Spike Lee), and her ex-husband (Isaiah Washington), who is still in love with her. Both of them worry—despite Girl 6's insistence to the contrary—that the "phone bone" job has distracted her from her dream of becoming a successful Hollywood actress. Girl 6 escapes her life by imagining herself as famous black women from the screen (small and big), including Carmen Jones, Thelma Evans from *Good Times,* Foxy Brown, and even a little girl making headlines on the local news after falling down an elevator shaft in a housing project. She is later forced to find a more tangible escape, however, when one of her callers begins to stalk her and threatens her life. She leaves New York for California, where she attends another audition. Again uncomfortable with the director's demands, she walks out of the audition, across the path of Dorothy Dandridge's star, and toward Grauman's Chinese Theatre.

At the beginning of the film, before she becomes Girl 6, Parks's protagonist has no clear identity. Lee says in the minidocumentary/DVD extra "The Making of *Girl 6,*" that her "character is kinda schizophrenic." She not only has no name (at least for the audience), but she constantly changes her public appearance, especially her hair and clothes. At the audition with Q.T., she has long straight hair pulled off her neck in an elaborate twist, and she wears a plain, low-cut dress. At her acting class, her hair is short, her clothes tight. When she passes out computer course flyers on the street, her hair is bobbed and red, but her clothes are not flashy: white jacket, black pants, button-down shirt (buttoned conservatively). Later, when she checks coats at a club, she wears a saucy white dress, and her hair is long and blonde. According to bell hooks, Girl 6's "constant changing of outfits, hairstyles, and so on, reminds viewers that femininity is constructed, not natural."[1] Like Booth in *Topdog/Underdog*, Girl 6 thinks she can change her self just by changing her clothes. The changing hair—an important cultural and historical symbol for African Americans in general and African American women in particular—suggests that Girl 6's black identity and especially her black female identity are fluid and exterior at the film's beginning.

The opening audition scene with Q.T. both reveals and unfolds the intricacies of this identity crisis. Parks took the monologue Girl 6 reads at this audition from *She's Gotta Have It* (1986), one of Lee's earliest films and a project that he wrote, directed, edited, and produced himself.[2] *She's Gotta Have It* takes the form of a documentary about a woman named Nola Darling who has three lovers who all know about each other and who all wish to be her only suitor.[3] Nola unabashedly admits that she loves sex. She wears her hair natural and short throughout. She shares a birthday with Malcolm X. The audience meets Nola in the film's first interview. The camera focuses on a figure tossing and turning under a white sheet on a large bed. Nola emerges and gives the monologue repeated in *Girl 6:* "I want you to know the only reason I am consenting to this is because I wish to clear my name. Not that I care what people think, but enough is enough. And if in the end it helps some other people out, well then that's fine too. I consider myself normal, whatever that means. Some people call me a freak. I hate that word. I don't believe in it. Better yet, I don't believe in labels. But what are you going to do, this was the deal." Nola clearly knows herself and wishes only for the world to know her as well. As *She's Gotta Have It* continues, men try to change her—and she briefly considers changing for one of those men—but she always comes back to her original, unapologetically sexual self.

Parks has portrayed Girl 6 as clearly longing for Nola's self-assurance, at least in her identity and possibly in her sexuality as well. When Girl 6 delivers Nola's monologue, her tone is painfully flat and unengaging, and Q.T. cuts her off at "enough is enough." She is obviously trying to appear sexy and smooth but only seems nervous and stiff. She wiggles, fidgets, and overgestures with her hands. When Q.T. tells her they are looking for someone who can "ooze sexuality," Girl 6 puckers her lips and moves into an overdone pinuplike pose. Q.T. then asks her to show him—and the black woman sitting with him—her breasts. Girl 6 hesitates, eventually complies, but then runs from the room. hooks has convincingly argued that, through scenes such as this, "the film reminds audiences that women's bodies are subordinated to patriarchal pleasure in ways that are similar in the movies and on the streets."[4] But Girl 6's reaction also suggests, and the rest of the film supports, that Girl 6 can talk about sex and can even pretend to be sexual, but she is uncomfortable with the physical elements of sexuality and intimacy. Charlene Regester has accounted for this by observing that "despite the fantasies appropriated by the film, Girl 6 is in conflict with her own image as a mature woman who is no longer a child."[5] Nola, of course, does not have this problem. Her breasts appear frequently in *She's Gotta Have It* and shots focused exclusively on one of her suitors interacting with her breasts often signify more extended moments of sexual intimacy, just as Girl 6's breasts come to represent her fear of such intimacy.

Both Girl 6's acting coach and her manager criticize her for leaving the audition. While the manager's anger seems rooted in the lost commission, the acting coach sees the move as part of Girl 6's failure to understand herself and "her art." The scene with the coach opens with Girl 6 again practicing Nola's monologue. After Girl 6 finishes the first sentence, the coach hangs her head, sighs, and mutters under her breath. She asks, "Where is the pain? . . . C'mon! It needs a bottom. Where's the bottom? What's this shallow shit? A bottom!" When Girl 6 responds that she "can't think," the coach screams and repeats three times, "Drop into the pain!" She goes on to say, "Acting is about doing and feelings. Drop into the pain!" When Girl 6 tries the monologue again, the coach stops her again and mocks the attempt. Girl 6, exasperated, tells her about Q.T. asking her to take off her shirt. Then this exchange follows:

COACH. So what! So what! Grow up! Grow up now!
GIRL 6. What are you talking about?
COACH. I am talking about you growing up. I am talking about you facing the reality of this business.
GIRL 6. Which is?
COACH. Which is . . . taking off your top bay-bee.
GIRL 6. That has nothin' to do with the work. You've taught me about the work.
COACH. It has plenty to do with the work. That's the business honey-bunch. Make it art! Turn it into something . . . special. Do you get it?
GIRL 6. Yes, I get it.

The coach's comments suggest that Girl 6 is so disconnected from herself that she does not even truly understand the implications of her chosen profession. While Girl 6, or any other actress, should certainly be allowed to choose roles that do not involve nudity, the coach's anger at Girl 6—and the skin-tight, nearly transparent outfit the aspiring actress is wearing at the time of the exchange—indicates that it is not modesty or morality that accounts for Girl 6's hesitation. Rather Girl 6's limited understanding of the intricacies of identity prevents her from seeing the potential beauty and creativity in that which initially seems negative or even ugly. Girl 6 cannot see how Nola's frustration with being misunderstood can translate into a revelation about how committed she is to finding happiness in her life on her own terms—or anything other than frustration with the rumors about her sexual perversion. And Girl 6 cannot see how Hollywood sexuality can be anything but perverted. While Hollywood certainly struggles with inappropriate representations of black female sexuality, as hooks's comments have suggested, to claim that all Hollywood nude scenes are lewd or demeaning seems a problematic assertion.

For the rest of the film, Girl 6 tries to understand herself more completely and find a truer sense of identity—ironically while working as a phone-sex operator exposed to sexual fantasies that even the most liberal ears might deem perverse. Phone sex, while certainly putting her on the path to such understanding, does so by showing her the effects of the absence of identity. On the phone she is only Girl 6 and the alter egos she makes up to please her callers, and she can only be black "if they request it."

She enters the field as a way to make some quick cash and because she thinks it will help her with her acting skills. Girl 6 seems surprised to find that talking about sex is easy for her. She hesitates only momentarily at her audition, and, at a training session with the other new girls, she describes her list of phone-sex alter egos in startling detail, including hair color, eye color, and the fact that her transsexual alter is "pre-op." When she finally hits the phones, her first call goes so well that she attracts the attention of the entire office.

Girl 6 continues to excel, finding the success she never experienced in her acting career. Two weeks after her first call, she already has a regular caller—her "first request"—waiting on the line when she arrives at work. Soon after, Girl 6 tells Jimmy that Lil, the madam, "says she ain't never seen nothin' like it. We had thirty eight phone calls last night, seventeen requests were for moi." This success seems to stem from her level of engagement with her callers. Most operators, even the new girls, distract themselves with drawing, reading, or smoking while they are talking to johns on the phone. Parks portrays Girl 6, however, as staying fully engaged in the fantasy. She is more creative and open in these scenes than she is in any of her acting scenes, and when one of her colleagues expresses concern about Girl 6's level of participation, her response indicates that she may not only be focused on the callers, but also relying on them to fulfill her needs for attention, intimacy, and even sexual pleasure:

DORIS. You know, you need to give yourself an activity of some sort, a magazine, a book, somethin', or else you're gonna get hooked girl.
GIRL 6. No, I'm concentratin'.
DORIS. Concentrating . . . Well . . . You comin' with 'em?
GIRL 6. *Laughs.* Please.
DORIS. You sure about that?
GIRL 6. I'm positive.

While she never explicitly answers Doris's question, the film suggests that Girl 6 is not yet a good enough actress to fake it.

Yet Parks seems to suggest that for Girl 6 being a phone-sex operator is not just about the sex. It is an opportunity to have a voice and for that voice to be heard. In the opening audition scene, Q.T. interrupts Girl 6 several times, snapping, "don't talk . . . listen." The acting coach also interrupts her monologue in order to criticize her performance. No one will stop to listen to her when she passes out computer fliers, and the extras coordinator on the movie set silences her pleas even to be allowed to use the bathroom. But in phone sex her voice is all anyone wants to hear. At their interview the madam tells Girl 6 she likes her "pipes." Many of Girl 6's callers, including her first, are just looking for "someone to talk to," and she, of course, is looking for someone who will listen.

While her initial motivation to begin the work was predominantly economic and, she claims, vocational—because she could practice acting and save the money she needed to move to Hollywood—her devotion to the job is emotional. In the men that call her and request to spend time with her on the phone, Girl 6 finds intimacy and companionship without commitment and without depth. She can take what she wants from and give what she wants to her caller, and she need only reveal the parts of her self—real or fabricated—that help make this exchange more pleasurable for her and the customer. In Parks's phone-sex world, then, Girl 6 can have what she perceives to be intimacy—which she cannot find in the real world—without confronting the shallowness of her identity or her fears of intimacy's physical elements. She can even have a lover for each identity she tries on.

Relationships are available to Girl 6 outside of the phone-sex world, but these relationships are complicated and demanding. Her ex-husband, like Booth in *Topdog,* survives and thrives off stealing. Her early interactions with him in the film suggest disappointment that the relationship left her scarred and may have even contributed to the self-questioning and fear of intimacy that plague her. Every time the ex appears he steals something; and before he steals, he touches, even caresses his mark, leading the viewer to wonder how the physical need to touch and possess what is not his might have manifested itself in his physical relationship with his wife. Even Jimmy, while seemingly a supportive friend, relies on Girl 6 financially. Also his support challenges her. After she has told him how much she has come to like phone sex and how fun it has become and starts talking about Bob Regular, one of her favorite callers, he interrupts to ask, "So when was the last time you went on an audition?"—a question that she tries to ignore and a question that none of her regular customers would ever ask.

Girl 6 takes her boss Lil seriously when she says during training, "It's not just sex. You're their friend." As Girl 6 talks to Jimmy about the men, she recounts their stories as if they are her close companions, defending them against Jimmy's criticism and describing their inner turmoil. The men become her surrogate friends, her community. Girl 6 works in a community of women, and these women—as seen when Doris expresses her concern that Girl 6 is getting too involved in the job—try to reach out to her and protect her. Parks shows these women laughing together, celebrating Girl 19's engagement, and sharing meals. But Girl 6 alienates herself even from them, fearing the commitment that comes with this community. When Lil becomes so concerned about this behavior that she forces Girl 6 to take a vacation, Girl 6 goes back to the first madam and becomes a "home girl." She then becomes totally isolated, and her apartment becomes a microcosmic phone-sex fantasy world. Jimmy tells her ex-husband that he never sees her, and when the ex attempts to visit, she opens the door briefly—without interrupting her phone call—smirks at him disgustedly, and shuts the door on him without a word, establishing that there is neither room nor need for him and his complications in her new world.

However, her relationships with the callers demand more from Girl 6 than she realizes, for while she does get to change who she is for each man, the changes are not just about clothes and hair. Girl 6 must change her desires, her boundaries. This behavior takes an emotional toll, and she begins to escape into her own fantasies, fantasies based on movies and television.

In the first fantasy, Girl 6 imagines herself as Dorothy Dandridge, playing the title character in *Carmen Jones* (1954). Parks made the ex-husband Joe, Carmen's obsessed lover, and the two reenact a vignette that combines dialogue from two scenes in the original film. Parks's choice of film is significant because, in *Notes of a Native Son* (1955), James Baldwin called *Carmen Jones* "one of the most important all-Negro movies that Hollywood has produced" because "the questions that it leaves in the mind relate less to Negroes than to the interior life of Americans."[6] But Baldwin took issue with the film's representations of sexuality: "The only reason . . . that the eroticism of *Carmen Jones* is more potent than, say, the eroticism of a Lana Turner vehicle is that *Carmen Jones* has Negro bodies before the camera and Negroes are associated in the public mind with sex. Since darker races always seem to have for lighter races an aura of sexuality, this fact is not distressing in itself. What is distressing is the conjecture this movie leaves one with as to what Americans take sex to be."[7]

By evoking *Carmen Jones,* then, Parks has highlighted *Girl 6's* connection not only to a history of sexualized black female stereotypes but also to a history of American prudishness about sex. *Girl 6* raises the same conjectures that Baldwin claimed *Carmen Jones* raises. Girl 6 idolizes Dandridge in general, but in this role in particular because of her effortless sexuality and power over Joe, a wholesome American soldier.

Baldwin also notes that when watching Dandridge's performance in *Carmen Jones,* "One feels—perhaps one is meant to feel—that here is a *very* nice girl making her way in movies by means of a bad-girl part."[8] At this point in the film, Girl 6 also struggles with this type of identity crisis, as indicated by her showing up to her first phone-sex interview in pig tails and a school girl uniform. She too wants to be a "good girl" but she keeps attaching herself to, and seeking success in, "bad girl" roles.

In the next media fantasy, Girl 6 is Lovely Brown in a scene based both on Pam Grier in *Foxy Brown* (1974) and Tamara Dobson in *Cleopatra Jones* (1973). These films can be read as both liberation and exploitation films. Both are a part of the blaxploitation genre, which names the group of films born from Hollywood's sudden interest in the 1970s in making money off black themes and black heroes/heroines. On Foxy Brown and Cleopatra Jones, critic Karen Ross noted that both "had bodies which were both athletic and sexually appealing and although they had to appear as powerful and threatening to accord with the conventions of the genre, they nonetheless remained vulnerable and feminine."[9] The women were thus the objects of both black and white male fascination, and in "the end," Ross argued, "the male gaze is more disempowering than the women's aggression is liberating, and in any case, their violence is usually directed against other women (as in *Cleopatra Jones*) so that the possibility of female solidarity was instantly closed off as potential threat. At the end of their labours, our heroines always returned home to the reassuring arms of their lovers."[10] Girl 6, of course, longs for both personal strength and intimacy with a male hero. She certainly does not attack the women in her community, but her relationships with them are noncommunal and somewhat adversarial: they are competing for callers, and she is winning.

While Girl 6's fantasy life seems remarkably active, Parks is careful to establish that everyone in the film fantasizes and thus, far from being pathological, fantasy—even sexual fantasy—can be "normal," if not healthy. This idea, of course, takes Parks's message back to Nola Darling's rejection of labels, particularly of the term "freak." At first, Girl 6 plays with the term, saying that her "girl-next door" character "Lovely Brown," the persona she puts on the most in the film, is "kinda freaky" during her training session with Lil and the other new girls. The more time that Girl 6 spends on the phone with her callers, however, the more she rethinks what it means to be a "freak," and she rejects its application to fantasy, as the following exchange with Jimmy reveals:

JIMMY. So what does that have to do with your acting career? What happened to that?
GIRL 6. I'm still an actress Jimmy.
JIMMY. How are you acting?
GIRL 6. What?
JIMMY. How are you acting? You're not on the stage, you're not in front of the camera. You're on the phone. How do you act talking on the phone to some—
GIRL 6. It *is* acting.
JIMMY. —some perverts? How is that acting?
GIRL 6. They're not perverts Jimmy, OK?
JIMMY. Oh, they're normal people right?
GIRL 6. Baby, let me tell you somethin', you can continue to live in that little fantasy world with the baseball cards and the autograph bull shit or whatever the fuck it is you do, but me, I got to eat and I got to pay my rent. Phone sex is acting. And if you don't like it, you can step.

If her phone-sex clients are not freaks, she cannot be a freak for entertaining them, and her job can be considered acting.

But after her favorite caller, Bob Regular, rejects her, Girl 6 returns to accepting the label. When her ex-husband observes, "I never knew you were such a freak," she curtly replies, "Maybe you just never brought it out in me." This exchange suggests that Girl 6 does not yet understand sexuality in the nonphone world and provides further evidence that her sexual relationship with her husband was at the least unfulfilling, if not unhealthy.

Indeed the emotional impact of the phone-sex career on Girl 6 becomes most evident when Bob Regular does not show up for their arranged meeting at Coney Island. While most of the callers' faces are fully visible in the film, Bob's remains obscured, suggesting that he represents potential—a type of man rather than any individual man. The film never mentions Bob and Girl 6 having phone sex; it shows them only talking about his mother. The loss of Bob Regular comes to represent the loss of Girl 6's hope that she will ever find a fulfilling, "normal" relationship, one not always about sex, in the nonphone world. The loss also marks the beginning of Girl 6's understanding that she needs more in her life than the sex-based phone relationships she has been experiencing. Here she reaches out to her ex-husband. The two go out to dinner; she demonstrates her sexy talk skills, and he tries to force his hand down her pants. As hooks noted, "Acting like the outraged Virgin, she sees no connection between her performance and his assumption that she will do anything to please him."[11] She has not considered that a fantasy could have real-life implications.

Her reaction, however, is not to withdraw from the phone-sex fantasy world, but to intensify her phone-sex experience by becoming a home girl, a change that promises a more visceral experience with the callers. The Madonna madam explains: "If you do decide to accept this mission, you must realize that your own private line is essential. I suggest getting an unlisted phone number that is inaccessible to Caller I.D. Choose a phone with a lightweight receiver. I suggest getting a headset. That way your hands are kept free. While office-bound fantasy girls are restricted by what they can say, a fantasy girl who works out of the home, a home girl, can experience complete and total freedom. You can invite your caller to fully experience his deepest, darkest, strangest, wildest desires. No inhibitions. No restrictions. Total freedom. No taboos."

Girl 6 indeed pushes the traditional boundaries. She gives the men her address so that she can receive their fan mail, and she locks herself in her apartment, totally immersing herself in the fantasy and trying to make it more real. Yet, with only one exception, Parks never allows the audience to see or hear the callers Girl 6 entertains at home; viewers hear only Girl 6 talking to them, making this new aspect of the job more personal—less about Girl 6 participating in a caller's fantasy than about her trying, now more futilely than ever, to fulfill her own need for intimacy.

During Girl 6's time as a home girl, Parks shows Girl 6 in her last TV fantasy. For this fantasy, Parks re-created Girl 6 as Thelma from *Good Times* (1974–79). However, as in the other fantasies, Parks combined two media images, and Thelma actually becomes the daughter of George and

Louise Jefferson from *The Jeffersons* (1975–85). In this fantasy a man tries to seduce naive Thelma on the phone. Louise, played by Lil, helps her to see the man's true intentions, and George, played by Jimmy, shoots the phone ("the tenth phone this month") with a shotgun. Thelma cries briefly after the shooting, but she soon laughs and dances with her mother and father, seemingly carefree. This scene is particularly important at this point in the film because Parks uses it to depict Girl 6's yearning for family and companionship as well as for protection. Lil and Jimmy look out for Girl 6's well-being more than anyone else in the film. However, she still closes herself off from both of them. In choosing to place herself with the Jeffersons, Girl 6 puts her character not in the Chicago ghetto, where Thelma and her family live in *Good Times,* but in a safe, affluent New York "deluxe apartment in the sky."

The Jeffersons represents African American success in Hollywood, given its nearly unprecedented ten-year run, but the show's legacy is complicated. For Robin R. Means Coleman, the show is part of an era in black comedy, spanning from 1972 to 1983, in which African Americans "remain in the separate Black world, one that is parallel to the White one. The characters, defined as assimilated hybrid minstrels, negotiate all of the situations whites do, yet separately and with overt references to their Blackness and difference."[12] However, Donald Bogle has argued that while George Jefferson "yearned for white signs and symbols of success and acceptance, and he lived by traditional capitalistic American values," he also "never wanted to be white. . . . For the African American audience . . . it was refreshing to see a middle-class black man who asserted his racial identity at every opportunity."[13] This certainty of identity—both familial and racial—likely draws Parks and her Girl 6 to this character and scenario.

Intriguingly, Parks did not make the women in *The Jeffersons* the focus of Girl 6's fantasy. When choosing a woman to play in the scene set on *The Jeffersons,* Parks turned to Thelma and *Good Times.* According to Bogle, Thelma is "the most overlooked and perhaps saddest character on the show." He continued, "Fortunately, she could exchange barbs but mainly her role was to react, not initiate much action. Mostly, the scripts called for her to stand around, looking sweet and vaguely yearning for something else."[14] Girl 6, trapped in a similarly stagnant role, connects with this longing for "something else," and in her case, much like Thelma's, that longing comes from a lack of identity and purpose. This fantasy is interrupted by Jimmy knocking on the door—like his character in *The Jeffersons* fantasy—to make sure Girl 6 is safe. Regardless of her attitude in the fantasy, however, Girl 6 lashes out defiantly at Jimmy for interrupting her work with his "bull shit."

Yet Jimmy's concerns end up being well founded. The aforementioned exception to the home callers' invisibility is Girl 6's last caller, "Mr. Snuff," who Lil cuts off in an earlier call to the office. As with Bob Regular, Parks ensures that Mr. Snuff's face is never clearly visible; he is always in shadows. He too is merely a representation, not of hope but of fear—fear of loneliness, fear of intimacy, fear of self-expression—the very fears that threaten to destroy Girl 6. He leaves a message on the answering machine for Girl 6's unlisted phone number, and when they talk later, the scene is red. The camera stays on Girl 6's face as she struggles with the conversation, appearing embattled and disoriented. When Mr. Snuff asks to come over, she tells him she would rather just stay on the phone. A very revealing exchange ensues:

MR. SNUFF. Don't you fuckin' perform.
GIRL 6. I'm not, I just—
MR. SNUFF. Don't you fuckin' perform me. I don't want that bullshit. I do the performing.
GIRL 6. I'm not performing for you.
MR. SNUFF. What are you doing?
GIRL 6. I just want to . . . I just want to love you.

And he just wants to kill her. All at once, the calls are no longer fantasy, and her real longings are revealed. Once she realizes his threats are also real, she lashes out at him, screams that she'll kill him, and runs upstairs to safety with Jimmy, finally relying on a real person and a real relationship to help her when she needs it.

This successful seeking out of protective intimacy in a time of vulnerability seems to signal a significant change in Girl 6. She is lying close to Jimmy the next morning, and she wakes him up to tell him that she is giving up the "phone bone" business and moving to Los Angeles. She even goes to visit the injured little girl she has obsessively watched on TV throughout the film and gives the child money and a kiss. And finally, as she is loading up the cab for the airport, she shares a passionate kiss—the only real intimate moment in the film—with her ex-husband, a signal that she will try to heal the wounds of the past.

However, the transformation is still not complete. Viewers still cannot know for sure who Girl 6 really is, and ultimately she has left one superficial business for another—trading phone sex for Hollywood. We only glimpse Girl 6's real identity when, after the kiss, her ex tells her, "Oh Judy, I'm going to miss you Judy." And she replies, "Judy . . . I always did like it when you called me that." As they kiss, phones fall from the sky. This oddity, combined with the Dandridge-esque audition fantasy that follows and the metadiscursive walk that reveals *Girl 6* playing at the Chinese Theater, gives viewers the sense that the entire movie has been a fantasy—with the main character putting herself into the role of Girl 6 because she saw the story in the movie. In such a case, her true identity is completely unknown and wholly constructed.

In the final audition scene, when another director asks Girl 6 to show her breasts, she launches again into Nola's monologue, this time finishing it. The problem, of course, is that it is *Nola's* monologue, *Nola's* declaration of self, not Girl 6's. Parks never gave Girl 6 the ability to define herself in her own words, and she is thus still relying on media images to find her self-definition. In the DVD extra "The Making of *Girl 6*," Lee stated that "by the end of the film, [Girl 6's] feet are firmly on the ground. She is triumphant." But Hollywood will never be real, and as long as Girl 6 defines herself by Hollywood's standards rather than face what her coach called "the reality of this business," she may never truly find herself.

Their Eyes Were Watching God

The March 6, 2005, broadcast of *Their Eyes Were Watching God,* drew more than twenty-four million viewers according to the *Washington Post,* making it "the most watched movie on any network since CBS's December–December romance 'One Special Night,' starring Julie Andrews and James Garner, more than five years [prior]," and Winfrey's most successful ABC film since 1997.[15] Sharon D. Johnson's feature on the film in *Black Issues Book Review* explained that Winfrey set out to "incarnate Hurston."[16] However, the success—even the extent—of this "incarnation" remains questionable.

The credits of the film version of *Their Eyes Were Watching God* (henceforth referred to as *Their Eyes* to differentiate it from Hurston's novel) list "Suzan-Lori Parks [new line] and Misan Sagay and Bobby Smith, Jr." as the authors of the film's screenplay, or teleplay, as some call it since the film first appeared on television. However, many critics—even literary-leaning critics such as Hurston's most recent biographer, Valerie Boyd[17]—as well as the user reviews on Amazon.com and Internet Movie Database, focus more on Winfrey's or star Halle Berry's role in the project. It is certainly almost impossible to determine, even with firsthand accounts of the creative process, who is responsible for creating or including specific elements of the story, but since Parks is given top billing as screenwriter,[18] including the film in her oeuvre seems appropriate. In addition, according to Regester, "As she made the transition from dramatist to screenwriter, Parks's screenplays brought to fore some of the very issues that prevail in her plays."[19] Thus the film version of

Their Eyes is a fitting companion for Parks's other works, such as *Venus, In the Blood, Fucking A,* and, of course, *Girl 6*—all works with extraordinary black female protagonists in situations that are simultaneously unique and ordinary, situating one woman's compelling story within a complex history of oppression of which many women have been a part.

Their Eyes opens with a bruised, dirty, and exhausted Janie (Halle Berry) hobbling into Eatonville under the town's critical gaze. Once home, she starts telling her story, giving her friend Phoeby an overview of life with her grandmother, marrying Logan Killicks, running off with Joe Starks, helping to build Eatonville, living under Joe's strict hand and watching him die, meeting and running off with Tea Cake, living in South Florida, weathering the storm, and, finally, shooting Tea Cake. Parks's *Their Eyes* shares with Hurston's novel, then, only some of the most basic plot points and broader themes that drive this plot: growth, love, and discovering individual identity.

The divergences between the text and the film are too numerous to list in their entirety, but there are among them particularly relevant changes in the treatment of race and community, in narrative voice, and in character motivation and development. These changes combine to make Parks's *Their Eyes* a completely new story with a particular emphasis on black female sexuality, specifically sexual autonomy and individual feminine identity. While these themes are certainly present in the text of Hurston's *Their Eyes Were Watching God,* the film makes them more central to the story—all the while downplaying other key issues and themes from the novel.

Certainly television time restraints and viewer tastes played a role in some of these edits. Yet, by revising *Their Eyes Were Watching God* for television and thus for a wider audience, Parks and her collaborators essentially presented a revised version of African American literary history, changing its scope and themes. The outcome can be read as paradoxical, for while they indeed introduced a valuable text and tradition to new audiences, they simultaneously remapped the historical value of that text and the tradition. While making African American literature more mainstream, such adaptation also creates an opportunity for the predominantly white power structures in the entertainment industry to control and reshape its message.

This reshaping manifests itself most clearly in a shift away from overtly racial content in the film. Gone, for example, is Janie's description of discovering her blackness when she sees herself in a photograph and realizes that she is the lone "real dark little girl." She explains, "But before Ah seen de picture Ah thought Ah was just like de rest" (9).[20] The film even trims Hurston's much-valued signature use of the black vernacular, an element that has been one of the most controversial features of the story since her novel appeared in 1937, just six years after James Weldon Johnson's preface to *The Book of Negro American Poetry* declared dialect "an instrument with but two full stops, humor and pathos."[21] Parks has attributed this revision to audience, explaining, "We took a step from the brilliantly rendered dialect and split the difference, retaining something like the dialect but putting in a voice that is hearable for the 2005 ear."[22] The 2005 ear's inability to hear and understand Hurston's vernacular suggests that the 2005 audience, black and white, has become disconnected from black vernacular culture, the very culture that Hurston's text seeks to celebrate.

By downplaying such racial elements, *Their Eyes* not only broadens its potential viewing audience but also narrows the focus of the story to the circumstances surrounding Janie's romances—her motivation for beginning and either remaining in or leaving each relationship as well as the effects that each relationship has on her identity and sexuality. Parks's film, for example, does not give the backstory about the rape of Janie's mother and her grandmother Nanny's encounter with the jealous white mistress, nor most of Nanny's related racial justification for wanting Janie to marry Logan Killicks. Nanny tells Janie in the text: "Honey, de white man is de ruler of everything as fur as Ah been able tuh find out. Maybe it's some place way off in de ocean where de black man is in power, but we don't know nothin' but what we see. So de white man throw down de load and tell de nigger man tuh pick it up. He pick it up because he have to, but he don't tote it. He hand it to his womenfolks. De nigger woman is de mule uh de world so far as Ah can see?" (14). Parks, however, includes only the last sentence of this justification, and in the place of Nanny's heartfelt and telling description of racialized and sexualized power imbalance appears instead a focus on economics—Logan Killicks's land holdings and position in the community.

In omitting this information, the film nearly vilifies Nanny (Ruby Dee) much as it does the other women in the story, portraying them as old-fashioned, closed-minded, and grasping at whatever power they can wield. Somewhat implied in this portrayal, of course—especially for the viewer who has read Hurston's text—is the exact sentiment that Nanny explains to Janie in her justification for the marriage to Logan Killicks: women are so stripped of agency by both white and black men that they must maximize any power they do have, even if it undermines their relationship with other women, as seen in Nanny's confrontation with her mistress in the novel. Without past access to Hurston's text, however, this implication is almost lost.

The film's massively altered depiction of Hurston's implied listener, Janie's friend Phoeby, only further separates the film and the text and de-textualizes the film's message about black female identity. In the text, Phoeby supports

Janie and kindly offers to be her mouthpiece in the community: "If you so desire Ah'll tell em what you tell me to tell 'em" (6). In Parks's film version, however, Phoeby seems friendly at first, but quickly moves on to chastising Janie:

PHOEBY. He dragged you down to his level and then—
JANIE. You all think he did me wrong.
PHOEBY. Janie, we all know he did you wrong.
JANIE. Well, I ain't studyin' what they think.
PHOEBY. You don't care what I think neither, do you? You left this town, runnin' off with that no count—
JANIE. Me and Tea Cake had us a real love—
PHOEBY. *the pitch of her voice rising*—And you got the nerve to come back up in here with no shoes on your feet and nothing but overalls on your back, making everything we believed in just look like dirt.
JANIE. Me and Tea Cake had us a real love—
PHOEBY. How could you do that?
JANIE. But you all couldn't see that—
PHOEBY. *crying* I used to look up to you.
JANIE. Phoeby, the only way you and this whole town ever seen me was as Mrs. Mayor Starks

Rather than listen to Janie and offer to speak for her, Phoeby interrupts and speaks over her as Janie tried to protest Phoeby's evaluation. The film's Janie could never say "mah tongue is in mah friend's mouf," as her textual counterpart does, for the film's Phoeby is not a sister but rather is another adversary (6). By erasing this oft-quoted sentence and by recasting Phoeby as yet another person to whom Jaime must explain herself, Parks's film deemphasizes the importance of the female community that Hurston's text privileges.

Parks's Janie finds community only twice in the film: during the brief time she spends building Eatonville with her neighbors—who as soon as the work is finished quickly refocus their energy on class-conscious jealousies—and then again much later in the film when she is in Florida with Tea Cake. Even here, however, the people are generally kind to the couple, but the film does not explore any of these relationships in detail. The film also does not give any glimpse of the color-induced jealousies that drive Tea Cake to strike Janie in Hurston's text, but rather portrays the two as soul mates, fulfilling each other spiritually as well as sexually. In shifting the focus away from Janie's relationship with Phoeby as well as the community in general, the film emphasizes feminine independence while nearly dismissing any possibility for redemptive female community. If audience is indeed the driving force behind the revisions from the text, then the implications for modern black community are troubling. The revisions suggest that class insecurity and fear distance women from each other, leaving only the occasional sexual partner for emotional support.

The production history of the film itself at first seems to contradict this message. Most of the primary players in the film are black women. Winfrey, of course, purchased the rights to the film (outbidding fellow executive producer and the only prominent man on the project, Quincy Jones), then spearheaded and produced the project.[23] Berry, by all accounts, was Winfrey's first and only choice to play Janie. Director Darnell Martin, who established herself in television by directing episodes of popular shows such as the *Law & Order* franchise, *Grey's Anatomy,* and *The L-Word,* is a pioneering independent filmmaker who is most famous for her first film, *I Like It Like That* (1994), which follows "a woman in the Bronx waging war with the forces that would hold her back."[24] For Parks, *Their Eyes* came on the heels of her Pulitzer win (2002) and the release of her much-anticipated first novel, *Getting Mother's Body* (2003).

Such a group of women collaborating to bring Hurston's work to the screen embodies, at least at first glance, the type of productive and redemptive community in Hurston's story. As Janie tells Phoeby both the story of her life before Eatonville and the story of the events that transpired after she left the town with Tea Cake, both women are transformed. Phoeby tells her friend, "Ah done growd ten feet higher from jus' listenin' tuh you Janie. Ah ain't satisfied with mahself no mo'" (192). Both enjoy the "finished silence" in which "for the first time they could hear the wind picking at the pine trees," and both think of love (192). Janie then realizes that Tea Cake "could never be dead until she herself had finished feeling and thinking" and she finds "peace" (193). Both telling and listening within the framework of this supportive black female community leads to healing.

While Parks's Phoeby also says she grows after listening to Janie, the two women do not then sit together as sisters to savor and share the communal experience. Instead the film's Phoeby runs out to get her husband, Sam, so they can go fishing, just like Janie and Tea Cake. Rather than bond with Janie, Phoeby wants to copy her. In Parks's film, class seems to separate Phoeby and Janie. Phoeby, like others in Eatonville, idolizes Janie and sees her leaving with Tea Cake as a fall, a relinquishing of status. And even among the women who created the film, class issues arise. While Parks and Martin are certainly not as wealthy and famous as Winfrey or Berry, they are still established in the creative class; they are well-respected artists who have excelled in their respective fields. Even so, Winfrey admits that she was concerned that Berry would not agree to do the project since Winfrey's request came almost immediately after Berry's Oscar win.[25] Class, then, continues to undermine female community even among the most powerful American black women, and the product of their collaboration reflects this anxiety.

Parks's film does leave some hope for community in that Phoeby is not the only listener: twenty-four million other sets of ears also heard the story. But while the film goes out of its way to chart Janie's transformations throughout the film, it would be difficult to measure such change in the viewer. Parks created changes in Janie through moments such as her fixation on the caterpillar she finds on Logan's porch, a creature that will inevitably metamorphose into a brilliant winged creature, just as Janie herself hopes to find beauty and liberation. In addition, Parks included three completely original baptismal scenes in which Janie swims and looks at the sky. In each scene, one following her betrothal to Logan Killicks, one after Joe's death, and one after Tea Cake's death, she washes away an old dream or an old burden and prepares to start again. In the first and third, a voice, Nanny's first, then Tea Cake's from beyond the grave, asks Janie what she is doing, to which she responds simply, "I'm watching God."

This departure from the meaning of Hurston's novel's original title reveals another instance of Parks moving away from a focus on the community and toward a more independent or autonomous feminine sensibility. "Their eyes" are no longer watching God, but "her eyes," or even more specifically, "Janie's eyes" are watching God. The change not only individualizes Janie's role in the film, but the context for this "watching"—a baptismal swim surrounded by nature—also creates a parallel relationship between Janie, nature, and the divine. Even into the early twentieth century, the Cult of True Womanhood and its call for purity, piety, domesticity, and submission still dominated cultural norms and expectations for women's behavior. In creating a balance among Janie, the natural world, and the divine, the film undermines these supposed standards governing a woman's behavior. Janie's sexuality and sexual desire are portrayed as perfectly natural. They do not evoke the wrath of God but instead allow her moments of quiet reflection on or perhaps even with him.

These moments differ significantly from those in Hurston's novel when people overtly watch God. As the roaring storm approaches near the end of the novel, Tea Cake, Janie, and their neighbors sit in their homes, "their eyes straining against crude walls and their souls asking if He meant to measure their puny might against His. They seemed to be staring at the dark, but their eyes were watching God" (160). Earlier in the scene, when their "eyes were questioning *God,*" Janie refers to God in very racialized terms: "Ole Massa," she says, "is doin' *His* work now. Us oughta keep quiet" (159). The text thus links God with patriarchy and unchecked power. Janie and others only watch him to anticipate his wrath, not to anticipate any kind of redemption. In Parks's *Their Eyes,* Janie and Teacake never watch or question God; they only cling to each other as the storm rumbles outside.

Parks's emphasis on the natural world in the film also contributes to a privileging of the visual in ways even beyond that expected when a text is adapted for the screen. This privileging is most obvious in the merging of Janie and the narrator's voices as well as in a general shift away from any narration, regardless of voice. Janie's character instead participates in every scene, and the voice heard is hers—fully engaged in the action if not herself describing it. The first voice in the film is Janie's—not in dialogue, but as Janie turned narrator, speaking in subtle dialect. She speaks, as Hurston's narrator does at the beginning of her text, about coming back from burying the dead. The voices from the porch soon swirl around her, and the new Janie, unlike her textual counterpart who speaks an unknown greeting to the women, tells the women to "go to hell" under her breath. And when Janie begins to tell Phoeby her story, there is minimal narration—again from Janie herself, before the action simply skips back to the past so that the audience can witness it firsthand. The audience, then, is never distanced from Janie or her emotions. Parks has allowed her viewers to witness Janie's sexual awakening, her disappointment and anger at being forced to marry Logan, her sadness at losing Joe's affection, her relief when he passes, and her longing for Tea Cake. Such witnessing creates a much more direct connection between Janie and the viewer, literally bringing Janie to life on the screen and giving her a voice, the very voice, as some have argued, she is ostensibly denied in Hurston's text.

Indeed, in her introduction to the Perennial Classics paperback edition of *Their Eyes Were Watching God,* Mary Helen Washington recalled a panel discussion about the novel at the 1979 MLA Convention. At this panel, she indicated, "[Robert] Stepto raised the issue that has become one of the most highly controversial and hotly contested aspects of the novel: whether or not Janie is able to achieve her voice in [the story]."[26] Stepto and others have looked to the courtroom scene near the end of the novel and "found Janie curiously silent in the scene, with Hurston telling the story in the omniscient third person so that we do not hear Janie speak—at least not in her own first-person voice."[27] They have found "that the frame story in which Janie speaks to Phoeby creates only the illusion that Janie has found her voice, that Hurston's insistence on telling Janie's story in the third person undercuts her power as speaker;" Washington, however, concludes that Janie's "silence reflects Hurston's discomfort with the model of the male hero that asserts himself through his powerful voice," and goes on to explain that "when Janie says at the end of her story that 'talkin' don't amount to much' if it's divorced from experience, she is testifying to the limitations of voice and critiquing the culture that celebrates orality to the exclusion of inner growth."[28] The lack of narrative voice and the privileging of the visual experience in Parks's *Their Eyes,* then, could also be read as a response to Hurston's declaration that "you got to *go* there to *know* there" (192).

Ironically *Their Eyes* leaves out the very scene that led to so much discussion about voice at the 1979 MLA panel. The courtroom scene's conspicuous absence would seem to indicate that the filmmakers found it as problematic as Stepto. However, leaving it out contributes to the film's revised message about autonomy and independence and ultimately gives the viewer more interpretive agency by leaving Janie's motive, and thus her defense, for shooting Tea Cake totally ambiguous. As seen in some of Parks's plays, such as *In the Blood,* an audience's access to written narration can radically change its understanding of a character's motivation. Such is the case here: Janie with narration and Janie without narration are completely different characters. Neither is more correct, or less real, but their differences are revealing, for they show an inevitable disconnect between oral and written communication—between spectacle and page.

Hurston's narrator, for example, implies that only self-preservation drives Janie to shoot Tea Cake. After he tries to shoot her once, Janie aims her own rifle at him "instinctively" (183). Hurston's narrator portrays the two lovers as animals engaged in a primal struggle for existence, for "the fiend in [Tea Cake] must kill and Janie was the only living thing he saw" (184). Here, and immediately after the shooting, the narrator, describing Janie as "just a scared human being fighting for its life," the narrator refers to her with the gender-neutral pronoun "it" (184). Once Janie knows she is safe, however, she again becomes "her sacrificing self with Tea Cake's head in her lap" (184); she is rehumanized. The implication here is that Janie did not have a choice to kill Tea Cake because if there had been a choice, her rational self would have chosen his life over hers. Instead some external force, be it fate or God, drove her to experience "the meanest moment of eternity," to choose survival and life over the "self-crushing love" she had for Tea Cake (128).

In the scene immediately before the shooting in Parks's film, however, Janie tells Tea Cake, "Fight it. Fight it. I know you can fight it. . . . Cause if you don't fight it, they gonna tie you down, and I ain't gonna let nobody tie you down." This sentiment paints the shooting as a mercy killing. By leaving open the possibility for autonomy in Tea Cake's shooting, Parks allows her version of Janie to choose life actively. The celebration of her life and the new beginning embodied in the baptismal scene that follows her return to Eatonville affirm this choice, making Janie's love for Tea Cake self-illuminating rather than "self-crushing." Hurston's Janie finds this same hope for the future in the last sentences of the novel as "she pulled in her horizon like a great fish-net. Pulled it in from around the waist of the world and draped it over her shoulder. So much of life in its meshes! She called her soul to come and see" (193). Both Janies, then, come to this self-love and independence at the end of their stories, even if not by exactly the same path.

Janie's transformation is clear—but what of the listeners, the audience? Although difficult to use as gauge of an audience's specific reactions to a film, viewer response—if available—is nevertheless worth considering in any revisionary experiment because it reveals the extent to which audiences are called back to, and reflect on, the original text.

User reviews are often poorly written and inaccurate, but they are nevertheless revealing. Most who posted reviews of the film had not read the book. These reviewers loved the adaptation and felt its impact. According to a March 7, 2005, review posted on the Internet Movie Database (IMDb), the film "teaches that material things are all right in their place"; yet they must sometimes be traded "for real living and true love." Some fans of the text applauded Winfrey, Parks, and the other collaborators for bringing *Their Eyes* to a wider audience. Most who had read Hurston's text, however, were disappointed. One particularly biting review posted to IMDb on March 9, 2005, explained, "I am a Black woman and I have read *Their Eyes Were Watching God* many times, most recently when I learned that Oprah Winfrey and ABC were presenting the television movie. . . . I watched the movie with four other Black people, two men and two women. No one had anything positive to say about the movie. I held on as long as I could, but after two hours, I had to agree with my fellow viewers: the movie was horrible. Shame on all involved who had any sort of creative control over this debacle. May Hurston haunt you until you know better."

The film's goal according to Winfrey, however, was to encourage people to read the book. As Henry Louis Gates, Jr., explained to *Black Issues Book Review,* "Some people come to a great novel through its filming, and some go to the film after reading the novel. . . . It doesn't really matter. More people overnight will know about Zora Neale Hurston and *Their Eyes Were Watching God* because of Winfrey's telefilm."[29]

Yet reviews from actual viewers show flaws in this logic. Shamontiel L. Vaughn from Chicago wrote in an Amazon review on May 12, 2006, that her first instinct was to buy the book after seeing the film; however, "after reading some of the reviews and finding out that so many readers didn't like the movie versus the book, I see that I never want to read the book. I was so content with that movie . . . and I don't want to let anything damper my satisfaction with it." Six days later, she posted an update to her review: "Curiosity got the better of me and I got the book. Now I'm really rolling my eyes because this book didn't have a THING on the movie. Tea Cake was a liar, a jerk, ridiculously macho, and he hit her . . . Even worse, Janie was a complete idiot in the book. Everything she did had to be approved by a man and she kept telling people she couldn't think well because she wasn't too smart. I like how much of the movie used the dialogue from the book, but I am so glad Oprah had a hand in this movie. She made Janie much stronger, intelligent, and got rid of that whole damsel in distress nonsense. If I had read the book first, I would've NEVER watched the movie."

Vaughn's comments suggest that the movie was powerful for her, perhaps even transformative, and that she felt a connection to the new Janie that she did not feel with the old. Still, her comments also reveal the inherent dangers of the revisionary experiment: in attempting to revise Hurston's story in ways that would not alienate 2005 viewers from the story, Parks's *Their Eyes* may have alienated Hurston's original story from these viewers, nullifying a literary sisterhood that might have been created between Hurston, Janie, and a new, broader twenty-first-century audience.

Another important issue about Parks's revision, the downplaying of racial elements in *Their Eyes*, also recurs as a topic among the viewer reviews. Many users may complain about the absence of racialized content, and some, especially on IMDb, notice that there are very few white characters in the novel. Indeed, there are even fewer white characters in *Their Eyes* than there are in the novel. Only three white characters appear in the film: Mr. Eaton, who donates the land to start Eatonville and then allows Joe to buy more and expand the town; the white boss in Florida; and the white doctor, who tries to get rabid Tea Cake the medicine that may or may not save him. Neither these white characters nor the power structures they represent cause any problems for the protagonists. Rather, Parks's film, like Hurston's text, "affirms and celebrates black culture,"[30] even without exploring how this culture triumphed and flourished in the midst of the very real racial politics that Hurston included in her text.

Again, the real-life story of *Their Eyes*'s production reveals an equally complicated relationship with racial themes and conflicting opinions about the role these themes play in the film. Parks, for example, claimed, "This is not a story about race. Our people just get to be. . . . It's a milestone, but what a milestone to reach."[31] Parks also pointed to what her perception of the universality of the film: "Women, African-American women, African-Americans, we Americans as a people haven't freed ourselves from the burdens of our history. . . . When you write about somebody trying to free themselves from the constraints of their society, it's what's going on next door. It's white guys trying to get free of the roles imposed on them too."[32] Winfrey, on the other hand, asserted, "I think it's really important for us to see African-Americans in a life that allows not only the history and legacy of the culture, but to show love. . . . And that's often not seen in a way that people can relate to."[33]

Meanwhile Berry also downplayed the racial elements in the film while she simultaneously affirmed that women in general, and black women specifically, face unique struggles in the film industry. She said of the film, "It's certainly not heavy-hitting. It's really a love story about a woman coming of age and finding love of herself and finding love in other people. It's not really that huge of a political statement as one might fear. So, there's no need to be afraid of it."[34] Yet she claimed in another interview, "I think the struggle for a woman of color to find good material is still very present and it's a struggle that I fight every day. . . . I think women have a hard time finding material in general, be you black, white, sky blue or pink. It's hard to find good characters to play, that really tell our story and embark on our journey in a real, full way."[35]

Each woman's approach to the film incorporates some element that can relate to black women, and each has sought only to broaden the audience of viewers for Hurston's story. Nevertheless, removing race seems an erroneous and dangerous method by which to do so. For Hurston's story is an American story because it is an African American story, not despite it. Furthermore Hurston's story, in which Janie faces inter- and intraracial politics as a black woman in an all-black town, reveals clear parallels to Berry's lack of scripts, Winfrey's lack of positive media images, and perhaps even the entire movie's lack of serious critical investigation.

Conclusion

Parks's *Girl 6* and her made-for-television *Their Eyes* both inevitably challenge film's ability to represent and shape black identity, culture, and history in general and black women's issues within these three topics specifically. Both also raise challenging questions about the future of black community and the efficacy of film in healing the divisive wounds that Hollywood itself has created, especially for black women, through problematic stereotypes of black identity and sexuality. Both films offer their examinations within the context of promising collaborations: Lee/Parks/Prince and Winfrey/Parks/Berry/Martin/Jones. Even so, the films offer little to reflect the positive implications of the collaborations—perhaps because these films must still cater to predominantly white audiences and a predominately white industry or perhaps because new issues, such as class and creative politics, have brought new complications.

Parks let both Janie and Girl 6, however, come out of their cinematic struggles stronger and more self-aware than when they began. While the films do not tell us exactly where the women end up, Janie will likely keep swimming and watching God, and Girl 6 likely will keep daydreaming and reading her monologue at auditions. Regardless of the politics of their creation—or how independent of politics the creation tried to be—the end of each story is left for the audience, and not Parks or even Hollywood, to determine. The women can still be only as free as the audience can imagine them to be.

CHAPTER 8

The Revisionary Revised

Essays and *365 Days/365 Plays*

Suzan-Lori Parks's essays, most notably those written in 1994 and collected in *The America Play and Other Works* (1995) as well as her 1999 essay "Tradition and the Individual Talent" demonstrate that she is ever aware of the literary, cultural, and historical implications of art in general and of her own art in particular. Her revisiting and revision of these essays—especially "From *Elements of Style*" (1994), an abbreviated version of which is reprinted at the beginning of *Venus* and all of Parks's subsequent plays, and "An Equation for Black People on Stage" (1994) revised into "new black math" (2005)—show that she believes art and its function to be vibrant, fluid, and eclectic. Her revision of her past literary creations, as seen in *Getting Mother's Body* and especially in *365 Days/365 Plays* (2006), proves her willingness to put her theory into action—a revolutionary act in itself for a writer or a theorist. Parks, beyond being a playwright or a novelist or a screenwriter, is a revisionary—a theorist with an ever-transformative vision of literature, especially her own literature, and its place in the world.

Like the famous theorists that came before her, Sterling Brown, James Weldon Johnson, Langston Hughes, Zora Neale Hurston, Henry Louis Gates, Jr., Barbara Smith, Houston A. Baker, Jr., bell hooks, and many others, Parks has written in her essays about the form and function of language ("From *The Elements of Style*"), about literary influence ("Tradition and the Individual Talent"), about the fine (or not so fine) line between protest art and "art for art's sake" ("Possession" [1994], "An Equation for Black People Onstage," and "new black math").

It may seem at first glance that Parks is simply walking well-worn roads, but as she asserted in the first paragraph of "new black math," some questions of aesthetics and poetics, especially those that are politically charged and intensely relevant to many artists' and many audiences' lives, are not ready to be left behind and classified as mere "literary history." She wrote: "10 years after writing the essay 'the equation for black people on stage'[*sic*] Im standing at the same crossroads asking the same questions. No sweat. Sometimes you can walk a hundred miles and end up in the same spot. The world ain't round for nothing, right? What is a black play? The definition is housed in the reality of two things that occurred recently and almost simultaneously: 26 August 05, playwright scholar poet-king August Wilson announces he is dying of cancer, and hurricane Katrina devastates the Gulf Coast. It feels like judgment day. What Im talking about today is the same and different. I was tidy back then. And now Im tidier. Tidier today like a tidal wave."[1]

This question, "what is a black play?" could just as easily be "what is black art?"—one of the same questions that defined the Harlem Renaissance and the Black Arts Movement. Parks has asserted that this question is still relevant, perhaps for some of the same reasons as it was in the 1920s and the 1960s, but now also for current reasons: the racial disparity evident in New Orleans and elsewhere after Hurricane Katrina and, more personally, the imminent death of August Wilson, who himself famously questioned the nature of black art and black theater in his 1996 speech "The Ground on Which I Stand."[2]

As the above excerpt from "new black math" demonstrates, Parks's theory is remarkable because it is relevant, accessible, and poetic. The essay goes on to list what a black play is and what it is not, sometimes with paradoxical results, confirming that literature and culture, even when approached from the most logical perspective, are never simple. In the first version of the essay, "An Equation for Black People on Stage," Parks used a similar quasi-mathematical style of reasoning and illustration, combined with her signature nontraditional type/format and iconoclastic diction. She wrote, "Let's look at the math:"

> BLACK PEOPLE + 'WHITEY'=
> STANDARD DRAMATIC CONFLICT
> (STANDARD TERRITORY)
> *i.e.*
> 'BLACK DRAMA' = the presentation of the Black as oppressed
> *so that*

WHATEVER the dramatic dynamics, they are most often READ TO EQUAL an explanation or relation of Black oppression. This is not only a false equation, this is bullshit.
so that
BLACK PEOPLE + X = NEW DRAMATIC CONFLICT
(NEW TERRITORY)
where x is the realm of situations showing African-Americans in states other than the Oppressed by/Obsessed with 'Whitey' state; where the White when present is not the oppressor, and where audiences are encouraged to see and understand and discuss these dramas in terms other than that same old shit.[3]

Similarly, in "From *Elements of Style*" Parks uses pictures combined with math problems to explain her theories. In one example, labeled "AMERICA" and meant to illustrate *The America Play* (1994), Parks drew a vertical line with arrows at both ends, an X, and a stick figure with a beard, bowtie, and hat. This was all set equal to parentheses that contain the basic outline of a house, marked "log cabin," and a triangle resting across the top of three rectangles, marked "big town." Also in the parenthesis are step-by-step directions:

Solve for X where X is the true measurement of the Great Man's Stature
Express X in terms of The Lesser Known
Express X in terms of Lucy and Brazil[4]

Outside of the parenthesis is another stick figure with a beard, bowtie, and hat (but no arms or legs). This figure also has a thought/speech bubble that contains the phrase "4 score and 7 years ago."[5] This innovative form of expressing a theory about unlocking the meaning of literature encourages nontraditional approaches to literary criticism as well as greater attention to literatures, such as Parks's, that rely on nontraditional elements, including misspelled words, pictures in the text, characters with their own languages, or stage directions that overstep their dramatic boundaries. And even if a text is completely linear, Parks's theories open up options for critical inquiries that challenge readers to more closely interrogate form, relationships among characters, and the role of the visual in a text.

Parks has not only revised traditional literary theory and some of the greatest literature in American letters; she has shown also that her approach to revision is "equal-opportunity" by revising her own work. In *Topdog/Underdog* (2002) she again cast a black Abraham Lincoln impersonator, just as she did in *The America Play;* and like its sister play *In the Blood,*

Fucking A revised Nathaniel Hawthorne's Hester Prynne. Parks's novel, *Getting Mother's Body,* is particularly significant, though, because in addition to revising William Faulkner's novels, it borrows and revises themes from multiple works in Parks's corpus, including the woman scorned and abandoned from *Venus* and *In the Blood,* abortion from *Fucking A,* and the mother's inheritance from *Topdog/Underdog.* In one of the most compelling examples of Parks self-revision in *Getting Mother's Body,* Homer Beede, a student and an aspiring race man, confronts a racist white sheriff and thinks to himself, "I want to kill him right now but I don't move. He might want to kill me too but he don't move either. The Negro-College-Going-Youth eyes the White-Just-Back-from-Fishing-Sheriff. If we was in a play these would be our parts. There's plenty of times a man has, in a situation just like this, forgot himself and just played his part" (167). This moment looks back to one of Parks's earliest plays, *The Death of the Last Black Man in the Whole Entire World,* which features characters with names such as Black Man with Watermelon, Black Woman with Fried Drumstick, Old Man River Jordan, and Ham. While Parks's play certainly problematizes these stereotypes, it nevertheless demonstrates how casting—by oneself, by others, or even by a playwright—can subsume identity and force characters into racially determined and deterministic paradigms. In *Getting Mother's Body,* Parks creates a character who chooses whether or not to play his part and a narrative space that allows him that freedom of choice.

Parks continues this self-revision in her collection *365 Days/365 Plays.* In this text Parks wrote a play a day for a year, beginning with November 13, since the idea for the collection came to her on November 13, 2002 (i).[6] Parks wrote of the experiment in the front matter, before the plays, "The plan was that no matter what I did, how busy I was, what other commitments I had, I would write a play a day, every single day, for a year. It would be about being present and being committed to the artistic process every single day regardless of the 'weather.' It became a daily meditation, a daily prayer celebrating the rich and strange process of a writing life" (i). Parks described the play-a-day process as sometimes being "torture," but she added, "that's when you find out who you are as a writer."[7]

Two years after finishing the plays, Parks worked with producer and friend Bonnie Metzgar "to set a production scheme in motion."[8] And a massive scheme it became: "After much logistical fine-tuning, a network of over 700 theatres emerged to form the year-long 365 Festival—hailed by many as the largest theatrical collaboration of all time—which began in November 2006. Theatres received a week's worth of plays to perform and were charged $1 per day per play licensing fee. The only rule: no admission fee."[9]

In the afterword to the plays, Parks and Metzger explained that their vision was to create "a nation-wide grassroots festival—a geographically diverse relay race which invites each theatre group to produce one week's worth of plays in its own style, creating a testament not only to the daily artistic process, but also to the incredible diversity and richness of the American theatrical landscape" (401). According to Deborah Geis, "no previous playwright has attempted such an ambitious project."[10]

In the text of *365 Days/365 Plays,* the plays are dated, one a day, through November 12 of the next year. Sometimes they are relevant to actual events—such as the invasion of Iraq on March 20, 2003, or Gregory Hines's death on August 9, 2003—that took place on or around those days. Other times the topic seems to come exclusively from Parks's imagination. But overall, Geis has observed, "Despite the huge number of short plays in the cycle, there is a distinct continuity in the styles and themes both from Parks's previous works and within the cycle itself."[11]

365 Days/365 Plays can thus be read as being about Parks as a writer, as it takes a literary journey through her daily thoughts—artistic, political, cultural, nonsensical, and various combinations thereof. Such a reading is underscored by the appearance of six pictures of Parks on the book's cover and spine. None of Parks's other works features her image so prominently. Her name is also larger on the cover than the name of the text, thereby privileging her authorial role in the work over the work itself. Such a privileging need not be seen as negative, however, for this focus on Parks's writing highlights her self-revisionary work within the text as well as asserts the greater cultural importance of the text: demonstrating how art can play a vital and formative role in the everyday lives of individuals—writers and readers.

Although every day of *365 Days/365 Plays* does not show Parks engaging her own work, her revisionary impulse surfaces consistently throughout the volume. As early as November 15, in an entry called "The Good-for-Nothing," we find a circuslike story reminiscent of *Venus.* A character called the Barker, much like The Mother-Showman, attempts to corral crowds to see The Good-for-Nothing, a woman who "dont work," "dont reproduce," "dont vote," "dont complain," and "dont even cause trouble" (7). As the crowd stands around watching her, a man laughs. The Barker then tells The Good-for-Nothing that her career is over, as talk of the laughing incident "will get around—its no use" (7). She then expresses concern about her future, and in a complete reversal of The Mother-Showman's attitude toward The Venus, the Barker responds, "Youve got a nice pair of legs. Maybe you could be a dancer. Yr also really good with numbers. You could be a banker or a loan shark" (8). Rather than deny the woman a creative outlet or a means of support, the Barker encourages The Good-for-Nothing, who is actually good for nothing "no more" (8). This new version of a familiar scene suggests a new trajectory for performance and performers. Whereas Parks's Venus grapples for her agency, this new character is encouraged to embrace the agency that she did not know she had.

This same entry, and many others like it, also employs Parks's use of stage directions as quasi-narrator, as seen in *In the Blood.* In "The Good-for-Nothing," the main action ends positively, the Barker tells The Good-for-Nothing, "Now yll make make something of yrself," and she replies, "Yes. Why not?" (8). Then, the stage directions explain, "They exit happily, going to dinner at the house of the Barker's friend: a woman he used to know, his ex-wife, actually, who after all these years is still very angry. She will slit his throat while he sleeps and spend the rest of her life in a woman's prison" (8). These stage directions add an element of tragedy and questioning: Will The Good-for-Nothing actually become something without the Barker's encouragement? What did the Barker do to his ex-wife to make her so angry? Is he not, after all, the benevolent man he appears to be in the dialogue?

While this section could be staged, the future tense suggests that it should not be since it would require showing multiple points in time: the dinner, the murder, the trial, the prison. Plus, all this would be difficult, if not impossible, to represent without dialogue. Thus the director would likely either leave this section out completely or have someone narrate it, thus introducing a new character and a new monologue that Parks did not write. If the director left it out, the play would end like *Getting Mother's Body,* happily and without complications. In a narrated version the director's choice of narrator would inevitably sway the audience's interpretation of the piece. If told by The Good-for-Nothing or the Barker, the story would become pure tragedy, the murder senseless. If told by the ex-wife, however, the action might become justified: the Barker's murder could be fitting revenge for the pain he caused a woman and thus prevent him from possibly doing the same to The Good-for-Nothing. "The Good-For-Nothing," therefore, even more so than *In the Blood,* is a completely different work on the page than on the stage. Parks seems in *365 Days/365 Plays,* then, to be further reinforcing the difference between the written and the performed and underscoring that to truly experience a play, one should both read it and see it.

In other segments, such as November 27th's "Hole," August 30th's "Holey Moley," and October 11th's "Another Deep Hole," Parks has continued to engage and refine her idea of "The Hole," a concept she introduced in *The America Play* and refined in *Getting Mother's Body.* Overall this continued attention to holes in *365 Days/365 Plays,* Geis has argued, "suggests the struggle to create the plays themselves: the need to keep 'digging' for more material, and the playwright's fear of having gotten herself into a 'hole' by taking on the project."[12] And while the many autobiographical elements of the collection support this reading, The Holes in *365 Days/365 Plays* also remain very abstract, while still taking on new characteristics, suggesting a deeper interpretive significance as well.

In "Hole," for example, a man digs a hole from which a woman emerges. The man and the woman become lovers, and the play suggests they will be happy, for "a closeness will emerge between them" (30). Yet the man, a hole digger by trade, finds his work problematic:

WOMAN. You've made a career of it. Hole digging.
MAN. That's the kicker. You think one would satisfy. Wrong.
Digging holes creates the need to dig holes.
WOMAN. Theres a word for that. A psychological term.
MAN. Dont tell me the term. I just want to be.
WOMAN. I feel the same way exactly. (30)

This exchange suggests that creating or uncovering a hole, symbolic of vulnerability or desire in Parks's previous work, simply causes more vulnerability or desire, and any attempt at understanding the psychological root of this "need to dig holes" feels—at least to the hole digger—unproductive. He cannot give up the work, and, in his vision of history, he has spent his "whole life" digging in the same place (29), indicating that "the play links a wholeness, a suggestion of a full and complete life, to the act of digging a hole."[13]

In "Holy Moley" a man who seems to understand this link tries to convince a woman that her obsession with a hole is ludicrous. She stares out the door of her house, sure that the hole is "out there," beckoning her "to cross the threshold" (304–5). After giving up his attempts to lure her away from the hole with talk of pie, the man tells the woman that inside there is "a holey mole" (305). The stage directions then continue, "The Woman comes to look. He points to nothing. She smiles. He smiles too" (305), suggesting that a person can be freed of a hole's hypnotic effects via love and creativity. Yet, here again, redemption is not complete because of the troubling gender dynamics. The man "has used subterfuge and trickery—rather than legitimate emotional connection—to draw the woman away from the door."[14] Thus the pair's—and especially the woman's—healing relies on a superficial, constructed reality.

Then finally, in "Another Deep Hole," two men encounter a hole that impresses them with its size. One measures the hole to confirm that "Its another deep hole," and the other puts up a sign next to it that reads: "ANOTHER

DEEP HOLE." Then, in the following segment, "Analysis," two unidentified characters talk about how one of them fell into "another deep hole" and is still in it. The one in the hole brought a sample of the hole, which is made of "Space." In her descriptions of these segments in the table of contents, Parks wrote that "every great gap should get a sign" (397), and "if you fall in, I hope there will be someone there for you" (398), respectively.[15] "Another Deep Hole," then, indicates that a person can be warned about a potential vulnerability, but even if he or she does give in, as in "Analysis" and "Holey Moley," redemption may come through companionship.

Although The Hole does receive much attention in *365 Days/365 Plays*, this attention seems minor compared to that which Parks gives to another of her favorite topics: Abraham Lincoln. Whereas in *Topdog/Underdog*, Parks explored Lincoln's legacy through two black brothers who eventually portray Lincoln's assassination as the inevitable result of a familial conflict exacerbated by racial politics and unstable identities, in *365 Days/365 Plays*, she wrote Lincoln himself and his family back into the drama.

In November 16th's "Mrs. Keckley & Mrs. Lincoln," for example, Parks explored racial politics through a humorous exchange between the mentally unstable Mary Todd Lincoln and her dressmaker Elizabeth Keckley as they get the First Lady ready to see a play, the same play during which her husband (who is never named in the segment) is murdered. Then in December 2nd's "Abraham Lincoln at 89," Parks imagined what might have happened if the president had not been assassinated, but merely injured badly enough to lose his mind. Mrs. Lincoln, Mrs. Keckley, "a respectable representation of the Local Population," and a host of dignitaries come to a birthday party (although it is not actually his birthday), who generally speaks in nonsense, save for when he announces, "Only when we cease to fight do we truly conquer," a sentiment that one of the locals finds ridiculous (37–38). This segment's overall feeling of ridiculousness and insanity suggests that had Lincoln survived the attempt on his life, his role in American history would have been altered drastically.

Lincoln comes up again in February 12th's "The Birth of Abraham Lincoln," in which Parks re-creates a scene with a "colored midwife" and baby Abraham's oddly overly concerned parents (121); February 17th's "The President's Day Sale," where impersonators line up in hopes of being purchased by "A Woman, very rich" (128); and March 25th's "A Promise Made in 1863 Isnt Worth Much These Days," a commentary on the shortcomings of the Emancipation Proclamation. The anachronism and sense of being "outside of time" in all of these plays "insinuates that the scene could have just as easily occurred 'here' and 'now' as happens in *Topdog/Underdog*."[16]

Through this use of time, Rebecca Rugg has explained, "There is a great leveling of the heroic and the pedestrian, with events of historic importance often refracted through the lens of the everyday. . . . Time's signature and direction shift throughout the plays in this cycle, even as they are organized by the steady, rhythmic punctuation of the calendar year."[17]

Beyond the revisions of her own works, *365 Days/365 Plays* is a pivotal work in Parks's corpus because it reinforces her role as both artist and theorist. Through *365 Days/365 Plays,* Parks both explored and demonstrated the role of art in the everyday lives of Americans, and ever revolutionary, she created an innovative way to bring this theory to "the people," to turn a personal project into a collective project, through the 365 Festival performances. As Parks and Metzgar explained in their afterword to *365 Days/365 Plays,* this festival "is not building a new community; it is revealing a community where it already exists—in theatres both grand and modest, in schoolrooms, storefronts, nursing homes, and alleyways" (401).

Parks and Metzgar suggested also that the festival might "encourage us to radically change the way that we produce/create/critique/enjoy/think about/talk about theatre and the world" (401). According to Philip C. Kolin, "*365* erases the entire spectrum of theatre—how it is created, coordinated, financed, marketed, staged, and received. Perhaps at its most productively radical, *365* assaults the hegemonies by which theatre has been controlled."[18] Such a grassroots effort is reminiscent of the rise of militant theater and nonprofit theater groups, such as the Negro Ensemble Company, Black Theatre Alliance, and New Federal Theatre, during and in the wake of the Black Arts Movement. But rather than advocate the "for us, by us" aesthetic of their predecessors, Parks and Metzgar wanted modern audiences, who are often plagued by artistic apathy, simply to embrace any aesthetic that allows for open-minded, democratic, relevant creative expression—especially in the theater.

Yet the goal may have also been fundamentally iconoclastic; as Rugg has suggested, 'The battle to determine the rightful subjects of drama has been long and has reflected the state of political thought from Aristotle to August Wilson and beyond; Parks's work stands as a serious contribution to that debate. . . . In her epic cycle, the window of narrative opportunity is open to all, and by writing these brief encounters with an unexpected, seldom-seen cast of characters, Parks continually fractures master narratives by reorienting the point of view. In this, her dramaturgy takes place in a lengthy history of anti-elitist and anti-Aristotelian dramaturgical experiments, which create arguments that the low are not inherently comic, nor the high the only source and subject of tragedy."[19]

This debate over "master narratives" emerged for Parks again when she participated in the Tony-award winning musical revival of *Porgy and Bess* (now called *The Gershwins' Porgy and Bess*), an abridged and revised adaptation of the 1935 work written by DuBose and Dorothy Heyward and Ira Gershwin with music composed by George Gershwin. *The Gershwins' Porgy and Bess* premiered at the American Repertory Theatre in Cambridge, Massachusetts, in August 2011 and moved to the Richard Rodgers Theatre on Broadway in December 2011. In his review of the Broadway production, critic Charles Isherwood labeled the show "the most controversial musical revival in recent memory."[20]

Officially Parks was the production's "Musical Book Adapter."[21] According to the *New York Times* preview of the Cambridge production, Parks was Director Diane Paulus's "chief writing collaborator," and together they "created scenes, invented biographical details and, in their most radical move, added a more hopeful ending."[22] As for the extent of the revisions, Parks told the *New York Times* in a video interview, "Sometimes I would rewrite a scene or sometimes just add a little bit of dialogue. Sometimes I would write something that hadn't been there before." Her task, she explained, was "taking this beautiful masterpiece, approaching it with love and respect and making it, oh, more real, more gritty, more accessible to contemporary audiences—not dumbing it down in any way, but just making it just more truthful to the African American experience."[23]

In this same interview, Parks detailed her revision of the context for one of the production's most famous songs, "I Got Plenty of Nothing," which she asserted has traditionally been a difficult piece for performers and audiences because they interpret it to be about blind happiness in the face of oppressive poverty. According to Parks, in the African American vernacular tradition "nothing" is often code for "something" unspeakable. In this case Parks added dialogue to suggest that, while living with Bess, Porgy's "nothing" is love, specifically sex. The song therefore became a celebration of intimacy and relationships.[24] Such a revision recalls Parks's earlier revisionary works, and the production's official study guide tied her moves here back to her signature Rep & Rev: "Putting the libretto of Porgy and Bess in the hands of Suzan-Lori Parks is like handing its sheet music to Miles Davis—the ensuing 'repetition and revision' maintains the essence of the original, but is enhanced by her signature style. It is a dialogue between the past and the present."[25]

But in a letter to the *New York Times* following the preview of the Cambridge production, the esteemed composer Steven Sondheim took issue with many of the collaborators' changes and intentions and especially with Parks's assertion that she was channeling Gershwin with her revisions.[26] She claimed that she wanted to "flesh out the two main characters so they are not cardboard cut-out characters" because "that's what George Gershwin wanted, and if he had lived longer . . . he would have gone back to the story of 'Porgy and Bess' and made changes, including to the ending."[27]

To this claim, Sondheim responded, "It's reassuring that Ms. Parks has a direct pipeline to Gershwin and is just carrying out his work for him, and that she thinks he would have taken one of the most moving moments in musical theater history—Porgy's demand, 'Bring my goat!'—and thrown it out. Ms. Parks (or Ms. Paulus) has taken away Porgy's goat cart in favor of a cane. So now he can demand, 'Bring my cane!' Perhaps someone will bring him a straw hat too, so he can buck-and-wing his way to New York."[28]

New Yorker critic Hilton Als, however, defended the production, asserting, "Paulus and Parks's approach ultimately has much less to do with the self-serving manipulation of a classic than it does with humanizing the depiction of race onstage."[29] Still, a revised version of the new musical arrived on Broadway. The most remarkable change was a new, less tidy, and more ambiguous ending—an ending that Paulus and her team maintain was not at all influenced by Sondheim's objections.[30] And the result, according to Ben Brantley, is that "the show is much improved, clearer and more fluid, than it was in Cambridge . . . even the new dialogue is inconspicuous."[31] In the production's study guide, Parks herself justified the work and her intentions, explaining, "It's not as if we are trying to put our thumbprints all over it; what we are doing is appreciating what is there, then trying to make what's there into a viable show for today's musical theatre stage."[32]

Parks's seamless melding of the literary, historical, political, and social in *365 Days/365 Plays,* as well as her essays, plays, novel, and screenplays, places her alongside W. E. B. Du Bois, Zora Neale Hurston, Langston Hughes, Lorraine Hansberry, Amiri Baraka, Nikki Giovanni, and many other great writers in the African American literary tradition who have demonstrated that art can and will change lives and change the world. They and she understand, as Parks asserted in "Possession," that literature does have the power to make and revise history, to write in those who have been forgotten, to take the "dis-membered" disremembered and put "the body back together" so it can sing and she can hear and capture its song in her texts. She wrote, "Through each line of text, I'm rewriting the Time Line—creating history where it is and always was but has not yet been divined," and thus she simultaneously has created her own well-deserved place in American history.

NOTES

Chapter 1—Understanding Suzan-Lori Parks

1. Suzan-Lori Parks, "Possession," in *The America Play and Other Works* (New York: Theatre Communications Group, 1995), 4.

2. Born Susan-Lori Parks, she decided to change her name because of a serendipitous "misprint." In an interview with writer John Marshall, Parks explained, "It was the result of a misprint. When I was doing one of my first plays in the East Village, we had fliers printed up and they spelled my name wrong. I was devastated. But the director said, 'Just keep it, honey, and it will be fine.' And it was." John Marshall, "A Moment with Playwright Suzan-Lori Parks," *Seattle Post-Intelligencer,* May 26, 2005, E1.

3. Richard E. Kramer, "A Production History of the Works of Suzan-Lori Parks," in *Suzan Lori Parks: Essays on the Plays and Other Works,* ed. Philip C. Kolin (Jefferson, N.C.: McFarland, 2010), 203–6; chronology, in *Suzan-Lori Parks: A Casebook,* ed. Kevin J. Wetmore and Alycia Smith-Howard (New York: Routledge, 2007), xiii–xi; Jodi Kanter, "Suzan-Lori Parks," in *Twentieth-Century American Dramatists: Fifth Series,* ed. Garrett Eisler (Detroit: Dictionary of Literary Biography, 2008), 160–68; Hilton Als, "Grace under Pressure," *New Yorker,* March 29, 2010, 102–3.

4. E. M. Forster, *Aspects of the Novel* (Middlesex, U.K.: Penguin Books, 1963), 108.

5. See R. Ely, "Writing, Computers, and Visual Impairment," in *Journal of Visual Impairment and Blindness* 83.5 (1989): 248–52.

6. Elizabeth Dyrud Lyman, "The Page Refigured: The Verbal and Visual Language of Suzan-Lori Parks's *Venus,*" *Performance Research* 7.1 (2002): 86.

7. Kimberly Benston, "Facing Tradition: Revisionary Scenes in African American Literature," *PMLA* 105.1 (1990): 99.

8. Frederick Douglass, *Narrative of the Life of Frederick Douglass, an American Slave, Written by Himself* (Boston: Bedford Books of St. Martin's Press, 1993), 56, 57.

9. Ibid., 57. Also quoted in Benston, "Facing Tradition: Revisionary Scenes in African American Literature," 100, 101.

10. Benston, "Facing Tradition: Revisionary Scenes in African American Literature," 101.

11. Ibid., 99–100.

12. Anna Julia Cooper, *A Voice from the South,* in *The Voice of Anna Julia Cooper,* ed. Charles Lemert and Esme Bham (Oxford: Rowman & Littlefield, 1998), 107.

13. Parks, "Possession," 4.
14. Ibid., 4–5.
15. Suzan-Lori Parks, "From *Elements of Style*," in *The America Play and Other Works* (New York: Theatre Communications Group, 1995), 6.

Chapter 2—"Three-ness" and "the Space in Between"

1. Suzan-Lori Parks, "Tradition and the Individual Talent," *Theater* 29.2 (1999): 28–29; Kevin J. Wetmore, "It's an Oberammergau Thing: An Interview with Suzan-Lori Parks," in *Suzan Lori-Parks: A Casebook,* ed. Kevin J. Wetmore and Alycia Smith-Howard (New York: Routledge, 2007), 128.
2. Shawn-Marie Garrett, "Figures, Speech and Form in *Imperceptible Mutabilities in the Third Kingdom,*" in *Suzan Lori-Parks: A Casebook,* ed. Kevin J. Wetmore and Alycia Smith-Howard (New York: Routledge, 2007), 1.
3. Ibid.
4. Ibid., 7.
5. Suzan-Lori Parks, *Imperceptible Mutabilities in the Third Kingdom,* in *The America Play and Other Works* (New York: Theatre Communications Group, 1995), 23–71. All parenthetical citations in this chapter refer to this edition.
6. W. E. B. Du Bois, *The Souls of Black Folk* (New York: Norton, 1999), 10–11.
7. Philip Kolin, "'You one of uh mines?' *Imperceptible Mutabilities in the Third Kingdom,*" in *Suzan-Lori Parks: Essays on the Plays and Other Works,* ed. Philip C. Kolin (Jefferson, N.C.: McFarland, 2010), 46.
8. James Frieze, "*Imperceptible Mutabilities in the Third Kingdom:* Suzan-Lori Parks and the Shared Struggle to Perceive," *Modern Drama* 41.4 (1998): 531.
9. Frieze, "*Imperceptible Mutabilities in the Third Kingdom,*"531.
10. Deborah Geis, *Suzan-Lori Parks* (Ann Arbor: University of Michigan Press, 2008), 45.
11. Liz Diamond, "Perceptible Mutability in the Word Kingdom," *Theater* 2.4 (1993) 24(3): 87.
12. Kolin, "'You one of uh mines?,'" 94.
13. Suzan-Lori Parks, "From *Elements of Style,*" in *The America Play and Other Works* (New York: Theatre Communications Group, 1995), 9.
14. Frieze, "*Imperceptible Mutabilities in the Third Kingdom,*" 528.
15. Mel Gussow, "Identity Loss in 'Imperceptible Mutabilities,'" *New York Times,* September 20, 1989, 24.
16. Garrett, "Figures, Speech and Form in *Imperceptible Mutabilities in the Third Kingdom,*" 6.
17. Kolin, "'You one of uh mines?,'" 51.
18. Garrett, "Figures, Speech and Form in *Imperceptible Mutabilities in the Third Kingdom,*" 12.
19. Geis, *Suzan-Lori Parks,* 46.
20. Garrett, "Figures, Speech and Form in *Imperceptible Mutabilities in the Third Kingdom,*" 14.
21. Geis, *Suzan-Lori Parks,* 47–48.
22. Kolin, "'You one of uh mines?'" 55.
23. Frieze, "*Imperceptible Mutabilities in the Third Kingdom,*" 528.
24. Kolin, "'You one of uh mines?,'" 59.

25. Ibid., 46.
26. Ibid., 49.
27. Garrett, "Figures, Speech and Form in *Imperceptible Mutabilities in the Third Kingdom*," 16.
28. Geis, *Suzan-Lori Parks,* xiii
29. Robert Brustein, "What Do Women Playwrights Want?" *New Republic* (April 13, 1992): 30.
30. Suzan-Lori Parks, *The Death of the Last Black Man in Whole Entire World,* in *The America Play and Other Works* (New York: Theatre Communications Group, 1995), 158–99. All parenthetical citations in this chapter refer to this edition.
31. Alice Rayner and Harry J. Elam, Jr., "Unfinished Business: Reconfiguring History in Suzan-Lori Parks's *The Death of the Last Black Man in the Whole Entire World,*" *Theatre Journal* 46.4 (1994): 452.
32. James Allen, *Without Sanctuary: Lynching Photography in America* (Santa Fe, N.M.: Twin Palms, 2000).
33. Rayner and Elam, "Unfinished Business," 453.
34. Geis, *Suzan-Lori Parks,* 70
35. Suzan-Lori Parks, "From *Elements of Style,*" in *The America Play and Other Works* (New York: Theatre Communications Group, 1995), 9.
36. Ibid., 72
37. Ibid., 64
38. Louise Bernard, "The Musicality of Language: Redefining History in Suzan-Lori Parks's *The Death of the Last Black Man in the Whole Entire World,*" *African American Review* 31.4 (1999): 694.
39. Heidi J. Holder, "Strange Legacy: The History Plays of Suzan-Lori Parks," in *Suzan-Lori Parks: A Casebook,* ed. Kevin J. Wetmore and Alycia Smith-Howard (New York: Routledge, 2007), 24–25.
40. Parks, "From *Elements of Style,*" in *Venus,* n.p.
41. Rayner and Elam, "Unfinished Business," 451.

Chapter 3—"Deliberate Calculation" in Money, Sex, and Black Plays

1. Suzan-Lori Parks, *Venus.* New York: Theatre Communications Group, 1997. All parenthetical citations in this chapter refer to this edition.
2. Suzan-Lori Parks, "new black math," *Theatre Journal* 57.4 (2005): 583.
3. Ibid., 576.
4. To differentiate between Parks's created character and the real Saartjie (Sarah) Baartman, this chapter refers to the play's protagonist as she is called in the play: "The Girl" and "The Venus." The play's use of the definite article for most character names is notable as it both universalizes and individualizes the character. In addition to fueling the paradoxical nature of the play, the use of the definite article highlights the fluidity of the Venus Hottentot's actual identity. Spellings of her real name varied almost ubiquitously across critical and historical sources, and as Elizabeth Dyrud Lyman has pointed out, "Saartjie herself, referred to variously as 'The Girl,' 'Venus,' and 'The Hottentot Venus,' is never named in a speech attribution or addressed by another character in her given name." Elizabeth Dyrud Lyman, "The Page Refigured: The Verbal and Visual Language of Suzan-Lori Parks's *Venus,*" *Performance Research* 7.1 (2002): 96.

5. Harriet A. Jacobs, *Incidents in the Life of a Slave Girl: Written by Herself*, ed. Lydia Maria Child (Boston: The author, 1861). All parenthetical citations in this chapter refer to this edition.

6. Jean Young, "The Re-Objectification and Re-Commodification of Saartjie Baartman in Suzan-Lori Parks's *Venus*," *African American Review* 31.4 (1997): 699–700.

7. Ben Brantley, "Of an Erotic Freak Show and the Lesson Therein." *New York Times*, May 3, 1996, C2.

8. Anne Davis Basting, "*Venus*," *Theatre Journal* 49.2 (1997): 225.

9. Harry J. Elam, Jr., and Alice Rayner, "Body Parts: Between Story and Spectacle in*Venus* by Suzan-Lori Parks." In *Staging Resistance: Essays on Political Theater*, ed. Jeanne Colleran and Jenny S. Spencer, (Ann Arbor: University of Michigan Press, 1998), 277.

10. The Venus does speak of her shame during her trial. In the following exchange The Chorus of the Court asks, "One more question, Girl, uh: / Have you ever been indecent?" The Venus responds [after a spell and a '*Rest*']: "Indecent?" The Chorus of the Court: "Nasty"; The Venus: "Never. / No. I am just me." The Chorus of the Court: "Whats that supposed to mean?!?!" The Venus: "To hide yr shame is evil. / I show mine. Would you like to see?" (76).

11. Young, "The Re-Objectification and Re-Commodification of Saartjie Baartman in Suzan-Lori Parks's *Venus*," 700

12. A chorus member early in the play indicates that The Venus's is "An ass to write home about. / Well worth the admission price" (7), which further connects this subversion to Parks's creation and to economics as well as echoes Parks in "new black math."

13. Elizabeth Brown-Guillory, "Reconfiguring History," "Reconfiguring History: Migration, Memory, and (Re)Membering in Suzan-Lori Parks's Plays." In *Southern Women Playwrights: New Essays in Literary History and Criticism*, ed. Robert L. McDonald and Linda Rohrer (Tuscaloosa: University of Alabama Press, 2002), 194.

14. The Venus's relationship to "home" is another paradoxical element in the play. She first seems eager to leave. Then, near the middle of the play, she tells The Baron Docteur, "I dont wanna go back inny more. / I like yr company too much. / Besides, it was a shitty shitty life" (105). And finally she ends the play thoroughly homesick: "I always dream of home / in every spare minute. / It was a shitty life but oh I miss it." (158).

15. Stephen Lucasi, "Saartjie's Speech and the Sounds of National Identification," *Mosaic* 42.2 (2009): 176.

16. Parks, "new black math," 576.

17. Ibid., 580.

18. Suzan-Lori Parks, "Tradition and the Individual Talent," *Theater* 29.2 (1999): 28–29.

19. Ibid., 29.

20. Aja Marneweck, "Staging Stereotype and Performing the Exotic Erotic: An Interrogation of Desire in the Texts of Parks and Kennedy." *South African Theatre Journal* 18.1 (2004): 53–54.

21. Elam and Rayner, "Body Parts," 272.

22. Parks, "Author's Notes," in *Venus*.

23. Kimbely D. Dixon, "An I Am Sheba Me Am (She Be Doo Be Wah Waaah Doo Wah) O(au)rality, Textuality and Performativity: African American Literature's Vernacular Theory and the Work of Suzan-Lori Parks." *Journal of American Drama and Theatre* 11.1 (1998): 54.

24. Brown-Guillory, "Reconfiguring History," 195.

25. Lyman, "The Page Refigured," 96.

26. Parks, "Tradition and the Individual Talent," in *The America Play and Other Works* (New York: Theatre Communications Group, 1995), 30.

27. The surveys were modeled on U.S. Census Bureau surveys in which approximately seventeen thousand adult subjects described their arts involvement via various media.

28. National Endowment for the Arts, *American Participation in Theatre* (New York: NEA, 1992), 2; *Research Division Report #45: 2002 Survey of Public Participation in the Arts* (New York: NEA, 2004), 16, 14.

29. Parks, "new black math," 578.

30. Sterling Brown, *Negro Poetry and Drama, and The Negro in American Fiction* (1937; New York: Atheneum, 1969), 139.

31. Aaron Bryant, "Broadway, Her Way," *Crisis* 109.2 (2002): 44.

32. Brown, *Negro Poetry and Drama, and The Negro in American Fiction,* 123

33. Harvey Young, "Choral Compassion: *In the Blood* and *Venus,*" in *Suzan Lori-Parks: A Casebook,* ed. Kevin J. Wetmore and Alycia Smith-Howard (New York: Routledge, 2007), 41

34. Elam and Rayner, "Body Parts," 269.

35. Basting, "*Venus,*" 225.

36. Parks, "new black math," 579.

37. Christoper Innes, "Staging Black History: Re-Imagining Cultural Icons," in *Race and Religion in Contemporary Theatre and Drama in English,* ed. Bernhard Reitz (Trier, Germany: Wissenschaftlicher Verlag Trier, 1999):106.

38. Parks breaks down the barrier between playwright, actor, and reader earlier in the play when The Brother speaks a description nearly verbatim (only the order is reversed) from the stage directions (10). Though this repetition would seem to align the writer, Parks, with The Brother (one of The Girl's most prominent exploiters), the inversion actually positions her in opposition to him.

39. Elam and Rayner, "Body Parts," 275.

40. Ibid., 276.

41. Parks, "new black math," 581.

42. Joanna Frank, "Embodied Absence and Theatrical Dismemberment," *Journal of Dramatic Theory and Criticism* 21.2 (2007): 170.

43. Bryant, "Broadway, Her Way," 44.

44. Suzan-Lori Parks, "An Equation for Black People Onstage," in *The America Play and Other Works* (New York: Theatre Communications Group, 1995), 19.

45. Parks, "new black math," 578.

46. Sanya Osha, "*Venus* and White Desire," *Transition* 2008.99 (2008): 90.

47. Sander Gilman, "Black Bodies, White Bodies: Toward an Iconography of Female Sexuality in Late Nineteenth-Century Art, Medicine, and Literature," *Critical Inquiry* 12.1 (1985): 204, 216.

48. Ibid., 216

49. S. E. Wilmer, "Restaging the Nation: The Work of Suzan-Lori Parks," *Modern Drama* 43.3 (2000): 443.

50. Parks, "new black math," 577.

51. Ibid., 577.

Chapter 4—What "Able" and "Angel" Mean to a Welfare Mother

1. Joseph Dalaker and Bernadette D Proctor, *Poverty in the United States: 1999* (Washington: U.S. Census Bureau, 2000), v. This line, which the Census Bureau calls the "poverty threshold," varies by the number of total people and the number of children in a family. For example, a single mother with one child's poverty threshold in 1999 was $11,483. A single mother with four children's poverty threshold was $19,578 (v–vii).

2. Ibid., v.

3. Suzan-Lori Parks, *The Red Letter Plays: In the Blood and Fucking A* (New York: Theatre Communications Group, 2001). All parenthetical citations in this chapter refer to this edition.

4. Nathaniel Hawthorne, *The Scarlet Letter: A Romance* (New York: W. W. Norton, 1988). All parenthetical citations in this chapter refer to this edition.

5. Lesley Ginsberg, "The ABCs of *The Scarlet Letter,*" *Studies in American Fiction* 29.1 (2001): 13

6. In John Edgar Wideman's *The Cattle Killing* (1996), Mrs. Trush teaches black children at the orphanage their letters. She says, "A. A for able. A for angel. A, children. Repeat after me. A for able. A for angel" (195). The fact that Wideman and Parks both were looking back to the same meanings for Hester Prynne's A at nearly the same time points to the particular significance of these meanings for modern black writers and black culture.

7. Deborah Geis, "Hawthorne's Hester as a Red-Lettered Black Woman? Suzan-Lori Parks's *In the Blood* and *Fucking A,*" *Journal of American Drama and Theatre* 16.2 (2004): 87.

8. Ibid., 80.

9. Leland S. Person, "The Dark Labyrinth of the Mind: Hawthorne, Hester, and the Ironies of Racial Mothering," *Studies in American Fiction* 29.1 (2001): 39.

10. Harriet Wilson, *"Our Nig"; or, Sketches from the Life of a Free Black* (1859; New York: Vintage, 1983). All parenthetical citations in this chapter refer to this edition.

11. Michael Winship, "Hawthorne and the 'Scribbling Women': Publishing *The Scarlet Letter* in the Nineteenth-Century United States," *Studies in American Fiction* 29.1 (2001): 3.

12. Geis, "Hawthorne's Hester as a Red-Lettered Black Woman?," 86.

13. Margo Jefferson. "'The Scarlet Letter,' Alive and Bitter in the Inner City." *New York Times,* November 23, 1999, E5.

14. Beth Maclay Doriani, "Black Womanhood in Nineteenth-Century America: Subversion and Self-Construction in Two Women's Autobiographies," *American Quarterly* 43.2 (1991): 208.

15. Harry J. Elam, Jr., "The Postmulticultural: A Tale of Mothers and Sons," in *Crucible of Cultures: Anglophone Drama at the Dawn of the New Millennium,* ed. Mark Maufort and Franca Bellarsi (New York: Peter Lang, 2002), 119.

16. Jon Dietrick, "'A Full Refund Ain't Enough': Money in Parks's Red Letter Plays," in *Suzan-Lori Parks: Essays on the Plays and Other Works,* ed. Philip C. Kolin (Jefferson, N.C.: McFarland, 2010), 94.

17. Lesley Ginsberg, "The ABCs of *The Scarlet Letter,*" *Studies in American Fiction* 29.1 (2001): 20.

18. Elam, "The Postmulticultural," 120.

19. Suzan-Lori Parks, "From *Elements of Style,*" in *The America Play and Other Works* (New York: Theatre Communications Group, 1995), 8–10.

20. Verna A. Foster, "Nurturing and Murderous Mothers in Suzan-Lori Parks's *In the Blood* and *Fucking A,*" *American Drama* 16.1 (2007): 79.

21. Sarah Wilkinson, "In the Blood: ADC." *Varsity* (November 3, 2006): 27.

22. Elam, "The Postmulticultural," 117.

23. Ibid., 123

24. Ibid.

25. Denis Donoghue, "Hawthorne and Sin," *Christianity and Literature* 52.2 (2003): 221.

26. Michael Feingold, "Hesterectomy," *Village Voice,* November 24, 1999.

27. Philip C. Kolin, "Parks' *In the Blood,*" *Explicator* 64.4 (2006): 247.

28. Ibid., 248.

29. Kennette Crockett, "*In the Blood:* By the First Black Female to Win the Pulitzer Prize for Drama." *Centerstage,* March 10, 2003.

30. Gwendolyn Brooks, "Lovers of the Poor," in *Blacks* (1960; Chicago: Third World, 1987), 287.

31. In his first sermon (scene 3), Reverend D, "preaching to no one in particular," alludes to Jesus's parable of the Good Samaritan (Luke 10:25–37) when he says, "There isn't a person on the street that hasn't passed me by at some point" (46). Later, as he is practicing his preaching, he quotes the famous passage "It is easier for a camel to go through the eye of a needle than for a rich man to enter the kingdom of God" (Matthew 19:24). The last time we see him, the stage directions indicate that "he carries a large neon cross" (101).

32. Elam, "The Postmulticultural," 123.

33. Geis, "Hawthorne's Hester as a Red-Lettered Black Woman?," 85.

34. Hester is also impregnated during her sexual encounters with these women (both of which also involve men), and the play suggests, through its doubling, that the woman is the parent of the resulting child. In addition, when Amiga tells Hester she is pregnant again, Hester replies, "Dont look at *me*" (68), implying that a child as a result of a homosexual union is possible, just not probable in that case. This blending of the supernatural and the homosexual is yet another theme that *In the Blood* shares with *Angels in America,* and Parks returns to the possibility of a child inheriting traits from her mother's lesbian lover in *Getting Mother's Body* (2003).

35. Kolin, "Parks' *In the Blood,*" 246.

36. Centers for Disease Control and Prevention, *CDC HIV/AIDS Fact Sheet: HIV/AIDS among African Americans* (Atlanta: Centers for Disease Control and Prevention, 2006), 3.

37. Centers for Disease Control and Prevention, *CDC HIV/AIDS Fact Sheet: HIV/AIDS among Women* (Atlanta: Centers for Disease Control and Prevention, 2006), 1–2.

38. Amy Schindler, "Angels and the AIDS Epidemic: The Resurgent Popularity of Angel Imagery in the United States of America" *Journal of American Culture* 22.3 (1999): 49.

39. Feingold, "Hesterectomy."

40. Daryl Ogden, "Cold War Science and the Body Politic: An Immuno/Virological Approach to *Angels in America,*" *Literature and Medicine* 19.2 (2000): 251.

41. Feingold, "Hesterectomy."

42. Ibid.

Chapter 5—Folding and Unfolding History, or, Identity Fabrication

1. Verna A. Foster, "Suzan-Lori Parks's Staging of the Lincoln Myth in *The America Play* and *Topdog/Underdog,*" *Journal of American Drama and Theatre* 17.3 (2005): 25.

2. Lucy Barton, "A Major in Costume," *Educational Theatre Journal* 2.1 (1950): 49.

3. Katy Ryan, "'No Less Human': Making History in Suzan-Lori Parks's *The America Play,*" *Journal of Dramatic Theory and Criticism* 13.2 (1999): 90.

4. Suzan-Lori Parks, *The America Play,* in *The America Play and Other Works* (New York: Theatre Communications Group, 1995), 158–99. All parenthetical citations in this chapter refer to this edition.

5. Suzan-Lori Parks, *Topdog/Underdog* (New York: Theatre Communications Group, 2002). All parenthetical citations in this chapter refer to this edition.

6. Foster, "Suzan-Lori Parks's Staging of the Lincoln Myth," 30.

7. Deborah R. Geis, *Suzan-Lori Parks* (Ann Arbor: University of Michigan Press, 2008), 103.

8. Ralph Ellison, *Invisible Man* (New York: Vintage, 1952), 153.

9. Houston A. Baker, Jr., *Blues, Ideology, and Afro-American Literature: A Vernacular Theory* (Chicago: University of Chicago Press, 1984), 193.

10. Nicole C. Matos, "'The Difference between the Two Bundles': Body and Cloth in the Works of Jamaica Kincaid," *Callaloo* 25.3 (2002): 847.

11. Sandy Alexandre, "Surfeit of Influence: Listening as Retreat and Antidote in *Topdog/Underdog,*" *Journal of American Drama and Theatre* 22.3 (2010): 64.

12. Suzan-Lori Parks, "From *Elements of Style,*" in *The America Play and Other Works* (New York: Theatre Communications Group, 1995), 3.

13. Ilka Saal, "The Politics of Mimicry: The Minor Theatre of Suzan-Lori Parks," *South Atlantic Review* 70.2 (2005): 63.

14. Parks explained at the bottom of the dramatis personae that "brackets in the text indicate optional cuts for production."

15. Haike Frank, "The Instability of Meaning in Suzan-Lori Parks' *The America Play,*" *American Drama* 11.2 (2002): 12.

16. Ellison, *Invisible Man,* 4

17. Geis, *Suzan-Lori Parks,* 105.

18. Matos, "The Difference between the Two Bundles," 850.

19. Mary Jane Lupton, "Clothes and Closure in Three Novels by Black Women," *Black American Literature Forum* 20.4 (1986): 409. Lupton borrows this term from Collette Dowling's 1987 book of the same title.

20. Iris Fanger, "Pulitzer Prize Winner Shakes Off Labels" *Christian Science Monitor,* April 12, 2002, 19.

21. Foster, "Suzan-Lori Parks's Staging of the Lincoln Myth," 34.

22. Jon Dietrick, "Making it 'Real': Money and Mimesis in Suzan-Lori Parks's *Topdog/Underdog*," *Modern Drama* 27.1 (2007): 54.

23. Geis, *Suzan-Lori Parks,* 112.

Chapter 6—As We Advance Living

1. Laura Miller, "On the Road Again: Suzan-Lori Parks's First Novel Involves a Pregnancy, a Journey, and an Unquiet Grave," *New York Times Book Review,* May 11, 2003, 10.

2. Suzan-Lori Parks, *Getting Mother's Body* (New York: Random House, 2003). All parenthetical citations in this chapter refer to this edition.

3. More subtle narrative clues also reveal the connection to *Light in August* (New York: Vintage, 1985). The most significant is the name *Beede* itself, for Faulkner uses "a shabby bead upon the mild red string of road" to symbolize movement, or lack thereof, in this novel (8).

4. Miller, "On the Road Again," 10.

5. Parks has underscored the importance of the blues aesthetic in *Getting Mother's Body* by releasing a companion CD (not mentioned anywhere in the front or back matter of the novel itself) of Willa Mae's songs, performed by Parks and her husband, blues musician Paul Oscher.

6. Glenda Dicker/sun, "Demeter, Persphone and Willa Mae Beede: Suzan-Lori Parks Gets Mothers Body," in *Suzan Lori Parks: Essays on the Plays and Other Works,* ed. Philip C. Kolin (Jefferson, N.C.: McFarland, 2010), 157.

7. In some cases such a focus leads to a redemptive reading of Faulkner's text, as demonstrated by critic Marc Hewson in his essay "'My Children Were of Me Alone': Maternal Influence in Faulkner's *As I Lay Dying,*" *Mississippi Quarterly* 53.4 (2000): 551–67.

8. In an interview with *Publishers Weekly,* Parks actually described herself as the novel's mother, and the book as child that would be born of her and that had its own will: "I'd been working on it for five years, and it was ready to be born." Natalie Danford, "*Getting Mother's Body,*" *Publishers Weekly* (January 27, 2003): 131.

9. Rosellen Brown, "Stumbling from Page to Stage," *New Leader* 86.3 (2003): 38.

10. Billy's words here echo those of Hester La Negrita's son Jabber in Parks's *In the Blood.* Both Jabber and Billy Beede believe that speaking something makes it more real, and that speaking a description, such as "mother"—or in Jabber's case, "slut"—actually makes that description more applicable to the subject being described. In both Jabber's and Billy's cases, not speaking the description protects them just as much, if not more, than their mothers, who are being described.

11. Brown, "Stumbling from Page to Stage," 38.

12. In *Venus* the Baron Docteur watches an on-stage play within the play; the stage directions indicate, "as if he's watching TV" (25).

13. Brown, "Stumbling from Page to Stage," 37.

14. Characters' names are not only printed at the beginning of each chapter in Parks's novel, but also on alternating pages throughout the text, on the running head where her (the author's) name would traditionally appear. Parks is known to exercise creative control over the printing of her texts (that is, the way they appear on

the page), and the versions of the texts cited in this chapter were both published by subsidiaries of the same publisher, Random House. Even if this move was not deliberate, it nevertheless subtly equates each character's voice with the authorial voice.

15. Brown, "Stumbling from Page to Stage," 37.

16. Haike Frank, "The Instability of Meaning in Suzan-Lori Parks' *The America Play,*" *American Drama* 11.2 (2002): 17–18.

17. Suzan-Lori Parks, "Possession," in *The America Play and Other Works* (New York: Theatre Communications Group, 1995), 5.

18. Suzan-Lori Parks, "An Equation for Black People Onstage," in *The America Play and Other Works* (New York: Theatre Communications Group, 1995), 21–22. This essay applies to Parks's prose as well as her plays because her mathematical paradigms appear frequently in *Getting Mother's Body.* Examples include Billy's adding up her potential income sources to fund her abortion (97) and Homer's algebra (220). This math also connects *Getting Mother's Body* back to Parks's *Venus* and that title character's focus on "calculation" (21–22).

19. Ralph Ellison, "The World and the Jug," in *Shadow and Act* (New York: Vintage, 1964), 139–40. This essay is included, serendipitously, in the section entitled "The Seer and the Seen."

20. Hilton Als, "The Show-Woman," *New Yorker* (October 30, 2006): 74–81. Baldwin, like Ellison, wrote at length about the nature of literary influence. Baldwin asserted in the introduction to the 1984 edition of his 1955 collection *Notes of a Native Son,* "My inheritance was particular, specifically limited and limiting: my birthright was vast, connecting me to all that lives and to everyone, forever. But one cannot claim the birthright without accepting the inheritance." Of the birthright Baldwin explained, "I am what time, circumstance, history, have made of me, certainly, but I am, also, much more than that. So are we all." Meanwhile, "The conundrum of color is the inheritance of every American, be he/she legally or actually Black or White." James Baldwin, *Notes of a Native Son* (Boston: Beacon, 1984), xii.

21. Harry J. Elam, Jr., "Editorial Comments: 'A Black Thing." *Theatre Journal* 57.4 (2005): x.

22. Ibid.

23. Ibid.

24. Alice Walker, "In Search of Our Mothers' Gardens," in *In Search of Our Mothers' Gardens* (New York: Harvest, 1984), 240.

25. One-leggedness is a recurring motif in *Getting Mother's Body.* In addition to June's injury, the Pink Flamingo on the motel's sign and Billy standing on one leg early in the novel also suggest a similar lack (14). Teddy and June refer to walking as taking the "eleven-bus," with the eleven representing two legs (42). One of these legs missing suggests a handicap vis-à-vis the ability to progress on a journey.

26. Suzan-Lori Parks, "From *Elements of Style,*" in *The America Play and Other Works* (New York: Theatre Communications Group, 1995), 9.

27. William Faulkner, *As I Lay Dying* (New York: Vintage, 1985), 140.

28. Faulkner, *Light in August,* 8.

29. Laz's central role as "resurrectionist" in *Getting Mother's Body* is reinforced by the biblical connections implied by his name. John 11:1–44 recounts the story of Jesus bringing Lazarus back to life after he had been dead and laid in the tomb for four days, an act that foreshadows Jesus's own resurrection, the central element in the Christian salvation narrative. In *Getting Mother's Body,* the first time we see Laz, he

is "rising from the dead" (13), and he later tells Dill's half sister Candy that he was given his name because he was "born not breathing" (216).

Chapter 7—"This film has been modified from its original version"

1. bell hooks, *Reel to Reel: Race, Sex, Class at the Movies* (New York: Routledge, 2002), 14.

2. In an interview with Charlie Rose, Lee claimed that idea for the story that became *Girl 6* "really came from thinking about *She's Gotta Have It,* and how in that film Nola Darling has three loves at the same time. Man, people thought that was cute and stuff like that, but that was before AIDS, and now ten years later, that kind of conduct or behavior, is dangerous. And ten years ago the phone sex business was not a multi-billion dollar industry you see. So, [with] these two things, it's really a look at how things have changed in the past ten years." Cynthia Fuchs, ed., *Spike Lee: Interviews* (Jackson: University Press of Mississippi, 2002), 117. And, in an interview with Joan Morgan of *Essence,* Parks talked about her experience as a phone-sex operator: "I actually was really good at phone sex. I have a very good phone voice and a very good imagination." Joan Morgan, "Wondering Who Flipped the 'Girl 6' Script? Meet Playwright Suzan-Lori Parks," *Essence* (April 1996): 74.

3. This film begins by scrolling across a black screen the famous opening lines of *Their Eyes Were Watching God,* with only subtle changes in capitalization and punctuation. Including this quotation connects all three films and their explorations of black female sexuality.

4. hooks, *Reel to Reel,* 12.

5. Charlene Regester, "The Unconscious and Metaphors in Suzan-Lori Parks's Screenplays of *Girl 6* and *Their Eyes Were Watching God,*" in *Suzan-Lori Parks: Essays on the Plays and Other Works,* ed. Philip C. Kolin (Jefferson, N.C.: McFarland, 2010), 175.

6. James Baldwin, *Notes of a Native Son* (1955; Boston: Beacon, 1984), 53.

7. Ibid.

8. Ibid., 50

9. Karen Ross, *Black and White Media: Black Images in Popular Film and Television* (Cambridge: Polity Press, 1996), 18.

10. Ibid., 19

11. hooks, *Reel to Reel,* 16

12. Robin R. Means Coleman, *African American Viewers and the Black Situation Comedy: Situating Racial Humor* (New York: Garland, 1998), 85.

13. Donald Bogle, *Prime Time Blues: African Americans on Network Television* (New York: Farrar, Straus and Giroux, 2001), 212.

14. Ibid., 203–4.

15. Lisa deMoraes, "ABC Execs Give Thanks to 'God'—and Halle," *Washington Post,* March 9, 2006, C07.

16. Sharon D. Johnson, "All Eyes on 'Eyes,'" *Black Issues Book Review* (March–April 2005): 42.

17. Valerie Boyd, "Their Eyes Were Watching Halle," *Essence* (March 2005): 132.

18. A *Boston Globe* article citing Harpo Films President and *Their Eyes* executive producer Kate Forte noted, "Three writers worked on the script but the person who 'cracked' it . . . was Suzan-Lori Parks." Suzanne C. Ryan, "'Eyes' Proved To Be a Tough Script To Crack," *Boston Globe,* 3, 2005, D1.

19. Regester, "The Unconscious and Metaphors in Suzan-Lori Parks's Screenplays," 169.

20. Zora Neale Hurston, *Their Eyes Were Watching God* (New York: Harper Collins, 1990). All parenthetical citations in this chapter refer to this edition.

21. James Weldon Johnson, preface, *The Book of American Negro Poetry (*New York: Harcourt Brace Jovanovich, 1983), 4.

22. Keith L. Alexander, "'Their Eyes,' Shining Bright," *Washington Post,* March 6, 2006, Y06.

23. Andrew Ryan, "Labour of Love," *Globe and Mail,* March 5, 2005, 2.

24. Felicia R. Lee, "A Woman's Journey Toward Herself," *New York Times,* March 6, 2005, A1.

25. Christian Toto, "Oprah's Gamble," *Washington Times,* March 3, 2005, B06.

26. Mary Helen Washington, introduction, *Their Eyes Were Watching God,* by Zora Neale Hurston (New York: Harper Collins, 1990), xii.

27. Ibid., xii–xiv.

28. Ibid., xiv–xv.

29. Johnson, "All Eyes on 'Eyes,'" 44.

30. Washington, introduction, xvi.

31. Lee, "A Woman's Journey toward Herself," 4,

32. Ibid.

33. Marisa Guthrie. "Berry Hopes to Open Some 'Eyes,'" *Daily News,* March 6, 2005, 3.

34. Alexander, "'Their Eyes,' Shining Bright," Y06.

35. Guthrie, "Berry Hopes to Open Some 'Eyes,'" 3.

Chapter 8—The Revisionary Revised

1. Suzan-Lori Parks, "new black math," *Theatre Journal* 57.4 (2005): 576.

2. August Wilson, "The Ground on Which I Stand," *Callaloo* 20.3 (1997): 193–503.

3. Suzan-Lori Parks, "An Equation for Black People Onstage," in *The America Play and Other Works* (New York: Theatre Communications Group, 1995), 10.

4. Suzan-Lori Parks, "From *Elements of Style,*" in *The America Play and Other Works* (New York: Theatre Communications Group, 1995), 14; The Great Man, The Lesser Known, Lucy, and Brazil are all characters in *The America Play.*

5. Ibid.

6. Suzan-Lori Parks, *365 Days/365 Plays* (New York: Theatre Communications Group, 2006). All parenthetical citations in this chapter refer to this edition.

7. Quoted in Damaso Reyes, "Public Theatre Debuts Suzan-Lori Parks's '365 Days/365 Plays,'" *New York Amsterdam News,* November 30, 2006, 20.

8. Jennifer Larson, "*365 Days/365 Plays:* A (W)hole New Approach to Theatre," in *Suzan Lori Parks: Essays on the Plays and Other Works,* ed. Philip C. Kolin (Jefferson, N.C.: McFarland, 2010), 124.

10. Geis, *Suzan-Lori Parks,* 158.

11. Ibid.

12. Ibid., 163.

13. Larson, "*365 Days/365 Plays,*" 128.

14. Ibid., 132.

15. Parks put the table of contents for *365 Days/365 Plays* at the end of the text and included a one- or two-sentence description of each play.

16. Larson, "*365 Days/365 Plays*," 129.

17. Rebecca Rugg, "Radical Inclusion 'Til It Hurts," *Theatre* 38.1 (2008): 54.

18. Philip C. Kolin, "Redefining the Way Theatre Is Created and Performed: The Radical Inclusion of Suzan-Lori Parks's *365 Days/365* Plays." *Journal of Dramatic Theatre and Criticism* 22.1 (2007): 80.

19. Rugg, "Radical Inclusion 'Til It Hurts," 74

20. Charles Isherwood, "A 'Porgy' for Theatergoers, Not for Fans of the Opera," *New York Times,* January 21, 2012, C1.

21. "Creative Team," The Gershwin's Porgy and Bess: Official Broadway Site, accessed July 21, 2012, http://www.porgyandbessonbroadway.com/creative.html

22. Patrick Healy, "It Ain't Necessarily 'Porgy,'" *New York Times,* August 7, 2011: AR1.

23. "Suzan-Lori Parks on 'Porgy and Bess,'" *New York Times* Video Library, August 10, 2011, accessed July 21, 2012, http://video.nytimes.com/video/2012/01/12/theater/100000001281743/suzan-lori-parks-on-porgy-and-bess.html.

24. Ibid.

25. "Study Guide," The Gershwin's Porgy and Bess: Official Broadway Site, accessed July 14, 2012, http://www.porgyandbessonbroadway.com/docs/PorgyBessStudyGuide LR-new.pdf, 13

26. "Stephen Sondheim Takes Issue with Plan for Revamped 'Porgy and Bess,'" *New York Times* Arts Beat, August 10, 2011, accessed July 21, 2012, http://artsbeat.blogs.nytimes.com/2011/08/10/stephen-sondheim-takes-issue-with-plan-for-revamped-porgy-and-bess.

27. Healy, "It Ain't Necessarily 'Porgy,'" AR1.

28. "Stephen Sondheim Takes Issue with Plan for Revamped 'Porgy and Bess.'"

29. Hilton Als, "A Man and a Woman: 'Porgy and Bess' Reimagined," *New Yorker*, September 26, 2011, Accessed July 21, 2012, http://www.newyorker.com/arts/critics/atlarge/2011/09/26/110926crat_atlarge_als.

30. Patrick Healy, "'Porgy': No New Scene, Some Hard Feelings," *New York Times,* November 15, 2011, C1.

31. Ben Brantley, "A New Storm's Brewing Down on Catfish Row," *New York Times,* January 13, 2012: C1.

32. "Study Guide," 13.

BIBLIOGRAPHY

Primary Works

PLAYS

365 Days/365 Plays. New York: Theatre Communications Group, 2006.

The America Play. In *The America Play and Other Works,* 158–99. New York: Theatre Communications Group, 1995.

Betting on the Dust Commander. In *The America Play and Other Works,* 73–90. New York: Theatre Communications Group, 1995.

"The Book of Grace." Unpublished, 2010.

The Death of the Last Black Man in Whole Entire World. In *The America Play and Other Works,* 158–99. New York: Theatre Communications Group, 1995.

Devotees in the Garden of Love. In *The America Play and Other Works,* 133–56. New York: Theatre Communications Group, 1995.

Fishes. Unpublished.

Fucking A. In *The Red Letter Plays: In the Blood and Fucking A,* 113–42. New York: Theatre Communications Group, 2001.

Imperceptible Mutabilities in the Third Kingdom. In *The America Play and Other Works,* 23–71. New York: Theatre Communications Group, 1995.

In the Blood. In *The Red Letter Plays: In the Blood and Fucking A,* 1–112. New York: Theatre Communications Group, 2001.

Pickling. In *The America Play and Other Works,* 91–98. New York: Theatre Communications Group, 1995.

"The Sinner's Place." Unpublished undergraduate thesis, Mount Holyoke College, 1984.

Topdog/Underdog. New York: Theatre Communications Group, 2002.

Venus. New York: Theatre Communications Group, 1997.

SCREENPLAYS

Act V. Unproduced.

Anemone Me. Unproduced.

Gal. Unproduced.

Girl 6. Directed by Spike Lee. 40 Acres and a Mule Filmworks, 1996.

God's Country. Unproduced.

The Great Debaters. With Robert Eisele. Directed by Denzel Washington. Harpo Films, 2007.

Their Eyes Were Watching God. With Misan Sagay and Bobby Smith, Jr. Directed by Darnel Martin. Harpo Productions, 2005.

NOVEL

Getting Mother's Body. New York: Random House, 2003.

ESSAYS

"An Equation for Black People Onstage." In *The America Play and Other Works,* 19–22. New York: Theatre Communications Group, 1995.

"From Elements of Style." In *The America Play and Other Works,* 6–18. New York: Theatre Communications Group, 1995.

"new black math." *Theatre Journal* 57.4 (2005): 576–83.

"Possession." In *The America Play and Other Works,* 3–5. New York: Theatre Communications Group, 1995.

"The Rear End Exists." *Grand Street* 14.3 (1996): 11–18.

"Tradition and the Individual Talent." *Theater* 29.2 (1999) 26–33.

Secondary Works

Alexandre, Sandy. "Surfeit of Influence: Listening as Retreat and Antidote in *Topdog/Underdog,*" *Journal of American Drama and Theatre* 22.3 (2010): 43–68.

Basting, Anne Davis. "*Venus.*" *Theatre Journal* 49.2 (1997): 223–25.

Bernard, Louise. "The Musicality of Language: Redefining History in Suzan-Lori Parks's *The Death of the Last Black Man in the Whole Entire World.*" *African American Review* 31.4 (1999): 687–98.

Brown-Guillory, Elizabeth. "Reconfiguring History: Migration, Memory, and (Re) Membering in Suzan-Lori Parks's Plays." In *Southern Women Playwrights: New Essays in Literary History and Criticism,* edited by Robert L. McDonald and Linda Rohrer, 183–97. Tuscaloosa: University of Alabama Press, 2002.

Diamond, Liz. "Perceptible Mutability in the Word Kingdom," *Theater* 24.3 (1993): 86–87.

Dicker/sun, Glenda. "Demeter, Persphone and Willa Mae Beede: Suzan-Lori Parks Gets Mothers Body." In *Suzan-Lori Parks: Essays on the Plays and Other Works,* edited by Philip C. Kolin, 156–68. Jefferson, N.C.: McFarland, 2010.

Dietrick, Jon. "'A Full Refund Ain't Enough': Money in Parks's Red Letter Plays." In *Suzan Lori Parks: Essays on the Plays and Other Works,* edited by Philip C. Kolin, 88–102. Jefferson, N.C.: McFarland, 2010.

———. "Making it 'Real': Money and Mimesis in Suzan-Lori Parks's *Topdog/Underdog.*" *Modern Drama* 27.1 (2007): 47–74.

Dixon, Kimberly D. "An I Am Sheba Me Am (She Be Doo Be Wah Waaah Doo Wah) O(au)rality, Textuality and Performativity: African American Literature's Vernacular Theory and the Work of Suzan-Lori Parks." *Journal of American Drama and Theatre* 11.1 (1998): 49–66.

Elam, Jr., Harry J. "The Postmulticultural: A Tale of Mothers and Sons." In *Crucible of Cultures: Anglophone Drama at the Dawn of the New Millennium,* edited by Mark Maufort and Franca Bellarsi, 113–28. New York: Peter Lang, 2002.

———, and Alice Rayner. "Body Parts: Between Story and Spectacle in *Venus* by Suzan-Lori Parks." *Staging Resistance: Essays on Political Theater,* edited by

Jeanne Colleran and Jenny S. Spencer, 265–82. Ann Arbor: University of Michigan Press, 1998.

Foster, Verna A. "Nurturing and Murderous Mothers in Suzan-Lori Parks's *In the Blood* and *Fucking A*," *American Drama* 16.1 (2007): 75–90.

———. "Suzan-Lori Parks's Staging of the Lincoln Myth in *The America Play* and *Topdog/Underdog*." *Journal of American Drama And Theatre* 17.3 (2005): 34–35.

Frank, Haike. "The Instability of Meaning in Suzan-Lori Parks' *The America Play*." *American Drama* 11.2 (2002): 4–20.

Frieze, James. "*Imperceptible Mutabilities in the Third Kingdom:* Suzan-Lori Parks and the Shared Struggle to Perceive," *Modern Drama* 41.4 (1998): 523–32.

Garrett, Shawn-Marie. "Figures, Speech and Form in *Imperceptible Mutabilities in the Third Kingdom*." In *Suzan Lori-Parks: A Casebook,* edited by Kevin J. Wetmore and Alycia Smith-Howard, 1–17. New York: Routledge, 2007.

Geis, Deborah. "Hawthorne's Hester as a Red-Lettered Black Woman? Suzan-Lori Parks's *In the Blood* and *Fucking A*." *Journal of American Drama and Theatre* 16.2 (2004): 77–87.

———. *Suzan-Lori Parks*. Ann Arbor: University of Michigan Press, 2008.

Holder, Heidi J. "Strange Legacy: The History Plays of Suzan-Lori Parks." In *Suzan-Lori Parks: A Casebook,* edited by Kevin J. Wetmore and Alycia Smith-Howard, 18–28. New York: Routledge, 2007.

Innes, Christopher. "Staging Black History: Re-Imagining Cultural Icons." In *Race and Religion in Contemporary Theatre and Drama in English,* edited by Bernhard Reitz, 95–107. Trier, Germany: Wissenschaftlicher Verlag Trier, 1999.

Kolin, Philip C. "Parks' *In the Blood*." *Explicator* 64.4 (2006): 245–48.

———. "Redefining the Way Theatre Is Created and Performed: The Radical Inclusion of Suzan-Lori Parks's *365 Days/365 Plays*." *Journal of Dramatic Theatre and Criticism* 22.1 (2007): 65–83.

———. "'You one of uh mines?' Imperceptible Mutabilities in the Third Kingdom." In *Suzan-Lori Parks: Essays on the Plays and Other Works,* edited by Philip C. Kolin, 48–64. Jefferson, N.C.: McFarland, 2010.

Larson, Jennifer. "*365 Days/365 Plays:* A (W)hole New Approach to Theatre." In *Suzan Lori Parks: Essays on the Plays and Other Works,* edited by Philip C. Kolin, 124–39. Jefferson, N.C.: McFarland, 2010.

Lucasi, Stephen. "Saartjie's Speech and the Sounds of National Identification." *Mosaic* 42.2 (2009): 171–89.

Lyman, Elizabeth Dyrud. "The Page Refigured: The Verbal and Visual Language of Suzan-Lori Parks's *Venus*." *Performance Research* 7.1 (2002): 90–100.

Marneweck, Aja. "Staging Stereotype and Performing the Exotic Erotic: An Interrogation of Desire in the Texts of Parks and Kennedy." *South African Theatre Journal* 18.1 (2004): 50–64.

Marshall, John. "A Moment with Playwright Suzan-Lori Parks." *Seattle Post-Intelligencer,* May 26, 2005, E1.

Osha, Sanya. "*Venus* and White Desire." *Transition* 99 (2008): 80–92.

Rayner, Alice, and Harry J. Elam, Jr., "Unfinished Business: Reconfiguring History in Suzan-Lori Parks's *The Death of the Last Black Man in the Whole Entire World*." *Theatre Journal* 46.4 (1994): 447–61.

Rugg, Rebecca. "Radical Inclusion 'Til It Hurts." *Theatre* 38.1 (2008): 53–75.

Ryan, Katy. "No Less Human': Making History in Suzan-Lori Parks's *The America Play.*" *Journal of Dramatic Theory and Criticism* 13.2 (1999): 81–94.

Saal, Ilka. "The Politics of Mimicry: The Minor Theatre of Suzan-Lori Parks." *South Atlantic Review* 70.2 (2005): 57–71.

Topdog Diaries: An Intimate Portrait of Playwright Suzan-Lori Parks. Directed by Oren Jacoby. Image Entertainment, 2004.

Wetmore, Kevin J., "It's an Oberammergau Thing: An Interview with Suzan-Lori Parks." In *Suzan-Lori Parks: A Casebook,* edited by Kevin J. Wetmore and Alycia Smith-Howard, 124–40. New York: Routledge, 2007.

Wilmer, S. E. "Restaging the Nation: The Work of Suzan-Lori Parks." *Modern Drama* 43.3 (2000): 442–52.

Young, Harvey. "Choral Compassion: *In the Blood* and *Venus.*" In *Suzan-Lori Parks: A Casebook,* edited by Kevin J. Wetmore and Alycia Smith-Howard. 29–47. New York: Routledge, 2007.

Young, Jean. "The Re-Objectification and Re-Commodification of Saartjie Baartman in Suzan-Lori Parks's *Venus.*" *African American Review* 31.4 (1997): 699–708.

INDEX

Actors Theatre of Louisville, 2
Act V (Parks), 2
agency, 5, 28–29, 117, 132; and complicity 27–28, 30–32; and economics, 29, 31; through language, 34, 46–7; in playwriting, 32, 35–36; and sexuality, 27, 37–38, 49; and subversion, 27–28
AIDS, 41, 54–56, 57
Alexander, Sandy, 65
America Play, The (Parks), 2, 58–82, 92–94, 129, 132; assassinations in, 67; and audience, 61–62, 71, 82; costumes in, 58–60, 62, 64, 67–68, 71–73, 75, 77–78, 82; inheritance in, 82; relationship to *Topdog/Underdog*, 59, 62; triple-consciousness in, 73; women in, 77–78. *See also* Great Hole of History, The
anachronism, 23, 91–92
Andrews, Julie, 115
Anemone Me (Parks), 2
Angels in America (Kushner), 3, 54–56
Annie John (Kincaid), 64
Apparatus Films, 2
Aristotle, 135
As I Lay Dying (Faulkner), 3, 83, 85, 87–91, 95, 97, 100
Aspects of the Novel (Forster), 3
audience: in *The America Play*, 61–64, 71, 82; expectations, 70, 77, 103; in *In the Blood*, 52, 57; participation, 36, 39; and race, 34–35, 113; reaction to costumes, 57, 59, 63. 72; reading versus viewing, 48, 102, 122; relationship to playwright, 32; and sexuality, 37; statistics on theatergoing, 34; of *Their Eyes Were Watching God*, 116–18, 123–26; in *Topdog/Underdog*, 58–59, 63–64, 72, 76–77; in *Venus*, 37–38
Autobiography of an Ex-Coloured Man, The (Johnson), 4
Autobiography of My Mother (Kincaid), 64

Baartman, Saartjie (Sarah), 3, 6, 26, 31–32, 38
Baker, Huston A., Jr., 63, 127
Baldwin, James, 1, 97; *Blues for Mister Charlie*, 83, 97; *Notes of a Native Son*, 83, 109–10
Baraka, Amiri, 136
Basting, Anne Davis, 35–36
Benston, Kimberly W., 4–5
Berry, Halle, 115–16, 119–20, 125–26
Betting on the Dust Commander (Parks), 1
Black Arts Movement, 128, 135
Black Boy (Wright), 4
Black Issues Book Review, 115, 123,
Black Theatre Alliance, 135
blaxploitation films, 110
blues, the, 86, 93
Blues for Mister Charlie (Baldwin), 83, 97
Bluest Eye, The (Morrison), 3
Bogle, Donald, 113
Book of American Negro Poetry, The (Johnson), 117
Book of Grace, The (Parks), 2
Boyd, Valerie, 115

Brantley, Ben, 28
Brooklyn Arts and Cultural Association (BACA), 2, 10, 20
Brooks, Gwendolyn, 53
Brown, Rosellen, 89–91
Brown, John, 36
Brown, Sterling, 127; *Negro Poetry and Drama*, 34–35
Brown-Guillory, Elizabeth, 31–33
Brustein, Robert, 20
Bryant, Aaron, 36

California Institute of the Arts (CalArts), 2
Carmen Jones (film), 3, 104, 109–11
Cattle Killing, The (Wideman), 3
Centers for Disease Control and Prevention (CDC), 55
Cheadle, Don, 2
Christianity, 29
Cleopatra Jones (film), 110
clothes. *See* costumes
Color Purple, The (Walker), 4, 99
community, 15, 21, 23, 41, 90, 97, 109–11, 116, 118–20, 125, 135
Cooper, Anna Julia; *Voice from the South, A* 5–6
costumes, 58–78, 82; in *The America Play*, 58–60, 62, 64, 67–68, 71–73, 75, 77–78, 82; in *Girl 6*, 104–5; and identity, 58–82; and invisibility, 63, 70, 72; 104–5; in *Topdog/Underdog*, 58–77; reflection of history in, 64, 75
Crisis, 35
Cult of True Womanhood, 120

Dandridge, Dorothy, 104, 109, 115
Death of the Last Black Man in the Whole Entire World, The (Parks), 2, 9, 20–25, 73, 90,130; structure of, 20
Dee, Ruby, 117
Def, Mos, 35
Devotees in the Garden of Love (Parks), 2
Diamond, Liz, 12
Dicker/sun, Glenda, 87
Dietrick, John, 47
disembodiment, 66
Diverse Works, 2
Dixon, Kimberly D., 33
Dobson, Tamara, 110
domesticity, 44,77, 120
Donoghue, Denis, 52
double-consciousness, 3, 9–12, 14, 20, 74, 94; relationship to triple-consciousness, 13
Douglas, Frederick, *Narrative of the Life of Frederick Douglass*, 4–5
dozens, the, 81
Du Bois, W. E. B., 14, 20, 136; *The Souls of Black Folk*, 3, 9–12

economics: and agency, 31; in *Girl 6*, 108–9; in *In the Blood*, 43–44; in *Their Eyes Were Watching God*, 117, 119; in *Topdog/Underdog*, 63, 78–79, 81; of playwriting, 33–34, 44; and sexuality, 38, 49; in *Venus*, 27–32, 37
Elam, Harry J., Jr., 20, 36, 49, 97–98
Eliot, T. S., 97
Ellison, Ralph, 81, 97–98; *Invisible Man*, 62–63, 69, 72; "The World and the Jug" 83, 96–97
Emancipation Proclamation, 6, 134
"Equation for Black People on Stage, An" (Parks), 96, 127–29
Euripides, *Medea*, 49

Father Comes Home from the Wars (Parks), 2
Faulkner, William 6, 130; *As I Lay Dying*, 3, 83, 85, 87–91, 95, 97, 100; *Light in August*, 3, 83, 85, 87–88, 91, 95, 97, 100
Feingold, Michael, 52, 56–57
feminism, 42–43, 96
"Fishes" (Parks), 1
For Colored Girls Who Have Considered Suicide When the Rainbow is Enuf (Shange), 14
Forster, E. M., *Aspects of the Novel*, 3
40 Acres and a Mule Filmworks, 2
Foster, Verna A., 59, 78

Foxy Brown (film), 104, 110
Frank, Haike, 68, 92
Frieze, James, 11–12
"From *Elements of Style*" (Parks), 7, 66, 99, 127–29
Fucking A (Parks), 2, 40–41, 55, 116, 129–30
Fuller, Margaret, 43

Gal (Parks), 2
Garner, James, 115
Garrett, Shawn-Marie, 10, 14–15, 19
Gates, Henry Louis, Jr., 123, 127
Geis, Deborah, 12, 45, 54, 62, 72, 131
Getting Mother's Body (Parks), 2, 7, 83–101, 119, 130, 132; as aesthetic shift, 85; compared to *As I Lay Dying*, 83, 85, 87–91, 95, 97, 100; compared to *Light in August*, 83, 85, 87–88, 91, 95, 97, 100; cultural literacy in, 94–95; journeys in, 84–5, 87, 100–101; metadiscourse in, 87; reflection in, 100–101; revision of The Great Hole of History in, 92–95; role of song in, 86–87, 93–94; structure of, 87–88, 91
Gershwin, George, 136
Gershwin, Ira, 136
Gilman, Sander, 38
Ginsberg, Leslie, 47
Giovanni, Nikki, 136
Girl 6 (film), 2–3, 103–16; compared to *She's Gotta Have It,* 105–6, 111, 115; costumes in, 104–5; metadiscourse in, 103, 115; sexuality, in, 103–12
God's Country (Parks), 2
Good Times (television show), 104, 112–13
Grauman's Chinese Theatre, 104, 115
Great Debaters, The (film), 2
Great Hole of History, The, 58–59, 67–68, 78, 82, 92; revised in *Getting Mother's Body*, 92–95, 101; revised in *365 Days/ 365 Plays*, 132–34
Greenlee, Sam, *The Spook Who Sat by the Door*, 64
Grier, Pam, 110
"Ground on Which I Stand, The" (Wilson), 128

Hansberry, Lorraine, 136
Harlem Renaissance, 128
Harpo Films, 2
Hawthorne, Nathaniel, 42, 44, 47, 52, 54; *The Scarlet Letter*, 3, 40–43, 48, 50–53, 55–57, 130; *The Marble Faun*, 51
Hines, Gregory, 131
history: and disembodiment, 17; in drama, 7, 6; inaccuracy in recorded, 61, 66, 71, 78; influence on identity, 2, 6, 16–17, 23, 42, 58–59, 61–62, 71–73, 92; malignancy of, 42; and memory, 64; revision of, 83–84, 95; recreation of 66–68; reflection in costume, 64, 75; role in artistic expression, 96–97; stasis in, 25; and stereotypes, 22–23; in *Venus*, 27; written, 71–72; *see also* anachronism; Great Hole of History, The
Holder, Heidi, J., 24
hooks, bell, 105, 112, 127, Howe, Irving, 96
Hughes, Langston, 97, 127, 136
Hurston, Zora Neale, 3, 23, 102–3, 115–26, 127, 136; *Their Eyes Were Watching God*, 3, 102, 116–26

identity: absence of, 107; adaptation of, 12; antithetical, 86; communal, 15, 21, 23, 90, 97, 111; and costumes, 58–82, 104–5; and creativity, 4, 45, 107, 133; and disembodiment, 11; evolution of, 24; fluidity of, 23, 25, 58, 76, 105; fragmentation of, 10, 13, 17, 20–22, 41, 65, 73; and freedom, 100; history's influence on, 2, 6, 16–17, 23, 42, 58–59, 61–62, 71–73, 92; and language, 9–10, 12–14, 16–17, 22, 25; in literary and visual culture, 5; loss of, 76; maternal elements of, 99; and memory, 14–15, 17–18, 58; metaphors for, 24; as performative, 68–70; racial, 1, 36;

identity (*continued*)
relational, 18; and revision, 5, 84; and sexuality, 49, 51, 116–17; suppression of, 76; and temporality, 14–15, 20–21, 61, 92; transference of, 68–70, 72, 78, 80, 82; and violence, 21. *See also* triple-consciousness
I Like It Like That (film), 119
illiteracy. *See* literacy
Imperceptible Mutabilites in the Third Kingdom, 2, 9–20, 69, 73; images of Middle Passage in, 10–11, 13, 17; role of language in, 13–15, 19; photographs in 15–16; structure of, 10; triple-consciousness in 9, 11, 15–20; wordplay in, 13, 18–21
Incidents in the Life of a Slave Girl (Jacobs), 3, 27, 46–7
inheritance: in *The America Play*, 82; and economics, 78; in *Getting Mother's Body*, 85–87, 94–96, 99; creative, 85, 87, 96–97, 99, 103; maternal, 79, 85–86, 94–96; paternal, 79, 82. 96; in *Topdog/Underdog*, 58, 78–79, 82, 130
Innes, Christopher, 35–36
In the Blood (Parks) 2, 40–57, 91, 116, 122, 129–30; 132; compared to *The Scarlet Letter*, 41–43; confessions in, 50–52, 56; connections to *Angels in America*, 55–56; economics in 43–44; interracial relationships in, 43; literacy in 44–48; storytelling in, 45–46
"In Search of Our Mother's Gardens" (Walker), 6, 83, 98
Invisible Man (Ellison), 62–63, 69, 72; *see also* invisibility
invisibility, 6, 55, 62–63, 67, 69–70 72

Jacobs, Harriet A., *Incidents in the Life of a Slave Girl*, 3, 27–30, 46–47
Jefferson, Margo, 45
Jeffersons, The (television show), 1, 3, 113
Jesus, 20, 52, 53
Jones, Quincy, 119, 126
Johnson, James Weldon, 127; *The Autobiography of an Ex-Coloured Man*, 4; *The Book of American Negro Poetry*, 117
Johnson, Sharon D., 115
Joseph Papp Public Theatre, 2, 28, 40
Juneteenth, 17

Keckley, Elizabeth, 134
Kincaid, Jamaica, 74; *Annie John*, 64; *Autobiography of my Mother*, 64; *Lucy*, 64
King Hedley III (Wilson), 97
King, Martin Luther, Jr., 74
Kolin, Philip C., 13–14, 52, 55, 135
Kushner, Tony, *Angels in America*, 3, 54–56

language, 1, 9, 45, 98, 127, 129; absence of, 82; and agency, 46–47; biblical, 17, 24; coded, 18–19; of disease, 56; of disembodiment, 22; evolution of, 12–13; fragmentation of, 11, 13, 19; and identity, 9–10, 12–14, 16–17, 22, 25; limits of, 10, 13; and media, 23; metaphorical, 9–10, 13, 24 56, 71–72, 100; performative, 14, 23, 33; and sexuality, 45; signification through, 13; struggles with, 13; and time, 9, 19; and triple-consciousness, 9, 24; unconventional, 9, 33, 36; vernacular, 31, 33, 87, 116–17; versus action, 76; versus images, 16, 71; and violence, 21; wordplay, 13, 18–21; written, 22, 47; *see also*, literacy
Lee, Spike, 34, 103–5, 115, 126
Light in August (Faulkner), 3, 83, 85, 87–88, 91, 95, 97, 100
Lincoln, Abraham, 3, 6, 58–82, 92, 129, 134–35
Lincoln, Mary Todd, 61, 134
literacy, 95; cultural, 47–48, 94–95; limiters of, 46; and self-expression, 44, 46; withholding, 46–49; *see also*, writing
Locomotive (Parks), 2
London Drama Studio, 1

Lucasi, Stephen, 31
Lucy (Kincaid), 64
Lupton, Mary Jane, 77
Lyman, Elizabeth Dyrud, 34
lynching, 16, 19, 21, 25, 69

MacArthur Foundation Genius Grant, 2
Madonna, 104, 112
Marble Faun, The (Hawthorne), 51
Marneweck, Aja, 33
Martin, Darnell, 119, 126
Matos, Nicole, 74
Means Coleman, Robin R., 113
Medea (Euripides), 49
memory: and costume, 64; destruction of, 18–19; healing through, 25; and history, 18, 2; and identity, 14–15, 17–18, 58; meaning created by, 16, 64; and narrative, 18; racial, 14–15, 19, 64; and time, 15, 18
Metzgar, Bonnie, 130–31, 135
Middle Passage, 10–11, 13, 17, 25
Miller, Laura, 83, 85
minstrelsy, 24, 63, 69, 113
Morrison, Toni: *The Bluest Eye,* 3; *Playing in the Dark: Whiteness and the Literary*
Imagination, 37
motherhood, 42, 52, 54, 56, 77–80, 86–88, 90, 94–95, 98–100

Narrative of the Life of Frederick Douglass (Douglass), 4–5
National Endowment for the Arts (NEA), 34
National Geographic, 96
Negro Ensemble Company, 135
Negro Poetry and Drama (Brown), 34–35
"new black math" (Parks), 26–27, 32, 36, 127–28, New Federal Theatre, 135
New Leader, 89
New York Times, 28, 45
New York Times Book Review, 83
New York Public Theatre, 2
New York Shakespeare Festival, 2, 40

Notes of a Native Son (Baldwin), 83, 109–10

Obie Award, 2, 10, 103
One Special Night (film), 115
Oscher, Paul, 2
Our Nig (Wilson), 43

page/stage dichotomy, 47–49, 76, 91, 122, 132, Parks, Suzan-Lori: on aesthetic, 9, 32–33, 38–39; advice for dramatists, 7; artistic agenda, 6; awards, 1–2; on black drama, 26–27, 128; childhood, 1; control over texts, 3, 33; creative process, 6–7; at Mount Holyoke, 1–2; narrative versus dramatic writing, 90–91; in New York, 1–2; radio plays, 2; revision of own texts, 127–36; screenplays, 2, 102–26; teaching, 2
Peabody, Elizabeth, 43
Person, Leland, 42
photography, 15–16
Pickling (Parks), 2
Playing in the Dark: Whiteness and the Literary Imagination (Morrison), 37
"Possession" (Parks), 1, 6, 95, 127, 136
Porgy and Bess (Parks), 136
poverty, 57, 74, 81; statistics, 40. *See also,* economics
Price, 103, 126
Pulitzer Prize, 2, 119

Radio Golf (Wilson), 97
Randle, Theresa, 103
Ray Charles Live! (Parks), 2
Rayner, Alice, 20, 36
Red Letter Plays, The. *See Fucking A; In the Blood*
Regester, Charlene, 106. 115
revision, 24, 85, 127; of *As I Lay Dying*, 83, 85, 87–91, 95, 97, 100; consequences of, 4–5, 85, 116, 124; creation through, 85, 88; of The Great Hole of History, 92–95, 101, 132–34; and identity, 5, 84; of *Light in August*, 83, 85, 87–88,

revision (*continued*)
91, 95, 97, 100; of Parks's work, 127–35; process, 6–8, 85–87; and the revisionary aesthetic, 3–8, 84–85, 90, 123–24, 127, 131; of *The Scarlet Letter*, 41–43; of screenplays, 102; of *Their Eyes Were Watching God*, 102–3, 115–26, 127. *See also* Rep & Rev
Rep & Rev, 13, 23, 29, 48, 99–100
Ross, Karen, 110
Rugg, Rebecca, 135
Ryan, Katy, 60

Saal, Ilka, 67
Scarlet Letter, The (Hawthorne), 3, 40–43, 48, 50–53, 55–57
Schindler, Amy, 55
sexuality: as agency, 27, 37–38, 49; black female, 27, 31, 107, 116; and economics, 38, 49; and expression, 108; in film, 103, 106–7, 109–11, 125–6; in *Girl 6*, 103–12; and class, 51; and identity, 49, 51, 116–17; and language, 54; morality of, 29, 57; and power, 51; self-indulgent, 53; on stage, 29, 37–38; as outlet, 96; as pathology, 38, 103; stereotypes of, 55, 103, 110, 125; in *Their Eyes Were Watching God*, 118, 120–21; in *Venus*, 27–38; white male, 27, 37–38
Shange, Ntozake, *For Colored Girls Who Have Considered Suicide When the Rainbow is Enuf*, 14
She's Gotta Have It (film), 105–6, 111, 115
"The Sinner's Place," (Parks), 1
slavery, 4, 10–11, 13, 16–17, 19, 23–24, 27, 29–31, 42–43, 46, 74, 92, 96
Smith, Barbara, 127
Souls of Black Folk, The (DuBois), 3, 9–11
Spook Who Sat by the Door, The (Greenlee), 64
stage directions, 15–16, 47–48, 64–65, 67, 73, 76, 79, 91–92, 129, 132–33
Stepto, Robert, 121–22
stereotypes, 33, 55, 69, 77, 125–26, 130; and history, 22–23; in popular culture, 23, 35, 103, 110, 113, 125–26; of sexuality, 55, 103, 110, 125; and triple-consciousness, 23

Tarantino, Quentin, 103
Their Eyes Were Watching God (Hurston), 3, 102, 116–26
Their Eyes Were Watching God (Parks), 2, 102–3, 115–26; audience of, 116–18, 123–26; baptisms in, 120–21, 123; compared to Hurston's text, 102–3, 115–26, 127; critical reception of, 102–3, 115; economics in, 117, 119; Parks's role in adaptation, 115; production history, 119, 124–25; sexuality in, 118, 120–21; vernacular in, 116–17; viewer response to, 123–24; voice in, 121–22
Third Kingdom, The (Parks), 2
3-Card Monty, 59, 72, 76, 80–81
365 Days/365 Plays (Parks), 2, 127, 130–36; holes in, 132–34, Lincoln in 134–35; production history of, 130–31; revision in, 131–32;
Ticknor, William D., 44
Topdog/Underdog (Parks), 2, 14, 50, 58–82, 86, 90–91, 105, 108, 129–30, 134; assassinations in, 66–67, 69; audience in, 58–59, 63–64, 72, 76–77; costumes in, 58–77; economics in, 63, 78–79, 81; inheritance in, 58, 78–79, 82, 130; relationship to *The America Play*, 59, 62; women in, 65, 77–78
"Tradition and the Individual Talent" (Parks), 127
trickster figure, 62
triple-consciousness, 73, 9–11, 13–21, 23–25; in *The America Play*, 73; and community, 21; evolution of, 24–25; relationship to double-consciousness, 13; and stereotypes, 23
Truth, Sojourner, 36
Turner, Lana, 110

Turner, Nat, 36
Two Trains Running (Wilson), 83, 97

United States Census Bureau, 40
United States Constitution, 17

Venus (Parks), 2, 26–39, 42, 116, 127, 130–32; as allegory for black playwrights, 32–38; audience in, 35, 37–38; critical debate over, 26–28; economics in, 27–32, 37' history in, 27; indictments in, 35–36; metadiscourse in, 27, 33; as revolutionary theatre, 36; sexuality in, 27–38
Venus Hottentot. *See* Baartman, Saartje
vernacular culture, 11, 31, 33, 87, 116–17
Village Voice, 52
violence, 11, 21, 42, 48, 56, 68–69, 81, 97, 110
Voice from the South, A (Cooper), 5–6

Walker, Alice, 4, 6, 98; *The Color Purple,* 4, 99; "In Search of Our Mother's Gardens," 6, 83, 98
Washington, Booker T., 53
Washington, Isaiah, 103–4
Washington, Mary Helen, 121–22
Washington Post, 115
Wideman, John Edgar, *The Cattle Killing,* 3
Wilkinson, Sarah, 49
Wilmer, S.E., 38
Wilson, August, 23, 97–98, 128, 135; "The Ground on Which I Stand," 128; *King Hedley III*, 97; *Radio Golf*, 97; *Two Trains Running*, 83, 97
Wilson, Harriet; *Our Nig*, 43
Winfrey, Oprah, 34, 102, 115, 119–20, 123–26
Winship, Michael, 44
Wolfe, George C., 2, 35
"World and the Jug, The" (Ellison), 83, 96–97
Wright, Richard, 97; *Black Boy*, 4
Wright, Jeffrey, 2, 35

X, Malcolm, 105

Yale Reparatory Theatre, 2
Young, Jean, 27, 30, 32